D1273013

# BANKS AND THEIR CUSTOMERS

## 3rd Edition

## *by*
## Margaret C. Jasper

Oceana's Legal Almanac Series:
*Law for the Layperson*

2004
Oceana Publications, Inc.
Dobbs Ferry, New York

Information contained in this work has been obtained by Oceana Publications from sources believed to be reliable. However, neither the Publisher nor its authors guarantee the accuracy or completeness of any information published herein, and neither Oceana nor its authors shall be responsible for any errors, omissions or damages arising from the use of this information. This work is published with the understanding that Oceana and its authors are supplying information, but are not attempting to render legal or other professional services. If such services are required, the assistance of an appropriate professional should be sought.

Library of Congress Control Number: 2004109193

ISBN: 0-379-11391-0

Oceana's Legal Almanac Series: Law for the Layperson
ISSN 1075-7376

To My Husband Chris

Your love and support
are my motivation and inspiration

-and-

In memory of my son, Jimmy

# Table of Contents

ABOUT THE AUTHOR........................................ ix

INTRODUCTION........................................... xi

## CHAPTER 1:
### OVERVIEW OF THE BANKING SYSTEM

THE DEVELOPMENT OF MODERN BANKING ......................... 1
THE MODERN DAY BANK ...................................... 2
  Commercial Banks........................................ 2
  Central Banks .......................................... 2
  Financial Intermediaries................................ 3
THE REGULATION OF BANKING ................................ 3
  Federal Reserve System.................................. 3
  Bank Powers ............................................ 3
    State Banks .......................................... 3
    National Banks ....................................... 4
  The Federal Deposit Insurance Corporation (FDIC)........ 5
DUTIES, POWERS AND LIABILITIES OF BANK DIRECTORS AND OFFICERS ... 6
BANKING UNDER THE UNIFORM COMMERCIAL CODE (UCC) ............ 7

## CHAPTER 2:
### UCC ARTICLE 3: NEGOTIABLE INSTRUMENTS

IN GENERAL .............................................. 9
TYPES OF NEGOTIABLE INSTRUMENTS .......................... 9
  Bank Check ............................................ 10
    Personal Check....................................... 10
    Corporate Check ..................................... 10
    Cashier Check ....................................... 10
    Travelers Check ..................................... 10
    Personal Money Order ................................ 11
    Bank Money Order/Teller Check ....................... 11
  Drafts and Notes ...................................... 11
    Drafts .............................................. 11

Notes . . . . . . . . . . . . . . . . . . . . . . . . . . . . . . . . . . . . . . . . . . . . . . . . . . . . . . . . . 12
Certificate of Deposit . . . . . . . . . . . . . . . . . . . . . . . . . . . . . . . . . . . . . . . . 13
NEGOTIABILITY . . . . . . . . . . . . . . . . . . . . . . . . . . . . . . . . . . . . . . . . . . . . . . 13
Written Form . . . . . . . . . . . . . . . . . . . . . . . . . . . . . . . . . . . . . . . . . . . . . . . . . 13
Signed by Maker . . . . . . . . . . . . . . . . . . . . . . . . . . . . . . . . . . . . . . . . . . . . . . 13
Unconditional Promise or Order to Pay . . . . . . . . . . . . . . . . . . . . . . . . . 13
Sum Certain . . . . . . . . . . . . . . . . . . . . . . . . . . . . . . . . . . . . . . . . . . . . . . . . . 14
Payable Upon Demand or Definite Date . . . . . . . . . . . . . . . . . . . . . . . . . 14
Payable to Order or to Bearer . . . . . . . . . . . . . . . . . . . . . . . . . . . . . . . . . . 14
ADDITIONS AND OMISSIONS . . . . . . . . . . . . . . . . . . . . . . . . . . . . . . . . . 15
Additional Terms or Language . . . . . . . . . . . . . . . . . . . . . . . . . . . . . . . . . 15
Omissions . . . . . . . . . . . . . . . . . . . . . . . . . . . . . . . . . . . . . . . . . . . . . . . . . . 15
Payee Name(s) . . . . . . . . . . . . . . . . . . . . . . . . . . . . . . . . . . . . . . . . . . . . . . 16
Discrepancies and Ambiguities . . . . . . . . . . . . . . . . . . . . . . . . . . . . . . . . 16
TRANSFERRING COMMERCIAL PAPER . . . . . . . . . . . . . . . . . . . . . . . . . 16
Assignment . . . . . . . . . . . . . . . . . . . . . . . . . . . . . . . . . . . . . . . . . . . . . . . . . 16
Negotiation . . . . . . . . . . . . . . . . . . . . . . . . . . . . . . . . . . . . . . . . . . . . . . . . . 17
Bearer Instrument . . . . . . . . . . . . . . . . . . . . . . . . . . . . . . . . . . . . . . . . . 17
Order Instrument . . . . . . . . . . . . . . . . . . . . . . . . . . . . . . . . . . . . . . . . . . 17
ENDORSEMENTS . . . . . . . . . . . . . . . . . . . . . . . . . . . . . . . . . . . . . . . . . . . . 17
Instrument Payable to Bearer or Order . . . . . . . . . . . . . . . . . . . . . . . . . 17
Types of Endorsements . . . . . . . . . . . . . . . . . . . . . . . . . . . . . . . . . . . . . . 18
Special Endorsement . . . . . . . . . . . . . . . . . . . . . . . . . . . . . . . . . . . . . . . 18
Blank Endorsement . . . . . . . . . . . . . . . . . . . . . . . . . . . . . . . . . . . . . . . . 19
Qualified Endorsement . . . . . . . . . . . . . . . . . . . . . . . . . . . . . . . . . . . . . 19
Restrictive Endorsement . . . . . . . . . . . . . . . . . . . . . . . . . . . . . . . . . . . . 19
LIABILITY OF PARTIES ON AN INSTRUMENT . . . . . . . . . . . . . . . . . . . . . 20
Contract Liability . . . . . . . . . . . . . . . . . . . . . . . . . . . . . . . . . . . . . . . . . . . 20
Primary Liability . . . . . . . . . . . . . . . . . . . . . . . . . . . . . . . . . . . . . . . . . . 20
Secondary Liability . . . . . . . . . . . . . . . . . . . . . . . . . . . . . . . . . . . . . . . . 21
Warranty Liability . . . . . . . . . . . . . . . . . . . . . . . . . . . . . . . . . . . . . . . . . . 22
DISCHARGE FROM LIABILITY . . . . . . . . . . . . . . . . . . . . . . . . . . . . . . . . . 23
Discharge by Payment . . . . . . . . . . . . . . . . . . . . . . . . . . . . . . . . . . . . . . . 24
Discharge by Cancellation . . . . . . . . . . . . . . . . . . . . . . . . . . . . . . . . . . . . 24
HOLDER IN DUE COURSE . . . . . . . . . . . . . . . . . . . . . . . . . . . . . . . . . . . . 25
Suspension of the Rule of Derivative Title . . . . . . . . . . . . . . . . . . . . . . . 25
The Shelter Doctrine . . . . . . . . . . . . . . . . . . . . . . . . . . . . . . . . . . . . . . . . . 26
Defenses . . . . . . . . . . . . . . . . . . . . . . . . . . . . . . . . . . . . . . . . . . . . . . . . . . . 27
Personal Defenses . . . . . . . . . . . . . . . . . . . . . . . . . . . . . . . . . . . . . . . . . 27
Real Defenses . . . . . . . . . . . . . . . . . . . . . . . . . . . . . . . . . . . . . . . . . . . . 27
Additional Requirements . . . . . . . . . . . . . . . . . . . . . . . . . . . . . . . . . . . . . 28
AUTHORIZED SIGNATURES . . . . . . . . . . . . . . . . . . . . . . . . . . . . . . . . . . 28
Holders in Due Course in Consumer Transactions . . . . . . . . . . . . . . . . . 29

# CHAPTER 3:
## UCC ARTICLE 4: BANK DEPOSITS AND COLLECTIONS

IN GENERAL . . . . . . . . . . . . . . . . . . . . . . . . . . . . . . . . . . . . . . . . . . . . . . . . . 31
AVAILABILITY OF FUNDS . . . . . . . . . . . . . . . . . . . . . . . . . . . . . . . . . . . . . . 32
  Cash Deposit . . . . . . . . . . . . . . . . . . . . . . . . . . . . . . . . . . . . . . . . . . . . . . . . 32
  Same Bank Items. . . . . . . . . . . . . . . . . . . . . . . . . . . . . . . . . . . . . . . . . . . . . 32
  Checks Drawn on other Banks. . . . . . . . . . . . . . . . . . . . . . . . . . . . . . . . . . 32
COLLECTING, DEPOSITORY AND PAYOR BANKS . . . . . . . . . . . . . . . . . . . . 32
  The Role of the Collecting Bank . . . . . . . . . . . . . . . . . . . . . . . . . . . . . . . . 33
  Role of the Depository Bank . . . . . . . . . . . . . . . . . . . . . . . . . . . . . . . . . . . 34
  The Role of the Payor Bank. . . . . . . . . . . . . . . . . . . . . . . . . . . . . . . . . . . . 34
    Wrongful Dishonor . . . . . . . . . . . . . . . . . . . . . . . . . . . . . . . . . . . . . . . . . 34
    The Midnight Deadline. . . . . . . . . . . . . . . . . . . . . . . . . . . . . . . . . . . . . . 35
    Final Payment. . . . . . . . . . . . . . . . . . . . . . . . . . . . . . . . . . . . . . . . . . . . . 35
TRANSFER WARRANTIES. . . . . . . . . . . . . . . . . . . . . . . . . . . . . . . . . . . . . . . 35
PRESENTMENT WARRANTIES. . . . . . . . . . . . . . . . . . . . . . . . . . . . . . . . . . . 36
BANK DEFENSES . . . . . . . . . . . . . . . . . . . . . . . . . . . . . . . . . . . . . . . . . . . . . 36
CHARGING THE CUSTOMER'S ACCOUNT . . . . . . . . . . . . . . . . . . . . . . . . . 37
  Forged Checks . . . . . . . . . . . . . . . . . . . . . . . . . . . . . . . . . . . . . . . . . . . . . . 37
  Altered Checks. . . . . . . . . . . . . . . . . . . . . . . . . . . . . . . . . . . . . . . . . . . . . . 37
  Postdated Checks. . . . . . . . . . . . . . . . . . . . . . . . . . . . . . . . . . . . . . . . . . . . 38
  Overdraft . . . . . . . . . . . . . . . . . . . . . . . . . . . . . . . . . . . . . . . . . . . . . . . . . . 38
  Old Checks . . . . . . . . . . . . . . . . . . . . . . . . . . . . . . . . . . . . . . . . . . . . . . . . 38
  Stop Payment Order . . . . . . . . . . . . . . . . . . . . . . . . . . . . . . . . . . . . . . . . . 38

# CHAPTER 4:
## UCC ARTICLE 4A: ELECTRONIC FUNDS TRANSFERS

IN GENERAL . . . . . . . . . . . . . . . . . . . . . . . . . . . . . . . . . . . . . . . . . . . . . . . . . 41
SECURITY PROCEDURES. . . . . . . . . . . . . . . . . . . . . . . . . . . . . . . . . . . . . . . 42
  Unauthorized Payment Orders . . . . . . . . . . . . . . . . . . . . . . . . . . . . . . . . . 42
  Erroneous Payment Orders. . . . . . . . . . . . . . . . . . . . . . . . . . . . . . . . . . . . 42
ACCEPTANCE OF ORDER. . . . . . . . . . . . . . . . . . . . . . . . . . . . . . . . . . . . . . . 42
MISDESCRIPTION OF BENEFICIARY. . . . . . . . . . . . . . . . . . . . . . . . . . . . . . 43
REJECTION OF ORDER . . . . . . . . . . . . . . . . . . . . . . . . . . . . . . . . . . . . . . . . 44
CANCELLATION AND AMENDMENT OF ORDER. . . . . . . . . . . . . . . . . . . . 44
PAYMENT OF ORDER . . . . . . . . . . . . . . . . . . . . . . . . . . . . . . . . . . . . . . . . . 44
DEBIT CARDS . . . . . . . . . . . . . . . . . . . . . . . . . . . . . . . . . . . . . . . . . . . . . . . . 45
THE CONSUMER CREDIT PROTECTION ACT: SUBCHAPTER VI—THE
ELECTRONIC FUNDS TRANSFER ACT . . . . . . . . . . . . . . . . . . . . . . . . . . . . 45
  Consumer Liability for Unauthorized Transfers. . . . . . . . . . . . . . . . . . . . 46

---

## CHAPTER 5:
## UCC ARTICLE 5: LETTERS OF CREDIT

IN GENERAL . . . . . . . . . . . . . . . . . . . . . . . . . . . . . . . . . . . . . . . . . . . . . . . . 47
PROCEDURE . . . . . . . . . . . . . . . . . . . . . . . . . . . . . . . . . . . . . . . . . . . . . . . . 47
ESTABLISHMENT OF THE LETTER OF CREDIT . . . . . . . . . . . . . . . . . . . . . . 48
   Advising Bank . . . . . . . . . . . . . . . . . . . . . . . . . . . . . . . . . . . . . . . . . . . . . 48
   Confirming Bank . . . . . . . . . . . . . . . . . . . . . . . . . . . . . . . . . . . . . . . . . . . . 49
   Liability of Issuing Bank . . . . . . . . . . . . . . . . . . . . . . . . . . . . . . . . . . . . . 49

## CHAPTER 6:
## SHOPPING FOR A BANK

IN GENERAL . . . . . . . . . . . . . . . . . . . . . . . . . . . . . . . . . . . . . . . . . . . . . . . . 51
NEW PROOF OF IDENTITY REQUIREMENT UNDER USA PATRIOT ACT . . . . . 51
TYPES OF BANK ACCOUNTS . . . . . . . . . . . . . . . . . . . . . . . . . . . . . . . . . . . . 52
   Savings Account . . . . . . . . . . . . . . . . . . . . . . . . . . . . . . . . . . . . . . . . . . . . 52
   Checking Account. . . . . . . . . . . . . . . . . . . . . . . . . . . . . . . . . . . . . . . . . . . 52
      Check Reporting Services . . . . . . . . . . . . . . . . . . . . . . . . . . . . . . . . . 52
   Title/Ownership of the Account. . . . . . . . . . . . . . . . . . . . . . . . . . . . . . . . 53
      Individual Account . . . . . . . . . . . . . . . . . . . . . . . . . . . . . . . . . . . . . . . 53
      Joint Account. . . . . . . . . . . . . . . . . . . . . . . . . . . . . . . . . . . . . . . . . . . . 53
      Corporate Account. . . . . . . . . . . . . . . . . . . . . . . . . . . . . . . . . . . . . . . . 53
      Trust Account . . . . . . . . . . . . . . . . . . . . . . . . . . . . . . . . . . . . . . . . . . . 53
      Fiduciary or Representative Accounts . . . . . . . . . . . . . . . . . . . . . . . . . 54
MAKING DEPOSITS. . . . . . . . . . . . . . . . . . . . . . . . . . . . . . . . . . . . . . . . . . . 54
   General Deposits . . . . . . . . . . . . . . . . . . . . . . . . . . . . . . . . . . . . . . . . . . . 54
   Special Deposit . . . . . . . . . . . . . . . . . . . . . . . . . . . . . . . . . . . . . . . . . . . . 54
CERTIFICATE OF DEPOSIT (CD). . . . . . . . . . . . . . . . . . . . . . . . . . . . . . . . . 55
INTEREST RATES . . . . . . . . . . . . . . . . . . . . . . . . . . . . . . . . . . . . . . . . . . . . 56
SAFE DEPOSIT BOXES. . . . . . . . . . . . . . . . . . . . . . . . . . . . . . . . . . . . . . . . . 56
   Access Procedures . . . . . . . . . . . . . . . . . . . . . . . . . . . . . . . . . . . . . . . . . 57
   Items You Should Place in a Safety Deposit Box . . . . . . . . . . . . . . . . . . 57
   Items You Should Not Place in a Safety Deposit Box. . . . . . . . . . . . . . . . 57
   Insurance. . . . . . . . . . . . . . . . . . . . . . . . . . . . . . . . . . . . . . . . . . . . . . . . . 57
   Further Safeguards . . . . . . . . . . . . . . . . . . . . . . . . . . . . . . . . . . . . . . . . . 58
   Abandonment . . . . . . . . . . . . . . . . . . . . . . . . . . . . . . . . . . . . . . . . . . . . . 58
SWITCHING BANKS . . . . . . . . . . . . . . . . . . . . . . . . . . . . . . . . . . . . . . . . . . 58
MAINTAINING BANK RECORDS . . . . . . . . . . . . . . . . . . . . . . . . . . . . . . . . 59
FORGOTTEN ASSETS. . . . . . . . . . . . . . . . . . . . . . . . . . . . . . . . . . . . . . . . . . 60

# CHAPTER 7:
## USING THE AUTOMATED TELLER MACHINE

IN GENERAL . . . . . . . . . . . . . . . . . . . . . . . . . . . . . . . . . . . . . . . . . . . . . . . . . . . 61
RESOLVING AN ATM PROBLEM. . . . . . . . . . . . . . . . . . . . . . . . . . . . . . . . . . 61
    Lost or Stolen ATM Card . . . . . . . . . . . . . . . . . . . . . . . . . . . . . . . . . . . . . . 61
    Statement Discrepancies. . . . . . . . . . . . . . . . . . . . . . . . . . . . . . . . . . . . . . 62
    The ATM Retained the Card . . . . . . . . . . . . . . . . . . . . . . . . . . . . . . . . . . 62
    The ATM Dispensed the Wrong Amount of Money . . . . . . . . . . . . . . . . . . 62
ATM DEPOSITS. . . . . . . . . . . . . . . . . . . . . . . . . . . . . . . . . . . . . . . . . . . . . . . . 62
ATM TRANSACTION FEES AND SURCHARGES. . . . . . . . . . . . . . . . . . . . . . . . 63
KEEP ACCURATE ACCOUNTING. . . . . . . . . . . . . . . . . . . . . . . . . . . . . . . . . . 63
SAFEGUARDS. . . . . . . . . . . . . . . . . . . . . . . . . . . . . . . . . . . . . . . . . . . . . . . . . 63

# CHAPTER 8:
## RESOLVING COMPLAINTS

IN GENERAL . . . . . . . . . . . . . . . . . . . . . . . . . . . . . . . . . . . . . . . . . . . . . . . . . . . 65
CONTACT YOUR BANK. . . . . . . . . . . . . . . . . . . . . . . . . . . . . . . . . . . . . . . . . . 65
PRIMARY FEDERAL REGULATORS . . . . . . . . . . . . . . . . . . . . . . . . . . . . . . . . 65
    Federal Deposit Insurance Corporation (FDIC) . . . . . . . . . . . . . . . . . . . . 65
    Office of the Comptroller of the Currency. . . . . . . . . . . . . . . . . . . . . . . . . 66
    Federal Reserve System. . . . . . . . . . . . . . . . . . . . . . . . . . . . . . . . . . . . . . 66
    National Credit Union Administration . . . . . . . . . . . . . . . . . . . . . . . . . . . 66
    Office of Thrift Supervision . . . . . . . . . . . . . . . . . . . . . . . . . . . . . . . . . . 67
FILING YOUR COMPLAINT LETTER . . . . . . . . . . . . . . . . . . . . . . . . . . . . . . 67
APPLICABLE LAW . . . . . . . . . . . . . . . . . . . . . . . . . . . . . . . . . . . . . . . . . . . . 68
    Credit Billing Disputes . . . . . . . . . . . . . . . . . . . . . . . . . . . . . . . . . . . . . . 68
        Rights . . . . . . . . . . . . . . . . . . . . . . . . . . . . . . . . . . . . . . . . . . . . . . . 68
        Responsibilities . . . . . . . . . . . . . . . . . . . . . . . . . . . . . . . . . . . . . . . . 68
    Debt Collection . . . . . . . . . . . . . . . . . . . . . . . . . . . . . . . . . . . . . . . . . . . . 68
        Rights . . . . . . . . . . . . . . . . . . . . . . . . . . . . . . . . . . . . . . . . . . . . . . . 68
        Responsibilities . . . . . . . . . . . . . . . . . . . . . . . . . . . . . . . . . . . . . . . . 68
    Credit Reports . . . . . . . . . . . . . . . . . . . . . . . . . . . . . . . . . . . . . . . . . . . . 69
        Rights . . . . . . . . . . . . . . . . . . . . . . . . . . . . . . . . . . . . . . . . . . . . . . . 69
        Responsibilities . . . . . . . . . . . . . . . . . . . . . . . . . . . . . . . . . . . . . . . . 69
    Equal Credit Opportunity . . . . . . . . . . . . . . . . . . . . . . . . . . . . . . . . . . . . 69
        Rights . . . . . . . . . . . . . . . . . . . . . . . . . . . . . . . . . . . . . . . . . . . . . . . 69
        Responsibilities . . . . . . . . . . . . . . . . . . . . . . . . . . . . . . . . . . . . . . . . 69
    Electronic Fund Transfers. . . . . . . . . . . . . . . . . . . . . . . . . . . . . . . . . . . . 70
        Rights . . . . . . . . . . . . . . . . . . . . . . . . . . . . . . . . . . . . . . . . . . . . . . . 70
        Responsibilities . . . . . . . . . . . . . . . . . . . . . . . . . . . . . . . . . . . . . . . . 70
    Funds Availability . . . . . . . . . . . . . . . . . . . . . . . . . . . . . . . . . . . . . . . . . 70
        Rights . . . . . . . . . . . . . . . . . . . . . . . . . . . . . . . . . . . . . . . . . . . . . . . 70

Responsibilities . . . . . . . . . . . . . . . . . . . . . . . . . . . . . . . . . . . . . . . . . . . . . . . . 71
STATE REGULATORY AGENCIES . . . . . . . . . . . . . . . . . . . . . . . . . . . . . . . . 71

## CHAPTER 9:
## WHAT HAPPENS WHEN YOUR BANK FAILS

IN GENERAL . . . . . . . . . . . . . . . . . . . . . . . . . . . . . . . . . . . . . . . . . . . . . . . . . . . . 73
FDIC DEPOSIT INSURANCE . . . . . . . . . . . . . . . . . . . . . . . . . . . . . . . . . . . . . 73
Coverage. . . . . . . . . . . . . . . . . . . . . . . . . . . . . . . . . . . . . . . . . . . . . . . . . . . . . . 73
Insurance Limitations . . . . . . . . . . . . . . . . . . . . . . . . . . . . . . . . . . . . . . . . . 74
Ownership Categories . . . . . . . . . . . . . . . . . . . . . . . . . . . . . . . . . . . . . . . . . 74
Single Accounts . . . . . . . . . . . . . . . . . . . . . . . . . . . . . . . . . . . . . . . . . . . . 74
Joint Accounts . . . . . . . . . . . . . . . . . . . . . . . . . . . . . . . . . . . . . . . . . . . . . 75
Self-Directed Retirement Accounts . . . . . . . . . . . . . . . . . . . . . . . . . . 75
Revocable Trust Accounts . . . . . . . . . . . . . . . . . . . . . . . . . . . . . . . . . . . 75
SAFE DEPOSIT BOXES . . . . . . . . . . . . . . . . . . . . . . . . . . . . . . . . . . . . . . . . . . 76
OBTAINING A LIEN RELEASE . . . . . . . . . . . . . . . . . . . . . . . . . . . . . . . . . . . 76
UNCLAIMED FUNDS . . . . . . . . . . . . . . . . . . . . . . . . . . . . . . . . . . . . . . . . . . . . 77
FDIC Unclaimed Funds Database . . . . . . . . . . . . . . . . . . . . . . . . . . . . . . 78
Claiming Held Funds . . . . . . . . . . . . . . . . . . . . . . . . . . . . . . . . . . . . . . . . . 78

## CHAPTER 10:
## ONLINE BANKING

OVERVIEW . . . . . . . . . . . . . . . . . . . . . . . . . . . . . . . . . . . . . . . . . . . . . . . . . . . . . 79
CONFIRM THAT THE ONLINE BANK IS LEGITIMATE . . . . . . . . . . . . . . . . . 80
VERIFY INSURANCE STATUS . . . . . . . . . . . . . . . . . . . . . . . . . . . . . . . . . . . . 80
STATISTICS . . . . . . . . . . . . . . . . . . . . . . . . . . . . . . . . . . . . . . . . . . . . . . . . . . . . 80
DEMOGRAPHICS . . . . . . . . . . . . . . . . . . . . . . . . . . . . . . . . . . . . . . . . . . . . . . 81
REGISTERING FOR ONLINE BANKING . . . . . . . . . . . . . . . . . . . . . . . . . . . . 81
ONLINE SERVICES . . . . . . . . . . . . . . . . . . . . . . . . . . . . . . . . . . . . . . . . . . . . . 82
ONLINE BILL PAYMENT . . . . . . . . . . . . . . . . . . . . . . . . . . . . . . . . . . . . . . . . 82
Automatic Bill Payment . . . . . . . . . . . . . . . . . . . . . . . . . . . . . . . . . . . . . . 83
Electronic Bills . . . . . . . . . . . . . . . . . . . . . . . . . . . . . . . . . . . . . . . . . . . . . . 83
MAINTAINING PRIVACY AND SECURITY . . . . . . . . . . . . . . . . . . . . . . . . . . 83
Securing Online Transactions . . . . . . . . . . . . . . . . . . . . . . . . . . . . . . . . . 84
Secure Browsers and Encryption Technology . . . . . . . . . . . . . . . . . . 84
Emptying the Cache . . . . . . . . . . . . . . . . . . . . . . . . . . . . . . . . . . . . . . . . 84
Cookies . . . . . . . . . . . . . . . . . . . . . . . . . . . . . . . . . . . . . . . . . . . . . . . . . . . 85
Javascript. . . . . . . . . . . . . . . . . . . . . . . . . . . . . . . . . . . . . . . . . . . . . . . . . . 85
Privacy Statements . . . . . . . . . . . . . . . . . . . . . . . . . . . . . . . . . . . . . . . . . . 86
The Gramm-Leach-Bliley Act (GLBA) . . . . . . . . . . . . . . . . . . . . . . . . . . 87
The Safeguards Rule. . . . . . . . . . . . . . . . . . . . . . . . . . . . . . . . . . . . . . . . 87
The Financial Services Modernization Act . . . . . . . . . . . . . . . . . . . . . . 88
SECURITY FAILURES AND IDENTITY THEFT . . . . . . . . . . . . . . . . . . . . . . . 89

# APPENDICES

APPENDIX 1: TWENTY-FIVE LARGEST BANKING COMPANIES RANKED BY CONSOLIDATED COMPANY ASSETS . . . . . . . . . . . . . . . . . . . . . . 91

APPENDIX 2: APPLICABLE SECTIONS—UCC ARTICLE 3: NEGOTIABLE INSTRUMENTS . . . . . . . . . . . . . . . . . . . . . . . . . . . . . . . . . 93

APPENDIX 3: SAMPLE PROMISSORY NOTE . . . . . . . . . . . . . . . . . 99

APPENDIX 4: APPLICABLE SECTIONS—UCC ARTICLE 4: BANK DEPOSITS AND COLLECTIONS . . . . . . . . . . . . . . . . . . . . . . . . . . . . . . 101

APPENDIX 5: SAMPLE NOTICE OF DISHONOR . . . . . . . . . . . . . . 107

APPENDIX 6: SAMPLE STOP PAYMENT ORDER. . . . . . . . . . . . . . 109

APPENDIX 7: APPLICABLE SECTIONS—UCC ARTICLE 4A: FUNDS TRANSFERS . . . . . . . . . . . . . . . . . . . . . . . . . . . . . . . . . . 111

APPENDIX 8: ELECTRONIC FUNDS TRANSFER ACT . . . . . . . . . . . 117

APPENDIX 9: APPLICABLE SECTIONS—UCC ARTICLE 5: LETTERS OF CREDIT . . . . . . . . . . . . . . . . . . . . . . . . . . . . . . . . . . . . 137

APPENDIX 10: THE U.S.A. PATRIOT ACT (H.R.3162)—SELECTED PROVISIONS. . . . . . . . . . . . . . . . . . . . . . . . . . . . . . . . . . . 139

APPENDIX 11: SAMPLE JOINT SURVIVORSHIP ACCOUNT SIGNATURE CARD 149

APPENDIX 12: SAMPLE CORPORATE BANKING RESOLUTION . . . . . . . 151

APPENDIX 13: DIRECTORY OF STATE CONSUMER PROTECTION AGENCIES 155

APPENDIX 14: FAILED FINANCIAL INSTITUTIONS (October 2000—April 2004) . . . . . . . . . . . . . . . . . . . . . . . . . . . . . . . . . . 161

APPENDIX 15: FEDERAL DEPOSIT INSURANCE CORPORATION—REGIONAL OFFICES. . . . . . . . . . . . . . . . . . . . . . . . . . . . . . . . . . . . 163

APPENDIX 16: TOP 25 ONLINE BANKS . . . . . . . . . . . . . . . . . . 165

APPENDIX 17: PROJECTED NUMBER OF ONLINE BANKING HOUSEHOLDS (2004-2008). . . . . . . . . . . . . . . . . . . . . . . . . . . . . . . . . . 167

APPENDIX 18: PROJECTED NUMBER OF ONLINE BANKING HOUSEHOLDS (2004-2008). . . . . . . . . . . . . . . . . . . . . . . . . . . . . . . . . . 169

APPENDIX 19: THE SAFEGUARDS RULE . . . . . . . . . . . . . . . . . . 171

APPENDIX 20: STATE IDENTITY THEFT LEGISLATION. . . . . . . . . . . 175

GLOSSARY. . . . . . . . . . . . . . . . . . . . . . . . . . . . . . . . . . . . . 219

BIBLIOGRAPHY. . . . . . . . . . . . . . . . . . . . . . . . . . . . . . . . . . 237

# ABOUT THE AUTHOR

MARGARET C. JASPER is an attorney engaged in the general practice of law in South Salem, New York, concentrating in the areas of personal injury and entertainment law. Ms. Jasper holds a Juris Doctor degree from Pace University School of Law, White Plains, New York, is a member of the New York and Connecticut bars, and is certified to practice before the United States District Courts for the Southern and Eastern Districts of New York, the United States Court of Appeals for the Second Circuit, and the United States Supreme Court.

Ms. Jasper has been appointed to the panel of arbitrators of the American Arbitration Association and the law guardian panel for the Family Court of the State of New York, is a member of the Association of Trial Lawyers of America, and is a New York State licensed real estate broker and member of the Westchester County Board of Realtors, operating as Jasper Real Estate, in South Salem, New York. She maintains a website at http://www.JasperLawOffice.com.

Ms. Jasper is the author and general editor of the following legal almanacs: AIDS Law; The Americans with Disabilities Act; Animal Rights Law; The Law of Attachment and Garnishment; Bankruptcy Law for the Individual Debtor; Individual Bankruptcy and Restructuring; Banks and their Customers; Buying and Selling Your Home; The Law of Buying and Selling; The Law of Capital Punishment; The Law of Child Custody; Commercial Law; Consumer Rights Law; The Law of Contracts; Copyright Law; Credit Cards and the Law; The Law of Debt Collection; Dictionary of Selected Legal Terms; The Law of Dispute Resolution; The Law of Drunk Driving; DWI, DUI and the Law; Education Law; Elder Law; Employee Rights in the Workplace; Employment Discrimination Under Title VII; Environmental Law; Estate Planning; Everyday Legal Forms; Executors and Personal Representatives: Rights and Responsibilities; Harassment in the Workplace; Health Care and Your Rights. Home Mortgage Law Primer; Hospital Liability Law; Identity Theft and How To Protect Yourself; Insurance Law; The Law of Immigration; International Adoption; Juvenile Justice and Children's Law; Labor Law; Landlord-Tenant Law; The Law of Libel and Slander; Living Together: Practical Legal Issues; Marriage and Divorce; The Law of Medical Malpractice; Motor Vehicle Law; The Law of No-Fault Insurance; Nursing Home Negligence; The Law of Obscenity and Pornography; Patent Law; The Law of Personal Injury; Privacy and the Internet: Your Rights and Expectations Under the Law; Probate Law; The Law of Product Liability; Real Estate Law for the Homeowner and Broker; Religion and the Law; Retirement Planning; The Right to Die; Law for the Small Business Owner; Social Security Law; Special Education Law; The Law of Speech and the First Amendment; Teenagers and Substance Abuse; Trademark Law; Victim's Rights Law; The Law of Violence Against Women; Welfare: Your Rights and the Law; What if it Happened to You: Violent Crimes and Victims' Rights; What if the Product Doesn't Work: Warranties & Guarantees; Workers' Compensation Law; and Your Child's Legal Rights: An Overview.

# INTRODUCTION

The business of modern banking is very complex and encompasses a number of services and the performance of a number of functions. It affects and directs many aspects of the economy of a country. Prosperous industrial societies need money, banks and financial institutions, which collect money and deposits from all elements of society and invest those funds in loans, securities and various other productive assets. These activities promote production, savings, investment and industrial development.

There are many different types of banks which serve varied needs such as large and small commercial banks, thrift and home financing institutions, mutual savings banks, savings and loan associations, cooperative banks, building and loan associations, homestead associations and savings and loan companies.

The banking industry is highly regulated. Consequently, it is subject to both federal and state statutes which provide for the powers and functions of banking and other financial institutions. An overview of those regulations, including those provisions of the Uniform Commercial Code that govern banking transactions, is set forth in this almanac.

Although the law of banking is complex and varied, this legal almanac discusses the law of banking as it applies to its individual customers. Everyone at one time or another has contact with or develops a relationship with a bank, whether through a checking account, savings account, mortgage, car loan, business loan, investments, or other financial matters. The customer encounters many issues in its dealings with a bank, some complex and some simple. The basic banking functions of depositing money, withdrawing money and securing a loan are well known. This almanac seeks to expand the customer's basic knowledge of how the banking system works, and provide the consumer with information concerning their rights and liabilities.

This almanac also discusses the increasingly popular method of banking online. Online banking is relatively easy, even for the least computer savvy individual. Instead of standing on long lines, banking customers are now able to do most of their banking from home on their personal computer. For example, one can now view statements and transactions, open and close accounts, purchase investment products, apply for a mortgage, transfer funds among accounts, pay bills, and much more, right from their computer.

Although proper use of the internet for banking purposes is secure if used properly, one drawback is the risk to one's privacy and the problem of identity theft if the user is not careful. This almanac also presents an overview of identity theft and privacy issues, and provides valuable tips on how to protect one's personal information.

The Appendix provides sample documents, applicable statutes, and other pertinent information and data. The Glossary contains definitions of many of the terms used throughout the almanac.

# CHAPTER 1:
# OVERVIEW OF THE BANKING SYSTEM

## THE DEVELOPMENT OF MODERN BANKING

Banking is an ancient industry dating back to at least the 13th century. These early banking systems dealt primarily in coin and bullion and their main functions were to change money. The early merchant bankers dealt in both goods and bills of exchange, and handled international accounts in trade. Early bankers also accepted deposits of money and valuables for safekeeping or transfer, and recorded loans between parties.

In England, banking practices developed whereby a bank customer could arrange to transfer their funds to another party by providing the banker with an order to do so. This was the forerunner of the modern check. Banks began to permit customers to write such checks in amounts exceeding their account balance, which was known as "bank money" or "credit" thus "creating money." Today, such accounts are known as "overdraft accounts."

During the colonial era in America, the short supply of money consisted mostly of gold and silver coins. Banks were eventually formed in America for the sole purpose of printing paper money to lend against mortgages on land. Credit was granted by wealthier asset holders who could afford to lend to borrowers. Borrowers were those people considered capable of using credit responsibly and repaying their loans.

These "private" banks, however, were risky, subject to fluctuations in value and based only upon the strength of private fortunes. To achieve stronger, more reliable banking activity, national banks were created which were quasi-public corporations. The growth of these institutions helped the economy to flourish, but it became apparent that regulations were necessary to reduce the risk of financial panic.

## THE MODERN DAY BANK

A bank is an institution that deals in money and negotiable interests, and provides other financial services. Its business basically consists of borrowing and lending. Banks accept deposits and make loans. A bank derives its profit from the difference in the interest rates paid and charged to its customers. The principal types of banking in the modern industrial world are commercial banking and central banking.

A bank's main liabilities are its capital and deposits. The deposits may be domestic or foreign, and its customers include corporations, private individuals, other banks, and even governments. The deposits may be repayable on demand or after the lapse of a period of time.

A bank's assets include cash, liquid assets, investments or securities, loans and advances made to customers, and the bank's own property, including the real property, furniture, etc.

A table of the 25 largest banking companies ranked by consolidated company assets is set forth at Appendix 1.

### Commercial Banks

A commercial bank deals in money and negotiable instruments, such as checks or bills of exchange. The bank also provides a variety of other financial services. The basis of the banking business is to "borrow" money from its customers, i.e., receive "deposits." The commercial bank uses these "loans" and, combined with the bank's own capital, the commercial bank makes loans and invests in securities. However, a bank must always have available cash on hand in order to pay its depositors upon demand, or when the amounts credited to the depositor become due. The bank makes its profit by borrowing at one rate of interest and lending at a higher rate, and by charging commissions for its services.

The amount of credit a bank extends may considerably exceed the sums it has on hand in cash, thus "creating money." A bank is able to do this because of public trust that the bank will honor its obligations in connection with the negotiable instruments, e.g. checks, that it circulates. This is the essence of commercial deposit banking.

### Central Banks

Another type of banking is carried on by central banks, bankers to governments, and "lenders of last resort" to commercial banks and other financial institutions. They are often responsible for formulating and implementing monetary and credit policies, usually in cooperation with the government. In some cases—e.g., the U.S. Federal Reserve

System—central banks have been established specifically to lead or regulate the banking system.

### Financial Intermediaries

Some financial institutions, which are often also called banks, such as finance companies, savings banks, investment banks, trust companies, and home-loan banks, do not perform the commercial banking functions described above. These institutions are also referred to as "financial intermediaries."

The basic function of the financial intermediary is to take the savings collected from private individuals and distribute those funds to others in the form of loans for building purposes or for the purchase of capital assets. These financial institutions cannot, however, "create money" like commercial banks because they cannot lend any more than is on deposit with the bank.

## THE REGULATION OF BANKING

Banks and bank accounts are regulated by both state and federal statutory law. Bank accounts may be established by national and state chartered banks and savings associations. All are regulated by the law under which they were established.

### Federal Reserve System

In the United States, the Federal Reserve System has evolved as the major banking and regulatory entity which has great influence over bank reserves, monetary expansion and interest rates. The Federal Reserve System was established in 1913. This was the true beginning of a central national bank system coexisting with decentralized banking institutions. The Federal Reserve Board was established with members from the executive branch of the government. Federal Reserve District Banks were established in every region. All national banks were to become members and state banks could become members.

Member banks had to purchase stock which capitalized and funded the Reserve Banks. The Federal Reserve Banks carried on lending operations to member banks and established reserves against its deposits. Banks were also permitted to buy and sell government obligations. This new system provided financial security to the nation.

### Bank Powers

#### State Banks

A state bank derives its powers from the state law creating the bank and from the bank's charter. Banks have express powers granted to them and powers implied from, and incidental to, these express powers.

The express powers usually include the power to:

1. Deal in real estate for bank buildings and loans;

2. Contract with customers;

3. Borrow money;

4. Act as agents;

5. Deal in drafts and notes;

6. Receive and transmit funds;

7. Buy, sell and exchange funds; and

8. Provide foreign credit for customers.

State banks usually have limited powers to act as guarantors or to buy or sell stock for their accounts. Some implied powers are to buy insurance on a car purchased with money loaned by advancing more funds.

Under the Federal Reserve Regulations, the state banks may also:

1. Act as government depositories;

2. Discount member-indorsed notes or drafts;

3. Make advances to member banks on notes for short time periods;

4. Deal in gold, and U.S. bills and notes; and

5. Establish discounts with other member banks.

### National Banks

The banking powers of the national banks are derived from the National Bank Act and other federal statutes. National banks can borrow money if the purpose is to pay debts or further their banking business. The lending limit is regulatory and is geared to the size of the bank's capital and surplus.

National banks can also:

1. Engage in the collection of notes, checks, bills of exchange and other evidences of debt;

2. Discount, purchase and negotiate notes, drafts and bills of exchange;

3. Seek recovery against the makers for nonpayment;

4. Rescind a transaction in cases of fraud;

5. Perform activities which are calculated to secure business and good will, such as income tax preparation assistance;

6. Extend guarantees to a debtor's creditors to keep the debtor in business, take over the debtor's business and otherwise protect its investments if the bank is faced with losses through debtor default;

7. Offer specialized credit, health, life and accident insurance in connection with their loans;

8. Issue letters of credit for their customers;

9. Accept assignments of judgments;

10. Accept bequests of personal property;

11. Make charitable contributions and set up charitable foundations; and

12. Lend money for the purchase of real estate.

Banks generally cannot acquire real estate except in foreclosure situations or for their own banking buildings. In addition, the real estate loans made by banks are heavily regulated and must be secured by a mortgage or lien on the real estate.

### The Federal Deposit Insurance Corporation (FDIC)

In 1933, a new law was passed establishing the Federal Deposit Insurance Corporation (FDIC). The FDIC is an independent U.S. government corporation created under the authority of the Federal Reserve Act of 1933. It is managed by a board of three directors. Two directors are appointed for six-year terms by the President, and the third director is the Comptroller of the Currency.

The FDIC was established after the disastrous collapse of the banking system in early 1933 and after state plans to insure depositors in the past had not proved successful. The FDIC was formed to insure and protect bank deposits through deposit insurance in the event of a bank failure, and to regulate certain banking practices. The FDIC also rehabilitates banks in trouble, passes on merger proposals, acts as a receiver, regulates bank advertising and rules on interest rates.

If a depositor's insured bank fails, FDIC insurance will cover the depositor's accounts, dollar for dollar, including principal and any accrued interest, up to the insurance limit. Since the start of the FDIC in 1933, no depositor has ever lost a penny of insured deposits. Historically, insured funds are available to depositors within just a few days after the closing of an insured bank.

The FDIC maintains its insurance fund by assessments on insured banks and from investments. Insured banks are assessed on the basis of their average deposits. All FDIC insured banks must meet high standards for financial strength and stability. The FDIC, along with other federal and state regulatory agencies, regularly reviews the operations of all insured banks to ensure these high standards are met.

The FDIC insures deposit accounts such as checking, NOW and savings accounts, money market deposit accounts, and certificates of deposit (CDs). FDIC insurance is discussed more fully in Chapter 9 of this almanac.

## DUTIES, POWERS AND LIABILITIES OF BANK DIRECTORS AND OFFICERS

The Board of Directors of a bank establishes policy, approves major transactions and supervises bank officers who operate the bank on a day to day basis. Directors owe the bank a fiduciary duty. Duties and liabilities are regulated by statute, common law rules, the bylaws and charters of the bank and generally accepted business practices. Bank directors have a duty to act with diligence, skill, and care as prudent persons in safeguarding the bank's and depositors' money and property, in complying with state and federal banking statutes and ensuring that the bank officers run the bank properly.

A bank director may be held liable for his breach of care and gross negligence if his actions or inactions cause a loss to the bank. They are not liable for good faith errors in judgment, but are liable for negligent failure to investigate borrowers who default. Directors and officers must also scrupulously avoid conflicts of interest with the bank such as competing with the bank and profiting from inside information or opportunities arising as a result of their position.

The president of the bank is usually the chief executive officer with power to bind the bank in ordinary, usual bank business. The vice president has limited powers of authority and derives these powers by express authorization from the president and the board of directors. The cashier of the bank usually has power over funds and securities of the bank, the books, payments, receipts and deposits. Any officer actually engaged in conducting the bank's business binds the bank. If an officer exceeds his authority, the bank may also be bound if another officer or director ratifies or accepts the act.

A bank is liable for the wrongs committed by its officers acting within the apparent scope of their authority. Officers and directors are primarily liable for their own wrongdoings such as accepting gifts or bribes for use of their influence, for making false reports regarding the status of the bank, for making illegal loans and for receiving deposits after a bank is insolvent.

## BANKING UNDER THE UNIFORM COMMERCIAL CODE (UCC)

The Uniform Commercial Code (UCC) refers to the set of laws drafted by the National Conference of Commissioners on Uniform State Laws (NCCUSL), in an attempt to promote certainty and predictability in the area of commercial law in order to facilitate commercial transactions. It was intended that such a comprehensive law would reduce the number of legal disputes arising out of commercial matters. Additions or revisions to the UCC are proposed by the NCCUSL and the American Law Institute (ALI).

The UCC is the primary source of commercial law in the United States. The NCCUSL recognized that it would be particularly advantageous if the UCC were uniformly adopted by all of the states with little or no revision or amendment. Although all of the states have adopted some form of the UCC, they have included a number of jurisdictional amendments.

The UCC has not been enacted as federal law; however, it is the governing law in the District of Columbia. The UCC provisions become the governing law in those jurisdictions which adopt its provisions, in whole or in part. However, where there is a federal law which conflicts with a UCC provision, the federal law will prevail over the UCC.

This legal almanac explores the UCC as it applies to banking law, and highlights general principles and important provisions. The UCC articles which primarily concern banks include the following:

1. Article 3: Negotiable Instruments—Article 3 is discussed more fully in Chapter 2 of this almanac.

2. Article 4: Bank Deposits and Collections—Article 4 is discussed more fully in Chapter 3 of this almanac.

3. Article 4A. Funds Transfers—Article 4A is discussed more fully in Chapter 4 of this almanac.

4. Article 5: Letters of Credit—Article 5 is discussed more fully in Chapter 5 of this almanac.

# CHAPTER 2:
# UCC ARTICLE 3: NEGOTIABLE INSTRUMENTS

## IN GENERAL

Negotiable instruments are mainly governed by state statutory law. Every state has adopted Article 3 of the Uniform Commercial Code (UCC), with some modifications, as their law governing negotiable instruments. Article 3 governs the relationship between parties who receive and transfer negotiable instruments, such as checks, drafts, notes, and certificates of deposit. Under the UCC, a negotiable instrument is generally defined as an unconditional promise or order to pay a fixed amount of money. To be considered negotiable, an instrument must meet the requirements stated in UCC Article 3.

Negotiable instruments do not include money, payment orders governed by UCC Article 4A, or investment securities governed by UCC Article 8. Secured transactions may also contain negotiable instruments; however, they are primarily covered under UCC Article 9. If there is a conflict between the UCC Articles, both Article 4 and 9 govern over Article 3. Checks are negotiable instruments but are mainly covered by Article 4 of the UCC. However, the United Nations Convention on International Bills of Exchange and International Promissory Notes would preempt Article 3 in the case of international transactions if the United States were to join the Convention.

Applicable provisions of UCC Article 3 are set forth at Appendix 2.

## TYPES OF NEGOTIABLE INSTRUMENTS

Negotiable instruments—also referred to as "commercial paper"—are widely used in today's society to serve as meaningful substitutes for money. There are a variety of negotiable instruments that serve this purpose, including bank checks, promissory notes, drafts, and certificates of deposit. Some of these are familiar and used often, while the others are used less frequently. This almanac is concerned primarily with bank checks, although the other types of negotiable instruments are also discussed.

### Bank Check

The bank check is the most familiar type of negotiable instrument. A check is commonly used in business transactions to pay for goods, and serves as a substitute for cash payments. A check may be safely sent through the mail between the parties whereas cash, unless sent by a registered and insured method, would be risky.

In any checking transaction, the customer typically deals with three parties: the drawer, drawee, and payee. Thus, a check is sometimes called a three-party instrument. For example, when paying a credit card bill with a check, the customer makes the check payable to the creditor. The customer who makes out and signs the check is known as the "drawer" of the check. The party to whom the "order to pay" money is given is the drawee—i.e., the bank where the checking account and funds are located. The party to whom payment is to be made is known as the "payee"—in this case, the creditor. There are different types of bank checks depending on the type of bank account the customer maintains, and the nature and capacity of the drawer.

### Personal Check

A personal check is the type of check drawn by an individual customer upon a bank in which the customer maintains an account. The personal check is commonly used for payment of debts.

### Corporate Check

A corporate check is a check having a corporation as the drawer. The president or other officers of the corporation who are so authorized by the corporate bylaws and resolutions may draw a check on behalf of the corporation. This check is drawn on corporate funds.

### Cashier Check

A cashier check is a check issued by a bank and drawn on itself. The bank is both the drawer and drawee of the check. They are also referred to as official checks, treasurer's checks and banker's checks.

### Travelers Check

Travelers checks are offered customers who intend to travel as an alternative to the risk of carrying cash. They are preferable to personal checks which may not be accepted, particularly when traveling overseas. Travelers checks are issued by well-known banks and agencies.

They are drawn as checks on the issuing bank or upon the issuing company, such as American Express.

The travelers checks are not activated until they are fully executed or signed. At the time of purchase, the customer pays money to the issuing bank or company. The travelers check itself is evidence that sufficient money has been paid. The checks are signed at the time of issue by the purchaser for identification and for later comparison to a countersignature. Execution is fully completed when the purchaser signs the instrument again before the payee—e.g., the merchant. The payee can then certify this signature by comparing it to the first signature. If both signatures match, the payee will accept the check.

The best feature of travelers checks is that if they are lost or stolen, the issuing bank or company has expedited procedures for replacing these checks. If the checks are lost or stolen and are either signed or unsigned, the issuer has an obligation to pay on those checks to someone who has received the traveler's check in good faith.

### Personal Money Order

A personal money order is a payment instrument issued by a bank, in a specified sum of money, for which the bank charges a small commission. The money order is a printed form that is an unconditional order to the bank to pay a specified sum of money to the order of a payee to be named. The amount of the money order is filled in by the bank. However, the money order is not activated until the purchaser fills in the name of the payee and signs the instrument as the drawer.

### Bank Money Order/Teller Check

Bank money orders or teller checks are signed by an officer of the bank. They are sold to the public as payment instruments and are activated when the purchaser completes the instrument by inserting the name of a payee. A bank money order or teller's check is payable on demand and is always drawn on a bank.

### Drafts and Notes

Drafts and notes are two types of negotiable instruments that are commonly used in business transactions to finance the movement of goods and to secure and distribute loans.

### Drafts

A draft is a type of negotiable instrument that orders a payment to be made. A draft is very similar to a check. It is also a three-party instrument that contains an unconditional order to pay. Both checks and drafts are order instruments since they contain an order or direction by the drawer to the drawee to pay the payee.

Both checks and drafts serve as payment devices and are used as a substitute for money. However, drafts commonly have the payee and the drawer as the same entity. This is because a draft is frequently used as a payment device for the sale of goods. For example, in exchange for goods sold, the buyer and seller may agree that the seller prepare a draft payable to the seller's order for the amount of the goods. The draft is drawn on the buyer who must pay for it when it is presented to him by the seller.

As stated above, a draft involves three parties, and is also known as three-party paper. The drawer is the person who signs the draft, or is otherwise identified in the draft as the person ordering payment to be made. The drawee is the person who is ordered by the drawer to make the payment. The payee is the person who is entitled to payment of the amount set forth in the draft, which is payable either on demand or at some definite time. The drawer of the draft is liable to make good on the draft if it is dishonored by the drawee when presented for payment by the payee.

Drafts are either sight drafts or time drafts. Sight drafts are payable on demand. A time draft is a draft payable at a fixed future date.

### Notes

A note is a type of negotiable instrument that "promises" that a payment will be made—known as a promissory note. As discussed below, a certificate of deposit (CD) is a type of note. A note involves two parties, and is also known as two-party paper. The note is issued by a maker, which unconditionally promises to pay to the order of the payee, a fixed amount of money, which is payable either on demand or at some definite time.

A sample promissory note is set forth at Appendix 3.

A distinction is drawn between a draft and a note in that a draft "orders" payment to be made, and a note "promises" that payment will be made. Promissory notes are either payable to "bearer"—i.e., anyone who has possession of the note—or payable to the order of a particular payee—i.e., order paper.

The principal function of a promissory note is to serve as a credit device—a means of borrowing money to be repaid in the future.

*Example: Buyer wishes to purchase a washing machine. However, due to limited funds, Buyer would like to make monthly installment payments on the appliance. For that purpose, Buyer may sign a promissory note, promising to make the monthly payments.*

### Certificate of Deposit

A certificate of deposit is a type of note issued by a bank which acknowledges that a sum of money has been received by the bank, and promises to repay that money at some definite time. The payee generally has the option of taking the sum of money at that time, or of rolling over the money—i.e., keeping the money on deposit with the bank for another fixed period of time. Fees may be assessed by the bank if the payee withdraws funds from a certificate of deposit prior to its maturity date.

A certificate of deposit is a two-party instrument. A CD, like a note, is an agreement between two parties for the payment of money. It is a written receipt by a bank for a special deposit of money and the bank's promise to repay it with interest on a specified date to a designated person or to bearer. A CD can be either negotiable or nonnegotiable. Generally, certificates for sums in excess of $100,000 are issued in negotiable form. Other CD's omit the words of negotiability and require the bank's consent for further transfer or negotiation.

## NEGOTIABILITY

To be considered "negotiable" an instrument must meet the requirements stated in Article 3 so that the holder of the instrument has a greater likelihood of being paid. This promotes the purpose of negotiable instruments as meaningful substitutes for money. In order for commercial paper to be negotiable, the following requirements must be met:

### Written Form

The instrument must be in written form and moveable. Thus, an oral agreement cannot be negotiated. The instrument need not be written on paper.

### Signed by Maker

The instrument must be signed by either the maker of the note or the drawer of the draft. The signature can be an "X" or any mark or a stamped signature so long as that mark is intended by the drawer to operate as his signature. The signature can be at the lower right hand corner of the instrument or in the body of the instrument.

### Unconditional Promise or Order to Pay

The instrument must contain an unconditional promise or order to pay. The language of a note must specify the "promise to pay" not just an acknowledgment of a debt.

*Example: The words "I promise to pay" are sufficient. However, the words "I owe you $100.00" are not a promise to pay and therefore destroy the negotiability of the instrument.*

The language contained in a draft or check must contain a specific "order to pay" given by the drawer to the drawee to pay the instrument when presented by the holder. It cannot be a mere request.

*Example: The words "pay to the order of," as on a check, are sufficient. However, the words "I wish you would pay" are merely a request and therefore an instrument with these words is not negotiable.*

The unconditional portion of this requirement means that the promise or order cannot be contingent on the terms of another agreement, transaction or event.

*Example: A note which states "I promise to pay Mary $50.00 on her graduation day" is nonnegotiable since the promise is conditioned on an event which may never take place.*

### Sum Certain

The instrument must be payable in a sum certain of money that can be calculated from the face of the instrument. Thus, if an instrument is payable in gold or beads, it is nonnegotiable.

### Payable Upon Demand or Definite Date

The instrument must be payable upon demand or at some future definite date. If a holder cannot determine from the face of an instrument when payment is due, then the instrument is nonnegotiable. A demand instrument is payable at any time if it states that it is payable on demand, payable at sight or it does not state a time for payment.

An instrument may also be payable at some future definite date. If the date for payment can be determined exactly from the face of the instrument, then the instrument is negotiable. However, if the date is dependent upon a future act or event, such as a wedding, then the instrument is nonnegotiable.

### Payable to Order or to Bearer

The instrument must be payable to the order of an entity or person, or it must be payable to the bearer or holder of the instrument. An order instrument must specifically identify the person or entity to be paid. A bearer instrument does not designate a specific payee and is payable to anyone who holds it.

## ADDITIONS AND OMISSIONS

As previously discussed, an instrument must meet certain legal requirements in order to be negotiable. Some instruments may contain additional terms or language, or may omit certain items. These factors must be assessed to determine the impact on the instrument's negotiability or on the rights and responsibilities of the parties to the instrument.

### Additional Terms or Language

A note is still negotiable even if it contains the following "additional" terms or language:

1. A default provision—e.g., a provision which states that the property securing the note may be sold if the maker fails to pay the note.

2. A protection of collateral provision—e.g., a provision which states that the maker promises to protect the property that secures the payment of the note.

3. An undated instrument. An undated instrument is considered dated as of the time it is issued. However, a postdated or antedated instrument is still negotiable.

4. The place where the instrument is drawn and/or where the instrument is payable—e.g., the drawer's name and address on a check, or the bank's name and address on the lower left portion of the check.

5. A reference to another writing—e.g. a mortgage or other security instrument referring to collateral.

6. A statement that the instrument is given in full satisfaction of a debt. This commonly is used in the endorsement of a check.

*Example: If A supplies services to B for a price of $100, but B believes the value of the services is only $50, B can write on the back of the check the words "By endorsing this check, A acknowledges full payment." This language does not destroy the negotiability of the check. A, however, has the right to write the words "under protest" and then endorse his name. This preserves A's right to pursue B for the additional $50.*

### Omissions

Certain missing terms may be completed or filled in by the holder of the instrument but only in keeping with the authority given to him by the drawer.

*Example: If a drawer is buying some lumber and forgets to fill in the lumber store as the payee, the store has the authority to name itself as payee.*

### Payee Name(s)

If an instrument is payable to two or more persons whose names are joined by the word "and," then the instrument is only payable to all of them and all the payees must endorse it before it can be negotiated. If the payees' names are separated by the word "or," then the instrument is payable to any one of them and only one person need endorse it before it can be negotiated.

If the payees' names are joined and separated by the words "and/or," then the instrument may be endorsed by any or all of them. If the names are not separated by any words or symbols, then the instrument is considered payable only to all of the payees.

If the payee is a corporation or describes a payee as holding an instrument for the benefit of a corporation, then the check is payable only to the corporation. Most banks will not cash a check payable to a corporation, but will only accept the check for deposit to the corporation's account.

### Discrepancies and Ambiguities

If an instrument contains a discrepancy between the written words of amount and the printed figures, the written words control unless the words are ambiguous.

*Example: If a check bears the figures "$1000.00" but the words are written "one hundred dollars and no/100," the check is for $100.00. However, if a check bears the figures "$842.00" but the words are written "eighty four-two and no/100," the check is for $842.00, since the words are ambiguous.*

If an instrument contains handwritten, typewritten and/or printed terms and there are discrepancies, the rules state that handwritten terms control both typewritten and printed terms and typewritten terms control printed terms.

## TRANSFERRING COMMERCIAL PAPER

There are two ways to transfer interests in commercial paper: (1) Assignment; and (2) Negotiation.

### Assignment

Assignment applies to non-negotiable instruments such as contracts. Assignment means that the owner of the instrument transfers all his right, title and interest in and to the instrument to the purchaser—nothing more. This transfer is accomplished through the use of words of assignment such as "I hereby assign, sell and grant."

### Negotiation

Another method used to transfer interests in commercial paper is by negotiation. Proper negotiation of a negotiable instrument can give the transferee a higher level of enforceability. Negotiation is effected by (1) delivery of the instrument to another, accompanied by (2) the transferor's endorsement such that the transferee becomes a holder. Both steps are necessary.

### Bearer Instrument

A bearer instrument is one that does not name a specific payee. The bearer is the holder of the instrument. All that is necessary for negotiation of bearer paper is to transfer physical possession of it to another holder. Since there is no specific payee, there is no requirement for an endorsement.

### Order Instrument

An order instrument, on the contrary, needs all the necessary endorsements plus transfer of physical possession in order to effect a proper negotiation.

## ENDORSEMENTS

An endorsement is a signature which is made on an instrument by the endorser. An endorsement is made in order to (1) negotiate—i.e., transfer—the instrument; (2) place a restriction on the payment of the instrument; or (3) incur endorser's liability on the instrument. Words may accompany the endorsement.

An endorsement transfers title to an order instrument merely by the holder signing his name on the instrument and delivering it to another party—i.e., the endorsee. Additionally, an endorsement carries the promise that, subject to certain conditions, the endorser will pay the amount of the instrument if the maker of the note or the drawer of the check or draft previously dishonored payment. By the process of endorsement, order instruments may become bearer instruments and vice versa.

The signature of a person as maker, drawer or acceptor of the instrument is not an endorsement. In addition, a signature would not be considered an endorsement if the accompanying words, terms of the instrument, or place of signature, etc., clearly indicate that the signature was made for a purpose other than endorsement.

### Instrument Payable to Bearer or Order

If an instrument is payable "to the bearer," it can be negotiated merely by transferring possession of the instrument. If an instrument is payable "to the order of [an identified person]," it cannot be negotiated by transfer of possession without the indorsement of that person.

An instrument is "payable to bearer" if:

1. The instrument states that it is "payable to bearer," or "payable to the order of bearer," or otherwise indicates that the person in possession is entitled to payment, and does not state an identified person as payee; or

2. The instrument states that it is "payable to cash," or "payable to the order of cash," or otherwise indicates that it is not payable to an identified person.

An instrument "payable to bearer" may become payable to an identified person if it is "specially" endorsed. As further discussed below, a special endorsement is one which identifies a person to whom the holder makes the instrument payable. Once specially endorsed, the instrument becomes payable to the identified person, and the instrument may be negotiated only by the endorsement of that person.

If the instrument is not "payable to the bearer," then it would be "payable to order." An instrument is "payable to order" if it names an identified person—e.g. "Payable to the order of John Doe." However, if the instrument is "payable to John Doe and bearer," it will be considered "payable to bearer."

An instrument payable to an identified person may become payable to bearer if it is endorsed "in blank." As set forth below, a blank endorsement, unlike a special endorsement, does not identify a specific person to whom the instrument is payable. Thus, the instrument then becomes payable to the bearer and may be negotiated by transfer of possession alone.

### Types of Endorsements

There are four types of endorsements—special, blank, qualified and restrictive.

### Special Endorsement

A special endorsement is one that names a particular person or entity—the endorsee—to whom, or to whose order the instrument must be paid or transferred. Negotiable instruments with special endorsements can be further negotiated only by the endorsement of the named endorsee. This type of endorsement provides protection in case the instrument is lost or stolen, since a finder or a thief cannot get any legitimate rights to the instrument.

An endorsement need not contain the words "Pay to the order of" although it is a good practice to use those words, especially if you are the payee and are depositing the check in your bank. Use of the words "for deposit only" are also recommended as further protection.

### Blank Endorsement

A blank endorsement is the equivalent of having bearer paper since it specifies no particular endorsee and may consist of a signature alone. A negotiable instrument endorsed in blank is payable to any bearer and may be negotiated by delivery alone. A finder or a thief of an instrument endorsed in blank may become a legitimate owner. The note can be properly negotiated to any number of people without any further endorsements being required.

### Qualified Endorsement

A qualified endorsement is relatively rare. It occurs when one party wants to specify the types of guarantees he is making on an instrument. A qualified instrument potentially limits or disclaims liability if the instrument is dishonored. The most common type is "without recourse" which disclaims particular types of liability. The endorser is saying that he will assume no responsibility to pay the instrument if the maker or drawer of the note will not pay. Without this qualified endorsement, if the maker does not pay, then the endorser must pay.

### Restrictive Endorsement

A restrictive endorsement is used to restrict payment. Types of restrictive endorsements include the following:

1. A conditional endorsement wherein a condition is placed on the endorsement is a restrictive endorsement.

*Example: "Pay to Mr. X when he paints my house." The note is not payable unless the conditions are met.*

2. If the endorsement attempts to restrict or prohibit any further transfer of the instrument, it is a restrictive endorsement.

*Example: "Pay to Mr. X with no further transfer."*

3. "For collection only," "For deposit only," and "Pay any bank" are all restrictive endorsements.

4. An endorsement stating that it is for the benefit of or in trust for a particular person is a restrictive endorsement.

If an instrument is made payable to a person under a misspelled name or a wrong name, the payee may endorse it in the misspelled or wrong name, in his proper name or in both the wrong and proper names.

## LIABILITY OF PARTIES ON AN INSTRUMENT

Liability on an instrument is predicated on the fact that the person's signature or an authorized signature appears on the instrument, e.g., a person may designate an agent as an authorized signatory.

There are two types of liability which may arise: (1) contract liability; and (2) warranty liability.

### Contract liability

Each party to a negotiable instrument assumes contractual liability to pay it to the holder. The extent of this liability depends on what capacity the person signed the instrument. Makers and acceptors are primarily responsible for the payment of an instrument. A holder must look first to those with primary liability. In contrast, drawers and endorsers are secondarily responsible for the payment of an instrument. A drawer and endorser are only liable after they receive timely notice that the primary party has refused to pay the instrument upon presentment—i.e., dishonored payment.

### Primary Liability

#### Liability of Makers

The maker of a note has an absolute obligation to pay the note after it becomes due, even if no demand for payment is made or the due date comes and goes.

#### Liability of Acceptors

Even though a drawer writes a check or draft, a drawer is not automatically responsible to pay. A drawer does not become obligated to pay a holder until the drawer has "accepted" the instrument. A drawee's acceptance constitutes his primary liability for payment of the draft.

When a bank is the drawee, its act of accepting a check in writing is called certification. A certified check bears an agreement signed by the drawer bank that the check will be honored when presented for payment. Only the drawer or holder can have a check certified. Certification must be written on the check and may consist of a signature alone, but usually has the word "certified" on it. By certifying a check, the bank agrees to pay the check as presented and becomes directly liable on the check.

Checks are frequently certified when a person is purchasing a home or a car. Although a drawer agrees to pay a check upon its dishonor, he and all prior endorsers are discharged if the drawee bank certifies the check at a holder's request. If the drawer requests the certification, he remains liable. An endorser is liable if he actually endorses after the check is certified.

### Secondary Liability

### Liability of Drawers and Endorsees

A drawer and an endorser are secondarily liable to pay a negotiable instrument unless they have expressly denied or disclaimed this responsibility. For example, a restrictive endorsement, "without recourse," relieves the endorser from secondary liability. Endorsers are also liable to any subsequent endorsers in the order in which they sign.

This secondary liability is only valid if the primary party is (i) asked to pay—i.e., presentment; and then (ii) refuses to pay—i.e., dishonor, and the drawer/endorser is given timely notice of that dishonor.

Presentment and notice of dishonor must be timely. The UCC states that if a holder, without excuse, fails to present on time, then all endorsers are discharged from liability. Drawers, on the other hand, are only released from liability if the drawee—i.e, the bank—becomes insolvent. Use of words such as "payment guaranteed" means that if the instrument is not paid when due, the signer agrees to pay it.

### Presentment

Presentment is a demand by the holder for payment or acceptance of a negotiable instrument upon the maker of a note or the drawee of a check. Obviously, if you are the holder of a negotiable instrument, you will have to make demand on it eventually. If it is demand paper, you can make demand at any reasonable time after you become the holder. If the paper is time paper, you can make demand on or after its due date. Presentment is not necessary for the person who is primarily liable.

Presentment may be in person, by mail or through a clearinghouse. If a presentment is made in person, that person has until the close of business that day to pay or dishonor. If a check is presented through the bank collection process, the bank has until midnight of the next business day to pay or dishonor.

### Dishonor

Dishonor means that the payer refuses to pay the instrument after proper presentment. If an instrument has been dishonored, then it is critical that you put all other parties—i.e., endorsers—on notice, or else they will not be liable. Notice of dishonor must be reasonable—e.g., oral or written, although written is the safest—and it must identify the instrument and state that it has been dishonored.

If a bank dishonors a check it has until midnight of the banking day immediately following the banking day the item was received to give notice of dishonor. This is known as the "midnight deadline." Individuals must give notice of dishonor before midnight of the third business day after they dishonor.

### Exceptions

As with most other rules, there are exceptions to this requirement. Presentment and dishonor may be waived by specific written words to that effect, e.g., a notation that "Presentment for Payment and Notice of Dishonor are Waived."

Similarly, if a party who is primarily liable is deceased or insolvent, then presentment is excused because it would be a wasted effort. Presentment is also excused when payment has been refused before presentment is required—e.g., a "stop payment order." However, notice of dishonor in both circumstances is still required to hold the secondary parties liable to pay.

Presentment and notice of dishonor are both excused if the holder's failure to act is beyond his control such as a mail delay, war, communications breakdown, etc.

### Protest

Although a formal statement of dishonor is not required, a holder may "protest" a check. A protest is a formal notice of dishonor which is (i) written; (ii) notarized; and (iii) identifies the negotiable instrument, the holder, and the fact that presentment was either made, excused or waived, and that it was dishonored for nonpayment. The protest can then be sent to all potentially liable parties to put them on notice of the dishonor.

### Warranty Liability

In contrast to contractual liabilities to pay as discussed above, only endorsers and others transferors have warranty liability on an instrument. A warranty is not a promise to pay the instrument but rather an implied promise made by each transferor to subsequent holders, and to the payor, that certain statements of fact about the instrument are true. When a warranty is breached, the transferor is liable to the holder for the amount the transferor paid for the instrument.

If there occurs a breach of warranty, the transferee is entitled to recover damages from the warrantor in an amount equal to the loss suffered as a result of the breach, however, recovery is limited to the amount of the instrument plus expenses and loss of interest.

Presentment warranties run with the instrument and are only in favor of the payor—i.e., the maker or drawee. The transferor warrants that he has good title to the instrument, that he has no knowledge that the signature of the maker or drawer is authorized, and that the instrument has not been materially altered.

Transfer warranties, on the other hand, are only given to the immediate transferee and, if he is also an endorser, to all subsequent holders. A person who transfers an instrument for consideration warrants to the transferee that (i) the warrantor is entitled to enforce the instrument; (ii) the signature is authentic and authorized; (iii) the instrument has not been altered; (iv) the instrument is not subject to a defense or claim in recoupment against the warrantor; and (v) the warrantor has no knowledge of any insolvency proceedings affecting the instrument.

A drawee bank cannot charge its customer's account for a check which has been forged. Normally, a person's unauthorized signature on an instrument, either by forgery or by an agent that has exceeded his authority, does not subject that person to liability. There are, however, three exceptions to this general rule:

1. When the unauthorized signature is adopted or ratified by the real person;

2. When the drawer is tricked into issuing an instrument with a fictitious payee or by an impostor; or

3. When a person's own negligence causes the unauthorized signature.

## DISCHARGE FROM LIABILITY

Discharge simply means that a person no longer has a legal obligation to pay an instrument. Discharge is a defense against a claim that payment is due and may either be a personal defense which is not effective against a holder in due course or a real defense.

If a party who is primarily liable pays an instrument, all other parties are discharged and he has no right to seek reimbursement from anyone else. In contrast, if a party who is secondarily liable pays, then he may obtain reimbursement from the primary party or from any other party who endorsed before him.

There are nine events that lead to a party's discharge of liability on an instrument:

1. When the holder is paid in full.

2. When the holder refuses an offer or tender of money to pay the instrument.

3. When the holder either cancels the instrument or when he, in writing, gives up his right to receive payment—i.e., cancellation and renunciation.

4. When the holder releases a party from liability without the consent of another party which impairs that party's right against the released party or when the holder impairs the security or collateral.

5. When a party who previously held an instrument takes it back from the current holder—i.e., acquisition.

6. When the instrument has been materially altered by fraud.

7. When there is an unexcused delay in presentment or notice of dishonor.

8. When a drawee certifies a check.

9. When a drawee agrees to pay a draft in a different amount from that written on the instrument.

### Discharge by Payment

If payment is made by or on behalf of a party obligated to pay on an instrument, to a person entitled to enforce the instrument, the instrument is deemed paid and the party is discharged. This is so even if payment is made with the knowledge of a claim to the instrument by another person.

Nevertheless, a party's obligation to pay on an instrument is not discharged if a claim to the instrument is enforceable against the party receiving the payment, and (i) payment is made with the payor's knowledge that payment is prohibited pursuant to injunction or other court order; or (ii) except for a cashier check, teller check or certified check, the person holding the claim indemnifies the payor against loss resulting from the payor's refusal to pay the person entitled to enforce the instrument; or (iii) the payor knows the instrument is stolen and makes the payment to the person seeking payment knowing he is in wrongful possession of the instrument.

### Discharge by Cancellation

A person who is entitled to enforce an instrument may discharge the obligation of a party to pay on the instrument by (i) an intentional voluntary act, such as surrendering the instrument to that party, or destroying, mutilating or otherwise canceling the instrument; or (ii) by agreeing not to sue or otherwise giving up his rights in a signed writing.

## HOLDER IN DUE COURSE

A holder in due course is a purchaser who takes title to an instrument, free of any defects or claims, and may acquire greater rights than the party who transferred those rights. This person is also known as a good faith purchaser. Since the purpose of a negotiable instrument is to serve as a meaningful substitute for money with free circulation in the marketplace, commercial paper can give the holder or bearer greater enforcement rights than a mere assignee under a contract.

Nevertheless, in order to have the rights of a holder in due course, the instrument must have appeared authentic when issued or negotiated to the holder, e.g. not forged or altered, and the holder must have paid value for the instrument in good faith without knowledge of any claims or defects in title, or that the instrument was dishonored.

*Example: Seller contracts with Buyer for goods to be shipped. Buyer pays Seller for the goods by check. Seller endorses the check to Seller's Bank. In the meantime, Buyer receives the goods but rejects them due to defects. Buyer then stops payment on the check with his bank—the "drawee bank." When Seller's Bank presents the check to the drawee bank for payment, the check is dishonored. When Seller's Bank notifies Buyer that the check was dishonored, Buyer claims that the goods were defective, thus, there was no consideration given for the payment. Buyer claims lack of consideration as a defense against both the Seller and the Bank.*

### Suspension of the Rule of Derivative Title

Ordinarily, the rule of derivative title, which is applicable in most areas of the law, does not allow a property owner to transfer rights in a piece of property greater than his own. When ordinary contracts are transferred, the person receiving the instrument—the assignee—steps into the shoes of the person transferring the contract—the assignor. The assignee only receives the same rights to payment as the assignor—no greater rights.

However, if an instrument is negotiable, this rule is suspended and the holder in due course—who does not have any knowledge of a defect in the title or claims against it—takes title to the instrument free of any defects or claims.

In relation to the suspension of the rule of derivative title, Article 3 provides for warranties to protect the parties in transactions involving negotiable instruments. The law insulates the holder against another person's claim that he is the owner of the instrument and against any claims which would deny the holder his right to be paid.

The following example clearly illustrates the difference between an assignee and a holder in due course:

*Example: Assume X agrees to paint Y's house for $1000. If X fails to paint the house, then Y does not have to pay. If X has assigned his right to payment from Y to Z, then Y still does not have to pay Z and Z cannot demand payment from Y because Y has a valid defense—i.e., his house was not painted—against both X and Z.*

However, the rules change with a holder in due course.

*Example: Assume Y signs a promissory note payable to the order of X for the $1000. If X negotiates this note to Z for reasonable value, then even if X does not paint Y's house, Y must still pay Z because Z is a holder in due course, and Y's personal defense is not applicable against Z.*

The requirements to be a holder in due course are:

1. You must give value—i.e. money;

2. You must take the instrument in good faith; and

3. You must take the instrument without knowing or being on notice that it is overdue or has been dishonored—e.g., that a stop payment has been ordered—or that anyone has a claim or defense against payments—e.g., that the check has obviously been altered.

### The Shelter Doctrine

Another way to obtain holder in due course status even if you cannot meet all the requirements for a holder in due course is through the "shelter doctrine." The shelter doctrine provides that a person who receives an instrument from a holder in due course, either by gift or purchase, automatically becomes a holder in due course.

Provided that one person on an instrument qualifies under all the rules as a holder in due course, the person who obtains the instrument after him acquires the status of a holder in due course.

The shelter doctrine has two exceptions:

1. If a transferee has himself been a party to a fraud or illegality affecting the instrument, then he cannot become a holder in due course; and

2. If a transferee was a prior holder of an instrument and had notice of a defense against that instrument, then he cannot re-acquire that instrument and improve his condition.

### Defenses

In most instances, a holder in due course will get paid and has a claim of title which is free from all claims of ownership by other people. Certain defenses or a party's assertion of his right to deny his obligation to pay can be raised against the holder of a note.

There are two types of defenses: (1) personal defenses; and (2) real defenses. Personal defenses are not effective against a holder in due course, but real defenses are effective against a holder in due course and will prevent him from getting paid.

#### Personal Defenses

Personal defenses do not deny the existence of a contract but state that because of some circumstance, the contract is unenforceable. The personal defenses include:

1. Failure of or failure to pay consideration;

2. Breach of contract;

3. Breach of warranty—e.g., failure of goods sold to be of reasonable quality;

4. Fraud in the inducement—e.g., a salesman's misrepresentation;

5. Payment of the note—i.e. payment has been already made even though note has not been marked "paid";

6. Failure to deliver the instrument;

7. Theft;

8. Restrictive endorsements.

#### Real Defenses

Real defenses deny the existence of a contract and render that contract null and void. The real defenses which can be asserted against a holder in due course are as follows:

1. Lack of a legal capacity to contract—e.g., an infant, minor or incompetent can disaffirm a contract.

2. Forgery of the signature of makers, drawers or endorsers.

3. Material and fraudulent alterations of the instrument, such as the amount, date and parties. However, a holder in due course can enforce an altered instrument according to its original terms or enforce an incomplete instrument as completed.

4. Fraud in the execution—e.g., where someone is induced into signing an instrument without knowing the character of the instrument, such as a note.

5. Void transactions—e.g., illegal deals such as gambling or usury, or deals consummated under extreme duress.

6. Discharge in bankruptcy

### Additional Requirements

In order for the Bank to enforce its rights, the following conditions must also apply:

1. The instrument must be negotiable, as set forth above.

2. The taker of the instrument must be a holder—i.e., the person in possession—if the instrument is payable to bearer, or the identified person if such person is in possession.

3. The holder who takes the instrument must be a holder in due course, as set forth above.

## AUTHORIZED SIGNATURES

A person is not liable on an instrument unless that person signed the instrument, or the instrument was signed by an authorized representative—i.e., an agent. If the instrument is signed by an agent, the person who is being represented is bound to the same degree as if they signed the instrument personally, even if they are not identified in the instrument.

If an authorized representative signs his own name to the instrument, as the authorized representative of another, the representative is not personally liable on the instrument provided the form of the signature shows clearly that it is made on behalf of the represented person identified in the instrument.

However, if the form of the signature does not clearly show that it is being made in a representative capacity, and the represented person is not identified in the instrument, the representative is liable to any holder in due course that took the instrument without notice that the representative did not intend to be liable.

An unauthorized signature is ineffective except as the signature of the unauthorized signer, in favor of a person who, in good faith, pays the instrument or takes it for value.

### Holders in Due Course in Consumer Transactions

Since the doctrine of holder in due course is so powerful, the Federal Trade Commission has modified the holder in due course rules which involve the sale or lease of goods or services to consumers.

Normally a purchaser who gives a note for a defective product has no defenses against a holder in due course who buys the note from the seller of this product. The FTC rules virtually eliminate holder in due course status through a credit contract which must contain a notice provision stating that a holder is subject to the claims and defenses a consumer may assert against a seller. The rule applies to contracts for the sale of services as well as tangible personal property.

Courts also deny holder in due course status to financial institutions that purchase notes from a seller where there is a close connection between the seller and finance company. In addition, many states have statutes which limit or prohibit the use of negotiable instruments in consumer transactions. Since a holder of a nonnegotiable instrument cannot be a holder in due course, the personal defenses of a consumer can be utilized.

# CHAPTER 3:
# UCC ARTICLE 4: BANK DEPOSITS AND COLLECTIONS

## IN GENERAL

Banks and bank accounts are regulated by both state and federal statutory law. Title 12 of the Code of Federal Regulations (CFR) contains federal agency regulations that concern banks and banking. Regulation J of the Federal Reserve comes into play if a check passes through the federal reserve system. Regulation CC extensively governs the availability of funds in a depositor's account and the process involving checks dishonored because of non-payment. Further, the timetable for making funds available for withdrawal after a check is deposited in a depository bank is governed by the Expedited Funds Availability Act.

Banking activities are also governed by a number of UCC Articles. This chapter is concerned with UCC Article 4, which sets forth the rights between parties with respect to bank deposits and collections. If there is a conflict among the Articles that deals with banking matters, Article 4 governs Article 3, but Article 8 governs Article 4.

UCC Article 4, which has been adopted at least in part in every state, "defines rights between parties with respect to bank deposits and collections." Part 1 contains general provisions and definitions; Part 2 governs the actions of the first bank—the depository bank—to accept the check and other banks— collecting banks—that handle the check but are not responsible for its final payment; Part 3 governs the actions of the bank that is responsible for the payment of the check—the payor bank; Part 4 governs the relationship between a payor bank and its customers; and Part 5 governs documentary drafts, which are checks or other types of drafts that will only be honored if certain papers are first presented to the payor of the draft.

Applicable provisions of UCC Article 4 are set forth at Appendix 4.

## AVAILABILITY OF FUNDS

After a customer has deposited money into their bank account, they will, at some point, want to use that money for their own benefit. However, the timing of their right to withdraw or use the money is governed by many rules, duties and liabilities.

The question of when you can withdraw the money you deposit depends on the form of the deposit. In other words, it depends upon whether you deposited cash, checks drawn in the same bank, or checks drawn on other banks.

### Cash Deposit

If the customer deposits cash, then the customer has the right to withdraw the money immediately.

### Same Bank Items

If a deposit contains a check drawn on the same bank into which the deposit is made, then the customer generally has the right to withdraw that depository item after the opening of the second banking day after the deposit was made.

### Checks Drawn on other Banks

If a deposit contains a check drawn on another bank, the money normally cannot be withdrawn until the check has been finally paid by the payor bank. This can take anywhere from 3 to 14 days depending on where the payor bank is located. Some banks have established their own time limits on when money can be withdrawn.

When you deposit a check drawn on another bank into your account, you are given a "provisional" credit which floats in your account until the check is paid and the credit becomes final. The amount of the provisional credit in your account is also called "uncollected funds" upon which you cannot draw.

## COLLECTING, DEPOSITORY AND PAYOR BANKS

The first bank to take an item is called a depository bank. The depositary bank may also be the payor bank, as discussed below. The other banks that subsequently handle the check, but are not responsible for its final payment, are called collecting banks.

The process of collection of a check begins when the check is deposited into a customer's account. When a depository bank or any other collecting bank receives a check, they have a duty to exercise ordinary care in timely presenting the check to the payor for payment or in sending the check to another collecting bank for presentment to the payor.

This ordinary care standard is also applicable in cases where the check is dishonored and notice must be given to all collecting banks.

A collecting bank has certain liabilities to its customers if it fails in any of its duties. If a bank, without excuse, fails to exercise ordinary care in handling an item, then a customer may recover damages in the amount of the item in question. The collecting or depository bank is liable for the payment of a check that has a forged endorsement, is materially altered or has a forged or unauthorized signature. Liability on a forged endorsement extends in favor of a drawee bank.

A depository/collecting bank is also liable if it fails to pay a check with a restrictive endorsement according to that endorsement. Damages are limited to the face amount of the check and may be reduced by proof that the actual loss is less. If there is a double forgery, i.e. both the signature and the endorsement are forged, the drawee bank is held liable for the payment of the check, not the depository bank.

### The Role of the Collecting Bank

While an item is in the process of collection, the collecting bank is an agent or sub-agent of the owner of the item—e.g., the payee who deposited the item—unless a contrary intent clearly appears. Any settlement given for the item is provisional until it becomes final. Because of the enormous volume of items which pass through collecting banks, it would be impossible to expect the bank to examine each indorsement, therefore, the fact of agency arises regardless of the form of indorsement on the item, or whether the item is indorsed at all. Nevertheless, any rights of the owner to the proceeds from the item are subject to the rights of the collecting bank.

The collecting bank is responsible for:

1. Presenting an item, or sending it for presentment.

2. Sending a notice of dishonor or nonpayment, or returning an item to the bank's transferor.

3. Settling for an item.

4. Notifying its transferor of any loss or delay in transit within a reasonable time after discovery.

In carrying out its functions, the collecting bank must exercise ordinary care. Ordinary care requires that the collecting bank take proper action following receipt of an item, notice, or settlement before its midnight deadline. The midnight deadline generally refers to midnight on the next banking day following the banking day on which the bank receives the item, notice, or settlement.

### Role of the Depository Bank

If a bank customer delivers an item to a depository bank for collection, the depository bank becomes a holder of the item provided the customer was the holder of the item, whether or not the customer actually endorses the item. If the bank satisfies all other requirements contained in UCC Section 3-302, the bank then becomes a holder in due course. The depository bank than warrants to the collecting banks, the payor bank and the drawer that the item was paid or deposited into the customer's account.

### The Role of the Payor Bank

The bank that is responsible for making payment on a check is called a payor bank. The payor bank may also be the depository bank. When a check is presented for payment to a payor bank, the bank can either pay the check or dishonor it. One of the major responsibilities of a bank is to pay its depositor's checks that are properly payable when there are sufficient collected funds on deposit in a customer's account to cover the amount of the check. If the bank refuses to pay a check that is properly payable the bank is liable to its customers for the damages that result from this wrongful dishonor.

### Wrongful Dishonor

Wrongful dishonor of an item is an improper and unlawful refusal by a bank to pay an item that is properly presented and otherwise properly payable.

If the bank pays a check that is not properly payable, then it must recredit its customers account for the amount of the check. If the dishonor is due to a mistake, the customer may recover only the actual damages it sustains. Some courts allow recovery of punitive and consequential damages.

Of course, there are instances when a bank may legitimately refuse to pay a check:

1. When there are insufficient or uncollected funds in the customer's account to cover the amount of the check.

2. When the check is subject to a stop payment order.

3. When the check is post dated.

4. When the check is presented more than six months after its date (stale-dated).

5. When the customer's account has been closed.

6. When the bank has properly effected a setoff against funds.

7. When the funds have been properly attached, restrained or garnished.

### The Midnight Deadline

The bank's responsibilities include making the decision to pay or dishonor a check within the midnight deadline. The bank accumulates all the checks received on one business day and defers posting the checks to its customers accounts until the next business day.

If the bank decides to dishonor a check, it must return the check to the presenting bank within this deadline. This is accomplished by mailing the check. If, however, a check is presented to a teller for immediate cashing, then it must be paid or dishonored by the close of business that day. Failure of the payor bank to adhere to this deadline results in strict liability for the full amount of the check.

A sample notice of dishonor is set forth at Appendix 5.

### Final Payment

Final payment of a check is significant since it marks the time when a depositor can withdraw the amount of the check from his account. Final payment occurs when the bank has paid the check in cash, has made a final credit to the account, completed the process of posting or recording the check to the drawer's account or if it fails to pay or dishonor a check within its midnight deadline.

An item is deemed "finally paid" if:

1. The payor bank pays the item in cash to the presenter;

2. The payor bank settles for the item without having a right to revoke the settlement; or

3. The payor bank makes a provisional settlement for the item, and fails to revoke the settlement within the statutory time period.

If, however, the payor bank settles for a demand, other than a documentary draft or immediate payment over the counter, before midnight of the banking day of receipt, the payor bank is entitled to revoke and recover the settlement.

### TRANSFER WARRANTIES

A customer or collecting bank that transfers an item and receives settlement or other consideration warrants to the transferee and to any subsequent collecting bank that:

1. The warrantor is a person entitled to enforce the item;

2. All signatures on the item are authentic and authorized;

3. The item has not been altered;

4. The item is not subject to any third party claims that can be asserted against the warrantor; and

5. The warrantor is unaware of any insolvency proceedings concerning the maker.

If the item is dishonored, the warrantor is obligated to pay the amount due on the item. A warrantor cannot disclaim liability under this section. Thus, if a person takes the item in good faith, he may recover damages from the warrantor in an amount equal to the loss suffered as a result of the breach. However, recovery is limited to the amount of the instrument plus expenses and loss of interest.

## PRESENTMENT WARRANTIES

If an unaccepted draft is presented to the drawee bank for payment or acceptance, and the drawee pays or accepts the draft, the presenter and any prior transferor of the draft warrants to the drawee that:

1. The warrantor is, or was, a person entitled to enforce the draft;

2. The draft has not been altered;

3. The warrantor has no knowledge that the signature of the drawer is unauthorized.

If there is a breach of warranty, the drawee is entitled to damages in an amount equal to the amount paid by the drawee less the amount the drawee received, or is entitled to receive, from the drawer, as well as expenses and loss of interest.

## BANK DEFENSES

Contributory negligence of a drawer is a defense the bank can assert against a drawer. For example, if the drawer wrote the check in a manner that facilitated an alteration that could not easily be detected, the bank is not liable for paying that check.

Negligence may also include the customer issuing an incomplete check or a check with enough space left on the amount line to permit the amount to be altered. However, the bank must also act in good faith and in accordance with reasonable commercial standards.

Another defense a bank can assert is the customers' failure to examine its bank statements. A customer has a duty to timely examine the monthly bank statements and canceled checks to discover any forgeries or alterations. Generally, the rule is that a drawee bank is strictly liable to its customers for the amount of any check it pays over its customer's forged signature.

A customer who fails to timely examine his statements and checks cannot hold his bank liable for forged or altered checks. The customer must examine his statement within fourteen days after the bank statement is made available to him either by receipt, or if the banks holds the statement and checks by his request or if the statement and checks are available for inspection.

If the customer fails to report any forgery within the fourteen day time period, the bank will not be liable for any other forged checks paid before the expiration of the fourteen days if the bank suffers a loss and the customer failed to exercise reasonable care.

If checks are paid by the bank after the expiration of the fourteen day period, the bank is not liable to its customers for the amount of the checks paid before the bank is notified. All is not lost however for the customer. Even if the customer is negligent in failing to discover and report forgeries, the bank may still be liable if the bank fails to exercise ordinary care when it paid the forged checks.

The bank must follow reasonable procedures to compare the customer's signature on file with the signature on the check. As a practical matter, banks usually only compare signatures on checks exceeding a certain base amount. This caveat is only available to a customer for a period of one year. If the forgery is not discovered within one year, then the customer must bear the loss.

## CHARGING THE CUSTOMER'S ACCOUNT

A bank may charge a customer's account for an item that is properly payable from the account. An item is "properly payable" if the customer authorizes the item, and it is in accordance with any agreement between the customer and bank. As set forth below, the bank has a duty to the customer to make sure that it only makes payments on genuine orders of the customer.

### Forged Checks

If the bank honors a check which bears a forged signature of the customer, the bank must credit the customer's account for the amount of the forged check.

### Altered Checks

If the bank honors a check which the payee altered by increasing the amount payable, the bank must credit the customer's account with the amount of the altered check, less the original amount.

*Example: If the bank honors a check written for $50, which is altered to reflect a payable amount of $500, the bank must credit the customer's account for $450, the amount of the altered check less the original amount.*

### Postdated Checks

Due to the automated check collection process, if a bank charges a customer's account for a check that is postdated—i.e., presented for payment before its date—the bank may still charge the customer's account unless it receives notice from the customer describing the postdated check.

### Overdraft

An overdraft results from the payment by the drawee bank of a drawer's check in a sum that is greater than the amount in his account. The UCC provides that a check is properly payable even though its payment will result in the creation of an overdraft in a customer's account. The bank, in effect has loaned money to its customer. However, a customer is not liable for the amount of the overdraft if he neither signed the item nor benefitted from its proceeds.

An overdraft may also occur by mistake or through a check kiting scheme. A check kiting scheme is where a bank depositor uses accounts at two banks to obtain money by cashing worthless checks at Bank A drawn on a Bank B account and then depositing enough cash at Bank B to keep the scheme afloat. As a general rule, the first bank to discover the scheme can avoid the kiting loss.

### Old Checks

An old or stale-dated check is a check that is presented for payment more than six months after its date. A bank is not obligated to pay a check which is presented for payment more than six months after its date, except for a certified check. However, a bank has the option to pay a stale-dated check if it does so in good faith. A bank will sometimes obtain the permission of the drawer of a check before paying a check that is stale.

### Stop Payment Order

A customer may order the bank to stop payment on any item, provided it gives the bank a description of the item in time for the bank to prevent taking action on the item. Since a check is an order given by a customer to his bank that directs the bank to pay money to the payee, the customer may revoke this order for any reason. This method of revocation is called a Stop Payment Order.

Once a stop payment order has been received, the bank's sole duty is to obey it. A check which has a valid stop payment order is not properly payable. A bank must receive a stop payment order in a manner and at a time that gives the bank a reasonable opportunity to act on the order before it pays the check. Consequently, a stop payment order is too late if the bank has accepted or certified the check, paid the check in cash, settled for the check or completed the posting process of the check.

A stop payment order may be given orally or in writing. An oral order is only binding on the bank for fourteen calendar days. If the customer confirms an oral order in writing, during the fourteen day period, the order is effective for six months. A written order is effective for six months unless renewed in writing within that period.

Generally, only the drawer has the right to stop payment on his checks. The only exception is a person claiming an interest in the account, such as a legal representative of a recently deceased person. A bank who pays a check over a valid stop payment order is liable to its customer only for the loss suffered from the payment of the check. The burden is on the drawer to establish his loss. The drawer also remains liable to a holder in due course.

A sample stop payment order is set forth at Appendix 6.

# CHAPTER 4:
# UCC ARTICLE 4A: ELECTRONIC FUNDS TRANSFERS

## IN GENERAL

A funds transfer is a series of transactions, beginning with the originator's payment order, made for the purpose of making payment to the beneficiary of the order. A funds transfer includes any payment order issued by the originator's bank, or an intermediary bank, which is intended to carry out the order. The funds transfer is completed when the beneficiary bank accepts the payment order for the benefit of the beneficiary. In most cases, the series of transactions is made electronically.

*Example: Buyer and Seller enter into a contract for the sale of goods. Instead of sending Seller a check, Buyer wants to have his Bank send the money to Seller's bank for credit to Seller's account. In order to accomplish this transfer of funds, Buyer must instruct his bank to carry out the transfer. Buyer's instruction is known as the payment order. Buyer is the originator of the payment order. Buyer's bank—the originator's bank—is known as the receiving bank because it "received" Buyer's payment order. Seller is the beneficiary of the payment order, and Seller's bank is known as the beneficiary's bank.*

When Buyer's bank executes the payment order by instructing Seller's bank to credit Seller's account, Buyer's bank also becomes the "sender" of a payment order with respect to Seller's bank, and Seller's bank becomes the "receiving bank" with respect to that order. In cases where additional banks handle the transfer between the originator's bank and the beneficiary's bank, those banks are called intermediary banks.

Funds transfers are governed by UCC Article 4A and Subchapter VI of the Consumer Credit Protection Act known as the Electronic Funds Transfer Act.

Applicable provisions of UCC Article 4A are set forth at Appendix 7.

## SECURITY PROCEDURES

Problems in funds transfers may arise if there is an error in the payment order, or an unauthorized payment order. In order to prevent such problems, a security procedure may be established by agreement between the customer and the receiving bank—i.e., the originator's bank—which would require some security device to be used, e.g, the use of algorithms or other codes, identifying words or numbers, encryption, or callback procedures.

### Unauthorized Payment Orders

If the receiving bank carries out the agreed upon security procedure, the payment order will be deemed effective as to the customer's order whether or not it was authorized by the customer, provided that: (i) the security procedure is a commercially reasonable method of providing security against unauthorized payment orders; and (ii) the receiving bank proves that it accepted the payment order in good faith and in compliance with the security procedure.

Nevertheless, if the customer can prove that the unauthorized payment order: (i) was not directly or indirectly caused by a person who had authority to act on the customer's behalf; or (ii) was made by a person who obtained access to the customer's transmitting facility or who obtained information facilitating a breach of the security procedure from a source controlled by the customer, the receiving bank is not entitled to enforce or retain payment even if the customer is at fault.

### Erroneous Payment Orders

If an accepted payment order was transmitted pursuant to a security procedure which was supposed to detect errors, and the payment order erroneously: (i) instructed payment to an incorrect beneficiary; or (ii) instructed payment in an amount greater than authorized; or (iii) duplicated a previous payment order, the sender is not obligated to pay the order if he proves that he or his agent complied with the security procedure. If the funds transfer is completed, the bank is entitled to recover any amount paid to the beneficiary to the extent the funds were erroneously paid.

## ACCEPTANCE OF ORDER

A receiving bank, not including a beneficiary's bank, is deemed to have accepted a payment order when it executes the order. Execution occurs when the receiving bank issues its own payment order, which is intended to carry out the payment order it originally received. A beneficiary's bank cannot execute a payment order, it can only accept it.

A beneficiary's bank is deemed to have accepted a payment upon the earliest happening of the following events:

1. The bank (i) pays the beneficiary; (ii) notifies the beneficiary that his account has been credited with the funds; or (iii) notifies the beneficiary of receipt of the order provided the notice does not indicate that the order is being rejected or the funds being held until payment is received by the sender; or

2. The bank receives payment of the entire amount of the sender's payment order; or

3. The opening of the next "funds-transfer business day" following the payment date of the order, provided: (i) the amount of the order is fully covered by a credit balance in an authorized account of the sender; or (ii) the bank has received full payment from the sender, unless there has been a rejection of the order as set forth in the statute.

Nevertheless, acceptance of the order cannot occur: (i) before it is received by the receiving bank; or (ii) if the beneficiary does not have an account with the receiving bank.

## MISDESCRIPTION OF BENEFICIARY

Acceptance cannot occur where a payment order received by the beneficiary's bank identifies a nonexistent or unidentifiable person or account as beneficiary.

If the name and account number contained in the payment order identify two different persons, the beneficiary's bank may rely on the account number as the proper identification of the beneficiary if the bank is not aware of the conflict.

In that case, if the beneficiary's bank pays the person identified by account number, and the originator is a bank, the originator is obligated to pay the order. However, if the originator is not a bank, and proves that the beneficiary was not entitled to payment, the originator is not obligated to pay the order unless the originator's bank can prove that, prior to acceptance, the originator received notice that payment of the order might be made by the beneficiary's bank on the basis of the account number alone. In any event, the originator's bank may be able to recover any amount paid to a person who was not entitled to receive payment, as provided in the statute.

If the beneficiary's bank pays a person identified by name, or knows that the name and account number identify different persons, no person has rights as beneficiary except the person paid by the bank, provided that person was entitled to receive payment. However, if no identified person has rights as beneficiary, acceptance cannot occur.

## REJECTION OF ORDER

A payment order is deemed rejected when the receiving bank transmits a notice of rejection to the sender orally, electronically or in writing. A rejection notice does not require any specific words provided it clearly indicates that the order is being rejected. Rejection is effective when the notice is given if it is transmitted by reasonable means—e.g., by a means agreed to between the parties. If the means of transmission is deemed unreasonable—e.g., any means other than that agreed to unless no significant delay resulted from noncompliance—rejection is effective when the notice is received by the sender.

## CANCELLATION AND AMENDMENT OF ORDER

The sender may transmit a communication to the receiving bank which cancels or amends the payment order orally, electronically, or in writing. The communication is effective if notice is received in time to give the receiving bank a reasonable opportunity to act prior to accepting the payment order.

If the receiving bank accepted the payment order prior to receiving the communication, cancellation or amendment is not effective (i) unless the receiving bank agrees; or (ii) unless otherwise authorized without agreement under a funds transfer system rule.

## PAYMENT OF ORDER

The day on which the amount of the payment order is made payable to the beneficiary by his bank is known as the "payment date." Although the payment date may be determined by the sender's instructions, it cannot occur before the order is received by the beneficiary's bank.

Once the beneficiary's bank accepts the order, the sender is obligated to pay the bank the amount of the order by the payment date. As it relates to a receiving bank other than the beneficiary's bank—e.g. an intermediary bank—the sender is obligated to pay the bank the amount of the order once the bank "accepts" the order; however, actual payment is not due until the bank "executes" the order—i.e., the receiving bank issues it own payment order intended to carry out the payment order it originally received.

Once the beneficiary's bank credits the beneficiary's account, payment to the beneficiary is deemed to have occurred when: (i) the beneficiary is notified of the right of withdrawal; (ii) the credit is lawfully applied to a beneficiary's debt; or (iii) funds are otherwise made available to the beneficiary.

## DEBIT CARDS

Most banks provide customers with debit cards, also known as ATM cards, so that the customer can access his or her accounts electronically during non-banking hours. In addition, many stores now accept debit cards for purchases in the same manner as credit cards. Debit card purchases or withdrawals are deducted directly from the bank account. There may be additional fees assessed for the use of debit cards.

ATM cards are discussed more fully in Chapter 7 of this almanac.

## THE CONSUMER CREDIT PROTECTION ACT: SUBCHAPTER VI—THE ELECTRONIC FUNDS TRANSFER ACT

The Electronic Funds Transfer Act (EFTA) was enacted as Subchapter VI of the Consumer Credit Protection Act for the purpose of providing a basic framework establishing the rights, liabilities, and responsibilities of participants in electronic fund transfer systems.

Electronic funds transfer systems under the EFTA include:

1. Automated Teller Machines, commonly referred to as ATMs, which permit customers to access banking services 24 hours per day;

2. Pay-by-Phone services;

3. Direct Deposit and Automatic Payment services; and

4. Point of Sale Transfer systems, which permit a consumer to pay for goods and services by transferring funds simultaneously out of the consumer's account and into the seller's account at the time of purchase.

The participants include the financial institution and the consumer. The EFTA defines a financial institution as: (i) a state or national bank; (ii) a state or federal savings and loan association; (iii) a mutual savings bank; (iv) a state or federal credit union; or (v) any other entity that directly or indirectly holds an account belonging to the consumer. The definition is broad so as to include any entity that may offer electronic fund transfer services to a consumer.

A consumer is defined as a natural person who uses electronic funds transfer systems.

### Consumer Liability for Unauthorized Transfers

Under the EFTA, there are three levels of liability that may be assessed against the consumer for unauthorized transfers.

1. If an unauthorized withdrawal is made from the consumer's account prior to the consumer being aware that his or her access card was lost or stolen, the consumer may be held liable for amounts withdrawn from the consumer's account prior to his or her notification to the financial institution, up to a maximum of Fifty ($50.00) Dollars.

2. If the consumer fails to notify the financial institution that his or her access card was lost or stolen within two business days of the consumer being aware of the loss, the consumer may be held liable for amounts withdrawn from the consumer's account prior to his or her notification to the financial institution, up to a maximum of Five Hundred ($500.00) Dollars.

3. If the consumer fails to report unauthorized transfers within 60 days of receiving a statement on which the unauthorized transfer appears, the consumer may have unlimited liability for amounts withdrawn from the consumer's account prior to his or her notification to the financial institution. The rationale for this apparently harsh rule is that the consumer would have to be unduly negligent for failing to notify the financial institution within that time period.

Applicable provisions of the Electronic Funds Transfer Act are set forth at Appendix 8.

# CHAPTER 5:
# UCC ARTICLE 5: LETTERS OF CREDIT

## IN GENERAL

The UCC defines a letter of credit as an engagement by a bank or other person, made at the request of the customer—e.g., the Buyer—that the issuer of the letter of credit—commonly the Buyer's bank—will honor drafts or other demands for payment by the Beneficiary—e.g., the Seller—provided the conditions specified in the letter of credit are met. Letters of Credit are governed by UCC Article 5.

Applicable provisions of UCC Article 5 are set forth at Appendix 9.

A letter of credit is commonly used in contracts for the sale of goods. However, the issuance of a letter of credit is not limited to the sale of goods. For example, a letter of credit may also involve the sale or transfer of other items under the UCC, such as investment securities. For purposes of this chapter, a sales contract for goods between a Buyer and Seller will be used to illustrate the letter of credit transaction.

A Seller may want some guarantee of payment if the Seller ships goods to the Buyer pursuant to a sales contract. The letter of credit gives the Seller some assurance that he will not have to incur considerable expense in retrieving the goods if the Buyer reneges on the deal, thus minimizing his risks.

## PROCEDURE

If the Seller requires a letter of credit in order to complete a transaction, a specific provision is included in the contract between the Buyer and Seller which sets forth the conditions which must be met before the Buyer's bank will pay the Seller for the goods.

Although no particular form of phrasing is required, a letter of credit provision generally states that the Buyer will arrange for a letter of credit with the Buyer's bank, to be issued in the purchase price amount, naming the Seller as the Beneficiary. To be valid, a letter of credit must be in writing and signed by the Issuer. If the Buyer fails to furnish the letter of credit within the required time, this constitutes a breach of the sales contract.

The letter of credit provision will also specify the required documentation the Seller needs to present to the Buyer's bank in order to receive payment for the goods. For example, the bank may require, among other things, an invoice, an inspection certificate, and/or an insurance policy covering the goods. In addition, the provision may require that the Seller comply with the conditions by a certain date. When the Seller presents his demand for payment to the issuing bank, he is warranting—i.e., making a representation—that he has complied with all of the terms set forth in the letter of credit.

In order to provide the Seller with a letter of credit, the Buyer enters into an agreement with the issuing bank, under which the Buyer agrees to pay the bank a service fee, and to reimburse the bank for payment made to the Seller under the letter of credit. Such reimbursement is made after the bank honors the request for payment by the Seller. The bank then surrenders the bill of lading to the Buyer, who presents the bill to the Carrier to obtain the goods.

If the bank is lending the Buyer the money to purchase the goods, the bank retains a purchase money security interest in the bill of lading and the goods.

### ESTABLISHMENT OF THE LETTER OF CREDIT

The letter of credit is deemed "established" as follows:

As to the Buyer, it is established as soon as either (i) the letter of credit is sent to the Buyer; or (ii) an authorized written advice of the issuance of the credit is sent to the Seller. Once an irrevocable credit is established as to the Buyer, it cannot be modified or revoked without the consent of the Buyer.

As to the Seller, it is established when he receives the letter of credit or an authorized written advice of its issuance. Once an irrevocable credit is established as to the Seller, it cannot be modified or revoked without the consent of the Seller.

#### Advising Bank

Once the letter of credit is issued, it is forwarded to the advising bank, which informs the Seller that the Buyer's bank has issued the credit. The advising bank is limited to this task, and does not play any role in honoring the letter of credit or issuing any payments under the credit.

### Confirming Bank

If, as an extra measure of protection, the Seller engages a confirming bank, that bank would become directly obligated to the Seller for payments under the credit as if it were the issuing bank. A confirmation must be in writing and signed by the confirming bank to be valid. In addition, any modification of the terms of the credit must also be signed by the confirming bank, if one is engaged.

### Liability of Issuing Bank

The issuing bank's responsibility is to make sure that the Seller has complied with all of the terms set forth in the letter of credit, e.g. presentation of required documentation. However, it is not the issuing bank's responsibility to make sure that the goods conform to the underlying contract between the Buyer and Seller, and it is not liable therefor.

If the Seller, or Seller's bank, presents the documentation required by the terms of the letter of credit, the Bank will honor the demand for payment. If the bank does not honor the demand, it will be liable to the Seller. In that event, the Seller may recover the face amount of the demand, together with incidental damages and interest, less any amount obtained by resale or other use of the goods.

If, however, the bank honors the request for payment, and it is determined that the documentation did not comply with the letter of credit terms, the issuing bank will be liable to the Buyer.

Nevertheless, the Buyer may obtain assurances that the goods conform to the contract in other ways. For example, one of the conditions in the letter of credit may be the issuance of an inspection certificate by a designated third party. In addition, if an insurance policy covering the goods is a condition, the Buyer's interests will also be protected.

# CHAPTER 6:
# SHOPPING FOR A BANK

## IN GENERAL

Selecting a bank to use for your financial affairs is a very important decision. One should take time to research the prospective bank before making a decision. Visit the branch you intend to use to do your banking. Ask questions. Is the staff knowledgeable, courteous and helpful? Were you given complete and satisfactory information concerning prospective products and services? If not, it is best to do your banking elsewhere to avoid future problems.

## NEW PROOF OF IDENTITY REQUIREMENT UNDER USA PATRIOT ACT

The U.S. Treasury Department and federal financial regulatory agencies have jointly issued new rules for customer identification pursuant to the USA Patriot Act of 2001. Under the new rules, which became mandatory on October 1, 2003, financial institutions are required to ask customers for proof of their name, address, date of birth, and social security number when opening a new account. Documentation, such as a driver's license or passport, must be provided for verification.

The text of the USA Patriot Act is set forth at Appendix 10.

Identification procedures may vary depending upon the type of account being opened and the policies of the financial institution. The financial institution must also check the customer's name to see whether it appears on any list of suspected terrorists or terrorist organizations. The new rules are in effect to prevent crimes such as money laundering, identity theft, and account fraud, that have been known to be a source of funds for terrorist operations.

## TYPES OF BANK ACCOUNTS

The most common types of bank accounts used by the average customer are the savings account and the checking account. Both types of accounts may provide for the payment of interest to the depositor.

### Savings Account

A savings account is usually a demand account. Savings accounts are governed by the federal Truth in Savings Act. Under the Truth in Savings Act, financial institutions are required to:

1. Disclose the Annual Percentage Yield (the "APY") on savings accounts.

2. Credit the entire deposit instead of crediting a portion of the deposit.

3. Refrain from advertising "free checking" with the savings account if there are any hidden charges or requirements, such as maintaining a minimum balance in the account to qualify.

### Checking Account

A checking account is also a demand account. Banks generally have a wide range of checking account types. Before opening an account, the customer should inquire about the various fees and obligations applicable to each type of checking account. One should consider which type of account meets their individual needs.

One factor to consider may be the number of checks the customer intends to write per month. Some banks offer low or no-fee checking; however, the customer can only write a limited number of checks from the account during the statement period. If the customer exceeds that number, additional charges may apply. If the customer regularly writes a large number of checks, he or she may prefer the type of account which carries a higher monthly fee, but permits unlimited check writing privileges.

### Check Reporting Services

Check reporting services are companies that monitor and report how a customer manages their checking account. Check reporting services protect financial institutions from losses associated with bounced or fraudulent checks. A single bounced check reported by one of these companies can make it difficult for a customer to open a checking account. Under the Fair Credit Reporting Act (FCRA), a bounced check or other wrongdoing reported to a check reporting service may stay on the customer's record for as many as seven years.

If a bank refuses to open a checking account for you based on an unfavorable report by one of these companies, you should ask for the contact information for the company that provided the unfavorable report. Request a copy of the report from the company to determine whether the information it contains is accurate. If the information is inaccurate, request that it be amended and resent to the bank which received the report.

If a financial institution was the source of the error, it is required by the FCRA to contact the check reporting service and have the record corrected. If you dispute the matter in writing, and the check reporting service refuses to amend the record to your satisfaction, you are entitled to add a written statement to your report.

To avoid this predicament, it is important to regularly balance your checking account to avoid bounced checks. In addition, do not close one checking account before opening a new one. Also, before closing an account, make sure all outstanding checks have been paid.

### Title/Ownership of the Account

When opening an account, one must designate the title in which the account is held.

### Individual Account

An individual account has only one person authorized to deposit or withdraw money. If the person is a minor, the bank must obtain authorization from a parent or legal guardian.

### Joint Account

A joint account exists when more than one person may withdraw money from a single account. A joint account which allows payment or delivery to either person or their survivor is a joint tenant account which gives the survivor title to the deposit.

A sample joint survivorship account signature card is set forth at Appendix 11.

### Corporate Account

A corporate account is authorized by a resolution authorizing a bank to pay checks signed by a corporate officer.

A sample corporate banking resolution is set forth at Appendix 12.

### Trust Account

A trust account involves a deposit by one person of his own money in his own name as trustee for another—e.g., "John Smith in trust for Jack Smith." This type of account creates a tentative trust which is revocable—i.e., able to be reversed—at will until the depositor dies. If the depositor dies before the beneficiary, the trust becomes irrevocable and title passes to the beneficiary.

### Fiduciary or Representative Accounts

A fiduciary or representative account is one in which the account holder deposits money in the account to be held for another. There are many types of fiduciary accounts, including receiver, trust, executor and attorney accounts.

## MAKING DEPOSITS

Deposits create contracts between the bank and depositor with the right of the bank to commingle deposited funds with other bank funds, and use the deposit until the funds are requested by the depositor. The common bank deposit is a demand deposit, e.g. a regular savings account deposit. A deposit can also be a "time deposit," which is placed on deposit for a specified time. A common type of time deposit is a Christmas Club account in which deposits are made in accordance with a plan that provides for regular deposits during the year and the withdrawal of the money for use at Christmas.

There are two categories of deposits: (1) General Deposits; and (2) Special Deposits. A deposit is considered to be a general deposit unless there is an agreement to be a special deposit.

### General Deposits

A general deposit is commingled with the other funds of a bank and is not capable of specific identification once deposited. A general deposit creates a debtor/unsecured creditor relationship between the bank and the depositor. Title to the general deposit passes from the depositor to the bank with the bank undertaking a duty to repay it with or without interest. The bank also bears the risk of loss.

### Special Deposit

A special deposit creates an agreement through which money or property is transferred to the bank with an understanding that the money or property is deposited for a special purpose, such as to pay a mortgage or bond, or that the specific item deposited is to be returned. The bank acts as a bailee/safekeeper. In this bailee/bailor relationship, title to the item deposited remains in the depositor. In addition, the risk of loss remains with the depositor absent the negligence of the bank, with the bank undertaking the duty of reasonable care of the item.

## CERTIFICATE OF DEPOSIT (CD)

A certificate of deposit (CD) is a type of general deposit under which the bank agrees to repay the depositor the amount of the deposit after an agreed period of time at a specified rate of interest. A CD typically offers a higher rate of interest than a regular savings account. Unlike other investments, a CD is eligible for federal deposit insurance of up to $100,000.

A CD is attractive for customers interested in a relatively low-risk investment that can be easily converted to cash. A CD is purchased for a fixed sum of money and a fixed period of time, e.g. 6 months, one year, etc., at a stated rate of interest. When the CD is redeemed, the customer receives the money they originally invested plus any accrued interest. If the customer redeems the CD before it matures, they may have to pay an "early withdrawal" penalty or forfeit a portion of the interest earned.

Some long-term, high-yield CDs have "call" features, meaning that the issuing bank may choose to terminate—i.e., call—the CD after only one year or some other fixed period of time. Only the issuing bank may call a CD. For example, a bank might decide to call its high-yield CDs if interest rates fall. On the other hand, if the customer invested in a long-term CD and interest rates subsequently rise, they are locked in at the lower rate for the term of the CD.

Before investing in a CD, it is important to find out certain information, as follows:

1. Maturity Date—It is important to determine the maturity date prior to investing in the CD. Ask for the maturity date in writing to make sure you do not mistakenly have your money tied up for longer than anticipated.

2. Call Features—Determine whether the CD is "callable"—i.e., whether it gives the bank the right to terminate the CD after a set period of time.

3. Interest Rate—Confirm the interest rate. The bank is required to give the customer a disclosure document that explains the interest rate on the CD, and whether the rate is fixed or variable. If the CD has a variable interest rate, determine when and how the rate can change.

4. Penalties—Determine the penalty for early withdrawal in case you must cash in the CD prior to the maturity date.

## INTEREST RATES

Until the early 1980's, interest rates on bank accounts were regulated and controlled by the national government. Interest payments on demand deposit accounts were generally prohibited and their was a ceiling placed on interest rates for savings accounts. Banks were also prohibited from offering money market accounts.

The Depository Institutions Deregulation Act of 1980 (DIDRA) eliminated the interest rate controls on savings accounts and the restrictions on checking and money market accounts were lifted nationwide by authorization of NOW and Super NOW checking accounts and the Garn-St Germain Depository Institutions Act.

National banks are subject to federal law with respect to the rates of interest they may charge on loans and discounts. A bank charging interest rates higher than the statutory mandate is guilty of usury and is subject to stiff penalties. The remedy to a customer is forgiveness of the entire interest due and recovery of twice the amount of interest actually paid.

The Federal Deposit Insurance Corporation (FDIC) has the power to promulgate rules governing advertising and payment of interest on deposits. The maximum rate of interest allowed to be paid on a time deposit is the lesser of the maximum rate set by the FDIC or the maximum rate authorized by the laws of the state in which the bank is located. Early withdrawals from a time deposit account are penalized by a forfeiture of interest.

Regular withdrawals from a savings account are not penalized. The maximum rates of interest which are allowed to be paid on deposits vary according to the characteristics of the account, including the amount and maturity date, and are fluctuating.

## SAFE DEPOSIT BOXES

One of the services a bank offers its customers is the ability to rent a safe deposit box. Most customers who rent safe deposit boxes do so in order to have a secure place to keep valuables and important documents. Also, some insurance companies charge lower insurance premiums on valuables kept in a bank's safe deposit box instead of at home.

A bank is treated as a bailee/safekeeper of a safe deposit box. Banks are held to a duty of exercising ordinary care in the offering of safe deposit boxes. They are not insurers of the property deposited. The safe deposit rental agreement usually limits the liability of the bank to willful acts. The bank may limit the persons who have access to the box, and the hours they may gain access.

### Access Procedures

Most banks have very strict safe deposit box access procedures, e.g., signature verification, restricted access, dual key access, etc. In addition, customers are not left unattended inside the vault, but are directed to viewing rooms outside of the vault where they can inspect their property in privacy.

### Items You Should Place in a Safety Deposit Box

There are certain valuable items and important documents which one may want to place in a safe deposit box. These may include originals of insurance policies; family records such as birth, marriage and death certificates; original deeds, titles, mortgages, leases and other contracts; stocks, bonds and certificates of deposit (CDs); valuable jewels, medals, rare stamps and other collectibles, negatives for irreplaceable photos, and videos or pictures of your home's contents for insurance purposes, in case of theft or damage.

### Items You Should Not Place in a Safety Deposit Box

There are certain items which should not be placed in a safe deposit box. For example, any item one may need in an emergency should not be in the safe deposit box, such as passports; medical care directives, e.g., a health care proxy; and funeral or burial instructions.

In addition, it is not advisable to have one's will located in the safe deposit box unless someone other than the customer has access to the box in case the customer dies. For example, if you choose to put your will in the safe deposit box, the person designated to oversee your financial affairs should have immediate access to the original will. Otherwise, some states will require a court order to open the safe deposit box, which can cause unnecessary time and expense.

The customer can jointly rent the box with a spouse, child or other person who will have unrestricted access to the box. It is not enough to merely give someone a key to the box because the bank may not allow them access, under state law, if they are not a joint-renter.

### Insurance

FDIC Insurance does not cover the contents of safe deposit boxes if they are damaged or stolen. By law, the FDIC only insures deposits in deposit accounts at insured institutions. Even though the customer is technically "depositing" valuables, including cash and checks, into the safe deposit box, these are not deposits under the insurance laws. A safe deposit box is strictly a storage space provided by the bank.

It is possible that the contents of the safe deposit box may be covered under homeowner's insurance, therefore, the customer should check his or her policy to determine whether coverage is available. The customer should keep a log of everything that is contained in the box, as well as photographs of any valuables, in case an item is lost and an insurance claim needs to be filed.

The bank would only be liable for damage or loss of the safe deposit box if it was negligent in the way it handled or protected the box. Because safe deposit boxes are stored in concrete and steel vaults with sophisticated security equipment, it is unlikely that a safe deposit box would be stolen. In addition, in order to gain access to the box, most banks have strict access procedures, discussed above.

### Further Safeguards

The customer should take additional steps to make sure their valuables are protected. The customer is generally given two keys to the safe deposit box. The keys to the box should be kept in a safe place, apart from each other, and apart from the house keys and car keys, and should not indicate the name of the bank where the box is located. If one of the keys is lost, the bank should be notified so they can be on alert in case someone tries to use the key. If both keys are lost, the customer will have to get a new box.

When visiting the bank, accompany the bank employee into the vault while he or she opens and closes the safe deposit box door with the key. Do not permit the bank employee to take the box out of your sight. Never leave the key in the box door. Do not open the box until you are alone in the privacy of the viewing area. Before leaving this area, make sure all valuables are returned to the box. When you return the box to the vault, make sure the box door is locked and take your key.

### Abandonment

If the customer does not pay the fee after a certain time period, as determined by state law, and the bank is unable to locate the customer, the safe deposit box may be declared abandoned and the contents turned over to the state's unclaimed property office. This may occur if the customer dies and nobody is aware that he or she had a safe deposit box.

## SWITCHING BANKS

For a number of reasons, a customer may wish to switch banks, e.g., if they are moving, or if another bank is offering a better deal. In order to make sure that the change goes smoothly, the following steps should be followed:

1. The existing checkbook should be balanced and all outstanding checks should have cleared before the checking account is closed.

This will ensure that no checks will be presented after the account is closed, resulting in unnecessary fees.

2. Open an account at the new bank before leaving the old bank so that you can continue banking activities, e.g. writing checks, etc., without interruption.

3. If your checks are being directly deposited, do not close the old account until you have confirmed that the direct deposits are being made to the new account.

4. If automatic payments are being made from the old account, e.g., to pay monthly bills, confirm when the payments will start being made from the new account before closing the old account.

5. If you are moving, give the old bank your new contact information, in writing, in case they need to reach you regarding your closed account.

6. Make a notation in your financial records that the old account was closed, and the date on which it was closed, so that individuals investigating your financial affairs in the future, e.g., heirs, will not waste time trying to track down a closed account.

7. Make sure any safe deposit box held at the bank is emptied and the keys returned to the bank.

## MAINTAINING BANK RECORDS

It is important to keep careful financial records for a number of reasons. For example, Federal tax rules require an individual to maintain receipts and other financial documents that support items on a tax return for as long as the IRS can assess additional taxes—e.g., up to three years from the date the tax return was filed and, in some cases, up to six years. The following items should be kept in a safe place for a reasonable period of time:

1. Canceled Checks—Checks that support tax return items, such as charitable contributions, should be held for at least seven years. Checks with no long-term significance should be held for approximately one year. Checks, receipts and documents relating to large purchases, such as the purchase of a home or car, should be kept indefinitely.

2. Transaction Receipts—Receipts for deposits, and ATM, debit and credit card transactions should be kept until the information appears on the statement and has been verified.

3. Bank Account Statements—Bank statements should be kept for up to seven years, e.g., for tax purposes.

4. Loan Documents—Loan documents should be kept for as long as the account is open.

5. Investment Statements—Documentation of the purchase or sale of stocks, bonds and other investments should be kept as long as the investment property is owned, and for seven years after the property has been sold or transferred, e.g., for tax purposes.

## FORGOTTEN ASSETS

Old family documents often contain evidence of bank accounts, safe deposit boxes and other investments. The FDIC receives many phone calls from people trying to find out information about old accounts. In most cases, the accounts had been closed long ago, however, occasionally, abandoned or forgotten assets are in the custody of the bank, a state government or the FDIC. If evidence of an old account or safe deposit box is discovered, one must first determine whether the financial institution is still in business. If the financial institution is still open, request a status report on the old accounts. If the account was not closed by the original owner, it is possible that the assets may still be available from the bank, or the assets may have been deemed abandoned and transferred to the state's unclaimed property office.

If a state has funds, and the individual provides satisfactory proof of ownership, the funds will be released. Even if a state has already sold an asset, the original owner or heirs generally have the right to claim the proceeds from the sale. If the bank was closed by the government, the deposits and safe deposit boxes may have been transferred to another institution or to the FDIC. In most cases, there is an acquiring institution for the failed bank's deposits and safe deposit boxes.

Information on bank failures and FDIC-insured funds is more fully discussed in Chapter 9 of this almanac.

# CHAPTER 7:
# USING THE AUTOMATED TELLER MACHINE

## IN GENERAL

ATM is short for "automated teller machine." ATMs have been around since the mid-1960s. The first ATMs were strictly for getting cash using a bank-issued ATM card. Depending on the bank, in addition to dispensing cash, today's ATMs can accept deposits and loan payments, transfer funds between accounts, provide account information, including copies of canceled checks, and much more. Some ATMs even dispense postage stamps. ATM cards may also be used to make purchases at stores, with the payment automatically coming from your bank account. Even if you are traveling in a foreign country, there will likely be an ATM somewhere that will be able to dispense cash.

## RESOLVING AN ATM PROBLEM

According to the FDIC, ATMs in the United States handle more than 10 billion transactions a year, and the overwhelming majority go smoothly. Nevertheless, an ATM user will occasionally encounter some type of problem which needs to be resolved, as set forth below.

### Lost or Stolen ATM Card

If your ATM card is lost or stolen, it is important to immediately report the loss to the bank that issued the card in order to limit your liability for unauthorized use. To limit your liability for any losses, it's important to immediately report the problem to your ATM card issuer. Your bank may ask you to sign an affidavit or other notice of the loss or theft.

Under the Electronic Funds Transfer Act (EFTA), if you report that your ATM card is lost or stolen within two business days after you realize your card is missing, your losses are limited to a maximum of $50 for any unauthorized use. If you wait more than two business days to report a lost or stolen ATM card, your potential liability can increase significantly—up to $500. If you wait more than 60 days after receiving a bank statement that includes an unauthorized transfer, the law doesn't require the bank to reimburse the customer for any losses due to unauthorized transfers made prior to notification.

Nevertheless, depending on the circumstances, if it is clear that you are an innocent victim of fraud, and you promptly reported the loss or theft of the card or an unauthorized transaction, many banks will voluntarily hold the customer to no liability.

### Statement Discrepancies

It is important to save all ATM receipts until you are able to reconcile them with your bank statement. If you find any errors, you must promptly report them to your bank. To be fully protected under the EFTA, the customer must notify their financial institution of any errors, orally or in writing, no later than 60 days after the bank sends the bank statement.

### The ATM Retained the Card

On occasion, an ATM will not return the card to the customer following the transaction. Sometimes this is due to a defect in the card. This may also happen if the bank suspects fraudulent activity, e.g., if the customer repeatedly enters the wrong PIN number. If this should occur, immediately contact the financial institution that issued the card. They will issue a replacement card.

### The ATM Dispensed the Wrong Amount of Money

Sometimes an ATM malfunctions and does not dispense the amount of cash requested. If the receipt states that you were given the amount of cash requested, instead of the actual amount dispensed, immediately contact your bank to report the problem. The bank will check the machine to see if it has more money than it should have, in which case the difference will be refunded.

## ATM DEPOSITS

When making a deposit at an ATM, record the transaction in your checkbook, including information about each check that was deposited. Keep the ATM receipt and verify the deposit by reviewing your account statement, checking your account online, or by calling your bank's customer service line.

If you believe some or all of your deposit was mishandled, immediately contact your bank and follow up with a letter. If a check is missing, you might have to ask the check issuer to stop payment. Funds deposited in an ATM are not immediately available for withdrawal, and are subject to the bank's funds availability policy and federal schedules.

## ATM TRANSACTION FEES AND SURCHARGES

ATMs are convenient, yet they can also be costly. For example, if you withdraw money from an ATM machine that is not owned by your bank, you can be charged a surcharge ranging from $1 to $4 per transaction. Federal law requires that an ATM alert a non-customer about a surcharge before a transaction is completed so the person can cancel the transaction if they wish.

Under the EFTA, ATM owners are required to advise the consumer about all ATM fees and any other matters regarding the ATM transaction. To avoid unnecessary fees, it is best to try and use your own bank's ATM whenever possible. Be aware that some banks also charge their own customers for ATM transactions. If you are unable to use a surcharge-free machine, you may incur two charges—one from the ATM's owner, and the second from your own institution.

In order to avoid surcharges altogether, consider asking for cash back when using your ATM card to make purchases at retail establishments.

## KEEP ACCURATE ACCOUNTING

It is important to record all ATM withdrawals and purchases in your check register. Failure to enter the information and account for the withdrawals can cause unnecessary overdrafts due to bad recordkeeping.

When using the ATM to check balances and transactions, do not rely on the balance reflected by the ATM machine. The ATM balance does not reflect deductions for checks written but not yet paid. The only way to know how much money is available is to accurately maintain your checkbook.

## SAFEGUARDS

ATM manufacturers and financial institutions try to make ATM use as safe as possible. They install sophisticated cameras, place ATMs in safe locations, provide adequate lighting, limit the maximum daily cash withdrawals, and employ other security measures. Nevertheless, thieves still target ATM users. In order to reduce the possibility of becoming a victim, the following safeguards should be followed:

1. Know where your ATM card is at all times, and do not keep your PIN number written down anywhere on or near the card. A thief who has both the ATM card and PIN number can quickly withdraw money

from your account. If possible, memorize the PIN number, and do not share the number with anyone. Destroy old ATM cards, cutting through the account number and magnetic strip before throwing the card away.

2. Only visit ATMs that are in safe, well-lit areas, particularly at night. If anyone is loitering at or near the ATM, stay away. Look around for unusual looking devices on or near the ATM that may be used to record or intercept your PIN number.

3. Protect your ATM card when you use it to make purchases at retail establishments. For example, if you give an employee your card and you notice that he or she swipes it through two devices instead of one, that second device could be recording your account information for use in making a fraudulent card. Report any suspicious activity to the bank that issued the card.

4. Be careful when using private ATMS. These ATMS are not owned by financial institutions but by non-banking companies and individuals. It is better to use an ATM at an FDIC-insured bank; however, if you must use a private ATM, only use ATMs at establishments you trust. Private ATMs have been known to be a source of fraudulent activity by dishonest owners who collect card numbers for use in making duplicate cards.

5. Withdraw the dispensed cash safely and immediately put the money in your wallet or pocket. Do not count the money at the machine. When using a bank's drive-up ATM, keep the engine running, the doors locked, and all of the windows rolled up.

# CHAPTER 8:
# RESOLVING COMPLAINTS

## IN GENERAL

If you have a complaint concerning your bank, there are a number of steps you can take to try and resolve the problem, as discussed below.

## CONTACT YOUR BANK

The first step in trying to resolve a complaint is to contact your bank directly. If your bank is a small, local bank, you should schedule a personal meeting with the branch manager. Often a face-to-face meeting will go a long way to resolving a problem, unlike a telephone call or letter-writing, which can be frustrating.

Most large banks have a customer service department that handles problem resolution. Call that department to discuss your concerns and find out what procedures you must follow to resolve your complaint. Get the name of the person you spoke with, and their mailing address, so you can send a follow-up letter confirming what was stated in the conversation, e.g., whether a refund will be issued, etc. Written notification is often required by the consumer protection laws.

## PRIMARY FEDERAL REGULATORS

If your attempts to resolve your complaint at the bank level are not successful, contact your bank's primary federal regulator. Following are the five Federal Regulators of Depository Institutions:

### Federal Deposit Insurance Corporation (FDIC)

The Federal Deposit Insurance Corporation (FDIC) supervises state-chartered banks that are not members of the Federal Reserve System, and insures deposits at banks and savings associations. Contact information for the FDIC is as follows:

Federal Deposit Insurance Corporation (FDIC)
550 17th Street, N.W.
Washington, DC 20429
(Tel) 800-934-3342/(Fax) 202-942-3427
E-mail: consumer@fdic.gov
Website: www.fdic.gov/

If your concern involves the FDIC, you should make that complaint to:

Federal Deposit Insurance Corporation (FDIC)
Office of the Ombudsman
550 17th Street, N.W.
Washington, DC 20429
(Tel) 800-250-9286/(Fax) 202-942-3040
E-mail: ombudsman@fdic.gov

### Office of the Comptroller of the Currency

The Office of the Comptroller of the Currency charters and supervises national banks. The word "National" appears in the name of a national bank, or the initials "N. A." follow its name. Contact information for the Office of the Comptroller of the Currency is as follows:

Office of the Comptroller of the Currency
Customer Assistance Unit
1301 McKinney Street, Suite 3710
Houston, TX 77010
(Tel) 800-613-6743/(Fax) 713-336-4301
E-mail: consumer.assistance@occ.treas.gov
Website: www.occ.treas.gov/

### Federal Reserve System

The Federal Reserve System supervises state-chartered banks that are members of the Federal Reserve System. Contact information for the Federal Reserve System is as follows:

Federal Reserve System
Division of Consumer and Community Affairs
20th Street and Constitution Avenue, NW
Washington, DC 20551
(Tel) 202-452-3693/(Fax) 202-728-5850
Website: www.federalreserve.gov/

### National Credit Union Administration

The National Credit Union Administration charters and supervises federal credit unions, and insures deposits at federal credit unions and many state credit unions. Contact information for the National Credit Union Administration is as follows:

National Credit Union Administration
Office of Public and Congressional Affairs
1775 Duke Street
Alexandria, VA 22314
(Tel) 703-518-6330/(Fax) 703-518-6409
E-mail: pacamail@ncua.gov
Website: www.ncua.gov/

### Office of Thrift Supervision

The Office of Thrift Supervision supervises federally and state-chartered savings associations, including federally chartered savings banks. The names generally identify them as savings and loan associations, savings associations or savings banks. Federally chartered savings associations have the word "Federal" or the initials "FSB" or "FA" in their names. Contact information for the Office of Thrift Supervision is as follows:

Office of Thrift Supervision
Consumer Affairs Office
1700 G Street, NW
Washington, DC 20552
(Tel) 800-842-6929
E-mail: consumer.complaint@ots.treas.gov
Website: www.ots.treas.gov/

If you are unsure about which Federal Regulator governs your financial institution, you can call the bank directly for this information, or obtain this information from the FDIC by telephone (800-934-3342 ) or online at (www.fdic.gov/).

### FILING YOUR COMPLAINT LETTER

The consumer does not have to know the law in order to file a complaint with a government agency. The agency is obligated to advise the consumer of his or her rights under the law, and whether those rights have been violated based on the facts presented.

When writing a complaint letter to a government agency, make sure to include the following information: (1) your name, address and telephone number; (2) the name and location of the institution; (3) a brief description of the problem and your efforts to resolve the problem, including the names of employees you contacted; and (4) the action you would like the institution to take to correct the problem. Attach copies of any supporting documents, such as letters, statements, etc.

The complaint letter should be signed by the person making the complaint. This authorizes the government agency to contact the institution on their behalf, and lets the institution know that the customer wants their information released.

## APPLICABLE LAW

The FDIC and other financial regulators can only become involved in issues that involve the laws and regulations where they have jurisdiction. Many disputes between financial institutions and their customers involve matters of state law or the Uniform Commercial Code and must be settled by other government agencies or a court.

Federal statutes that shield a consumer from many banking-related problems also impose obligations on the consumer. Following is a list of consumer rights and responsibilities:

### Credit Billing Disputes

#### Rights

The Fair Credit Billing Act (FCRA), part of the Truth in Lending Act (TILA), protects consumers against inaccurate credit card bills, including unauthorized purchases, and allows consumers to withhold payments on defective goods until the matter is settled.

#### Responsibilities

To be fully protected, if you detect an error in your monthly statement, you must report the problem to the creditor in writing, and your complaint must be received within 60 days after the creditor sent you the statement being questioned. If a credit card is lost or stolen, the consumer's liability for unauthorized purchases is generally limited to $50 per card if a report of the loss is made in a timely manner.

### Debt Collection

#### Rights

The Fair Debt Collection Practices Act (FDCA) governs when and how a debt collector can attempt to collect money owed on a loan, bill or other personal or household debt in order to ensure that debt collectors treat the consumer fairly and without harassment.

#### Responsibilities

Within five days after a debt collector contacts you, he or she must send you a written notice stating the amount you allegedly owe, the name of the creditor, and what actions you should take if you believe you don't owe the money. After you receive that notice, you have 30 days to dispute any or all of the debt. If you dispute the bill, the debt collector can't contact you again to collect the money until he or she has provided you with proof of the debt, such as a copy of a bill.

## Credit Reports

### Rights

Credit bureaus are firms that gather and distribute credit reports. These reports are used by lenders, insurance companies, employers and others who have a legitimate right to learn about someone's credit history and reliability. The Fair Credit Reporting Act (FCRA) sets procedures for how your credit history is collected by credit bureaus and is shared among lenders. The law also enables you to have errors in your credit file corrected.

### Responsibilities

It is the consumer's responsibility to find out what is contained in their credit record and challenge the completeness or accuracy of any information contained in their file. To request a copy of a credit report, the consumer may call any of the nation's three major credit bureaus at these toll-free numbers:

Equifax—(800) 685-1111
Experian—(888) 397-3742
Trans Union—(800) 888-4213

If you believe that a credit bureau is distributing inaccurate information even after you brought that matter to its attention, you may file a complaint at any time with the Federal Trade Commission (877-382-4357), the federal regulator of credit bureaus, or bring a civil lawsuit to recover damages within two years of the alleged violation.

## Equal Credit Opportunity

### Rights

The Equal Credit Opportunity Act (ECOA) makes it unlawful for a creditor to discriminate against any loan applicant on the basis of race, color, religion, national origin, sex, marital status, age or certain other characteristics. The ECOA applies to credit cards, mortgages and other types of loans.

### Responsibilities

If you believe you've been denied credit illegally, you should first try to resolve the issue with the creditor. However, if that fails, you may file a complaint with the creditor's primary federal regulator, as set forth above. You also can bring a civil lawsuit against the creditor, but your case must be filed within two years of the alleged violation.

### Electronic Fund Transfers

#### Rights

The Electronic Funds Transfer Act (EFTA) provides a basic framework of the rights, liabilities and responsibilities of financial institutions and consumers when it comes to errors in the handling of electronic deposits or withdrawals. This would include transactions performed at an ATM or on a home computer, or by pre-arranged direct deposit or automatic payment programs at the bank.

#### Responsibilities

The consumer's responsibilities under the law depends on the particular situation, as follows:

#### Pre-Authorized Electronic Payments

If you want to discontinue a pre-authorized electronic payment from your bank account to a third party, you must send a written notice to the financial institution that must be received at least three days before the scheduled date for the payment you want discontinued.

#### Lost or Stolen ATM Card

If your ATM card is lost or stolen, your losses are limited to $50 if you report your ATM card lost or stolen within two business days of discovering the loss. If you wait between two and 60 days of discovering the loss, you can be liable for up to $500 of any unauthorized withdrawals. In general, if you wait more than 60 days after receiving a bank statement that includes an unauthorized electronic transfer, the law does not require your bank to reimburse you for any losses. You are not responsible, however, for any funds withdrawn after you notify your bank about a lost or stolen ATM card or debit card. If your bank concludes there's been no error with an electronic transfer, but you disagree with that determination, you may file a complaint with the appropriate federal or state government agency.

### Funds Availability

#### Rights

One way depository institutions protect against bad checks is by putting a hold on certain checks when they are deposited. The Expedited Funds Availability Act sets the time periods and other requirements governing when institutions must make deposited funds available to their customers for withdrawal or payment.

### Responsibilities

If you believe your financial institution isn't making deposited funds available within the required time period, you can file a complaint with the institution's primary federal regulator, as set forth above. You may also file a lawsuit against the institution, but you must do so within one year of the alleged violation.

## STATE REGULATORY AGENCIES

Some banking matters may involve state laws. For assistance, the reader is advised to contact the appropriate state financial institution regulatory agency for their state, or contact the state Attorney General. Consumers can also contact their state consumer protection agency for further guidance.

A directory of state consumer protection agencies is set forth at Appendix 13.

# CHAPTER 9:
# WHAT HAPPENS WHEN YOUR BANK FAILS

## IN GENERAL

The Federal Deposit Insurance Corporation (FDIC) was created by Congress in 1933 to make the savings of millions of Americans secure. The FDIC protects depositors' funds in the event of the financial failure of their bank or savings institution. The FDIC does not protect against losses due to fire, theft, or fraud, which are subject to other protections such as hazard and casualty insurance.

The FDIC is often appointed as receiver for failed financial institutions. When an institution is closed by its chartering authority, the FDIC makes payment of insured deposits to all of the failed institution's depositors as soon as possible, usually on the next business day after the closing. Those depositors who have funds in excess of the insurance limits receive the insured portion of their funds. They also may receive a portion of their uninsured funds either at that time, or as the assets of the failed institution are liquidated.

A list of failed financial institutions from October 2000 through April 2004 is set forth at Appendix 14.

## FDIC DEPOSIT INSURANCE

### Coverage

The FDIC insures deposit accounts such as checking, NOW and savings accounts, money market deposit accounts, and certificates of deposit (CDs). The basic insurance limit is $100,000 per depositor per insured bank. If a depositor has $100,000 or less in all of his or her deposit accounts at the same insured bank, those funds are fully insured.

The FDIC insures both principal and interest, up to the insurance maximum. For example, if an individual had an account with a principal balance of $95,000 plus $4,000 accrued interest, the total amount would be insured by the FDIC. If, however, the principal balance on the account was $100,000, the accrued interest on that account would not be insured because the additional amount was over the insurance limit.

The FDIC does not insure funds invested in stocks, bonds, mutual funds, life insurance policies, annuities, or municipal securities, even if these products were purchased from an insured bank. The FDIC also does not insure U.S. Treasury bills, bonds, or notes. These items are backed by the full faith and credit of the United States government.

Insured banks usually display the FDIC sign. To find out whether a particular bank is insured by the FDIC, or to obtain more information about FDIC deposit insurance coverage, a consumer can contact their regional FDIC office, or FDIC headquarters, as follows:

Federal Deposit Insurance Corporation
Office of Consumer Affairs
550 Seventeenth Street, NW
Washington, DC 20429
(Tel) 1-877-ASK-FDIC/1-877-275-3342
Website: www.fdic.gov/

A directory of FDIC Regional Offices is set forth at Appendix 15.

### Insurance Limitations

All funds held in the same type of ownership accounts at the same institution are added together before deposit insurance is determined. The total amount of funds held in the same type of ownership accounts are only insured up to the applicable maximum. However, if the funds are in different types of ownership accounts, or are deposited in separate institutions, they would then be separately insured.

For example, if a depositor has deposits in one insured bank totalling more than $100,000, depending on the ownership category of the account, each may be separately insured up to the limit of $100,000.

### Ownership Categories

The most common ownership categories are (1) single accounts; (2) joint accounts; (3) self-directed retirement accounts; and (4) revocable trust accounts.

### Single Accounts

A single account is a deposit account owned by one person and titled in that person's name alone. This account category does not include deposits held in individual retirement accounts (IRA) because an IRA is protected under a separate category.

All single accounts at the same insured bank are added together and the total is insured up to $100,000. If the depositor has a savings account and a certificate of deposit (CD) at the same insured bank, and both accounts are titled in the depositor's name alone, the two accounts are added together and the total is insured up to $100,000.

*Example: John has savings of $65,000 in his savings account and $45,000 in a CD at the same insured bank. The two accounts total $110,000, leaving a total of $10,000 over the insurance limit.*

### Joint Accounts

Joint accounts are deposit accounts owned by two or more people who have equal rights to withdraw money from the account. Each person's share of each joint account, with the same or different co-owners at the same insured bank, is added together and the total is insured up to $100,000. If the depositors have joint checking and savings accounts at the same insured bank, their portions of the two accounts are added together and insured up to $100,000.

*Example: John and James have $250,000 in a Certificate of Deposit at an insured bank. Each individual's share of the joint account is considered equal unless otherwise stated in the bank records. Therefore, John and James each own $125,000 in the joint account category, making a total of $50,000 ($25,000 each) over the insurance limit.*

### Self-Directed Retirement Accounts

Self-directed retirement accounts are deposits made in retirement accounts at an insured bank, for which the depositor has the right to choose how the money is deposited or invested, such as an IRA. All self-directed retirement accounts at the same insured bank are added together and the total is insured up to $100,000. Naming beneficiaries on a self-directed retirement account does not increase the insurance coverage.

### Revocable Trust Accounts

Revocable trust accounts are deposits held in either a payable-on-death account or a living trust account. Payable-on-death (POD) accounts are the most common form of revocable trust deposits. These informal revocable trusts are created when the account owner signs an agreement stating that the funds will be payable to a beneficiary upon the owner's death. Living trusts are formal revocable trusts created for estate planning purposes. The owner controls the funds in the trust during his or her lifetime. Upon the owner's death, the trust generally becomes irrevocable.

If certain conditions are met, revocable trust accounts are insured up to $100,000 per owner for each "qualifying" beneficiary, including the owner's spouse, child, grandchild, parent, or sibling. Adopted and stepchildren, grandchildren, parents, and siblings also qualify. In-laws, cousins, nieces and nephews, friends and organizations do not qualify. Living trust coverage is based on the interests of qualifying beneficiaries who would become entitled to receive trust assets when the trust owner dies, or if the trust is jointly owned, when the last owner dies. This means that, when determining coverage, the FDIC will ignore any trust beneficiary who would have an interest in the trust assets only after another living beneficiary dies.

The account title for a revocable trust account must include a term such as "payable on death," "in trust for," "living trust," "family trust," or similar language or an acronym (such as "POD" or "ITF") to indicate the existence of a trust relationship. In addition, for POD accounts, the beneficiaries must be identified by name in the bank records.

## SAFE DEPOSIT BOXES

The contents of a safe deposit box are not insured by the FDIC or by the bank where the box is located. Some banks may make a very limited payment if the box or contents are damaged or destroyed, depending on the circumstances. In the event of a bank failure, in most cases an acquiring institution would take over the failed bank's offices, including locations with safe deposit boxes. If the FDIC conducts a payoff because no acquirer can be found, boxholders would be sent instructions about removing the contents of their boxes.

## OBTAINING A LIEN RELEASE

A lien is a claim on property, such as a home or car, to ensure payment of a debt. For example, when you borrow money to purchase a car, the lender files a lien on the vehicle with the state. This insures that in the case of default on the loan, the lender can take the car back. When the debt is fully repaid, a release of the lien is provided by the lender. It is very important that the release of lien is filed. The lien is then removed from the records and a clear title issued, showing the owner's free and clear title to the property.

Usually, the consumer would obtain the lien release from the bank that gave them the loan for the property. However, if the lender bank has failed, the consumer cannot go to the bank for the lien release. In that case, the FDIC may be able to provide the consumer with a lien release of the property under the following circumstances:

1. The lienholder is a financial institution that failed and has been placed in FDIC receivership.

2. The loan was paid off before the Institution failed.

3. The loan was paid off to the FDIC after the Institution failed.

A request for a lien release from the FDIC must be made in writing, and must provide all of the details concerning the transaction. The request should be mailed to the FDIC at the following address:

Federal Deposit Insurance Corporation
1910 Pacific Ave
Dallas, Texas 75201
Attn: DRR Customer Service Center

In addition, the lien release request can be e-mailed (cservicefdic dal@fdic.gov) or faxed (703-812-1082) to the FDIC.

## UNCLAIMED FUNDS

When a failed financial institution with federal deposit insurance is liquidated, the FDIC resolution division is responsible for paying:

1. Unclaimed insured deposits up to $100,000;

2. Dividends declared on excess deposits over the $100,000 insured amount;

3. Dividends declared on general creditor claims; and

4. Funds distributed to the shareholders of the failed institution.

In many instances these funds remain unclaimed because:

1. The insured deposit is never claimed from the assuming financial institution;

2. The dividend check on the excess deposit amount is not cashed;

3. The dividend check on the general creditor claim is not cashed;

4. The check to the shareholder is not cashed; or

5. A valid address is not on file and the dividend check has been returned to the FDIC.

According to the FDIC, some people never claim their insured deposits and end up forfeiting their money under federal law. Individuals have 18 months from the date a bank fails to claim their insured funds from the FDIC. At the end of that period, the FDIC sends any unclaimed deposits to the state unclaimed property office. The customer may be able to recover these funds from the state for 10 years; however, if they fail to do so within that time period, any unclaimed money is returned to the FDIC's deposit insurance funds and is no longer available to be claimed. The contents of any safe deposit box left unclaimed with the FDIC is sent to state unclaimed property offices.

### FDIC Unclaimed Funds Database

The FDIC maintains an online database of unclaimed funds for consumers to search to determine whether they are entitled to any unclaimed insured deposits or undelivered dividend checks being held by the FDIC. However, as receiverships are terminated, under federal law, unclaimed insured funds can no longer be claimed, and data is removed from the FDIC website. Dividends, however, for uninsured portions of a deposit might be claimed post-termination if a dividend check was returned for a bad address.

### Claiming Held Funds

If the consumer determines that the FDIC is holding funds in their name from a financial institution, they should complete an FDIC Claimant Verification form, which is available online, including the FDIC reference number obtained from the online database, have the form notarized, and mail it to the following address:

Federal Deposit Insurance Corporation
1910 Pacific Avenue
Attention: Unclaimed Funds
FDIC-Liability Accounting Unit, 8th Floor
Dallas, Texas 75201

An FDIC representative will contact the claimant within 30 days of receipt of the FDIC Claimant Verification form. Notification will either be in writing, by phone, or by receipt of check.

# CHAPTER 10:
# ONLINE BANKING

## OVERVIEW

Online banking refers to the use of a personal computer to carry out a variety of banking transactions while online over the internet. Online banking was first offered to customers in 1995 by a small number of institutions. Since that time, online banking has gained worldwide popularity, and many banks now offer their customers the ability to do their banking over the internet.

A table depicting the top 25 online banks is set forth at Appendix 16.

Studies have indicated that there is substantial customer demand for computer banking services and banks have found that it is important to offer this service in order to stay competitive. As more individuals become computer savvy and have access to the internet, the advantages of online banking becomes more attractive. Banking over the internet is fast and convenient. In fact, a customer can access their banking information from virtually anywhere in the world.

Online banking also offers many advantages for the bank. The bank has an opportunity to generate revenue, increase productivity, and attract new customers online. Online banking helps the bank to sell its products such as credit cards, loans, certificates of deposit, and other financial services. Online banking is also very cost-effective. According to one study, the cost of a full-service teller transaction is $1.07, while the cost of an internet-based transaction is one penny.

As use of the internet continues to expand, more banks are using websites to offer products and services. Although the internet offers the potential for safe, convenient ways to shop for financial services and conduct banking business 24 hours a day, the consumer must make sure they are dealing with a legitimate institution, as set forth below.

## CONFIRM THAT THE ONLINE BANK IS LEGITIMATE

Whether you are dealing with a traditional bank or an online bank that has no physical offices, you must make sure that it is legitimate and that your deposits are federally insured. Read key information about the bank posted on its website. Most bank websites have an "About Us" section or something similar that describes the institution. You may find a brief history of the bank, the official name and address of the bank's headquarters, and information about its insurance coverage from the FDIC.

Be aware of copycat websites that deliberately use a name or website address very similar to, but not the same as, that of a real financial institution. The intent is to lure you into clicking onto their website to obtain personal information, such as your account number and password. Always check to see that you have typed the correct website address for your bank before conducting a transaction.

## VERIFY INSURANCE STATUS

To verify an online bank's insurance status, look for the familiar FDIC logo or the words "Member FDIC" or "FDIC Insured" on the website. Also check the FDIC's online database of FDIC-insured institutions. A positive match will display the official name of the bank, the date it became insured, its insurance certificate number, the main office location for the bank, and its primary government regulator. If your bank does not appear on this list, contact the FDIC. Some bank websites provide links directly to the FDIC's website to assist you in identifying or verifying the FDIC insurance protection of their deposits.

You must also determine whether the online bank uses different names for its online and traditional services, in which case you would be dealing with the same parent bank. This means, for example, that to determine your maximum FDIC insurance coverage, your deposits at the parent bank will be added together with those at the separately named online bank, and will only be insured for up to the maximum amount covered for one bank.

Not all banks operating on the internet are insured by the FDIC. Many banks that are not FDIC-insured are chartered overseas. If you choose to use a bank chartered overseas, it is important for you to know that the FDIC may not insure your deposits.

## STATISTICS

According to the American Bankers Association, approximately 625 of the nation's 9,000 consumer banks currently offer some form of online banking, and a recent survey found that more than six and a half million people now bank online. As reported by The Online Banking Report, twenty percent of internet users now access online banking services, a total that is expected to reach 33 percent by 2006. By 2010, it is expected that over 55 million U.S. households will use online banking and bill payment services.

Tables setting forth the projected number of U.S. households using online banking services and online bill payment service are set forth at Appendix 17 and 18 respectively.

## DEMOGRAPHICS

The internet also targets a valuable demographic. The majority of people using the internet are in the middle to high income bracket, and studies indicate that 50% of the people online are either in professional or managerial positions. These customers are also the ones who want to have the convenience of online banking for home or business use.

Small business owners are another group of individuals looking to the internet to manage their business banking more efficiently. Business-to-business commerce increased forty-fold, from $8 billion in 1997 to $327 billion in 2002. Banks will play a significant role in this new technology by offering online banking products which allow the business banking customer to perform numerous transactions from their computer, including payroll and bill payment options.

## REGISTERING FOR ONLINE BANKING

In order to sign up for online banking, the customer must access their bank's website. It is usually quite easy to search for the bank's website using a search engine if the customer does not already have the website address—also known as a Uniform Resource Locator (URL). The bank website explains the procedure of setting up the online banking account in detail.

Although most bank websites are designed to be very "user-friendly," customers who are not computer proficient, or who experience difficulty registering, usually have the option of telephoning an 800-number where they can receive technical support. Most bank websites also offer online technical support and customer service.

In order to take advantage of online banking, the customer needs a computer and a modem. The customer accesses the internet through their internet service provider (ISP), and types in the bank's URL, which takes the customer to the bank's webpage, at which point the customer must "log into" their account. After providing their account number and other identifying information, the customer will be directed to choose a username and a password which they will use to access their accounts electronically. Online banks require the customer to have a username and password to make sure nobody else can access the account.

Banks that do not offer web-based services provide the customer with online software that enables the customer to directly dial into the bank's system with a modem using a designated personal identification number (PIN) and password. This is generally known as PC banking. The advantage of PC banking is the customer does not need an internet account with an ISP to access their banking information, thus eliminating the monthly ISP. Nevertheless, most banks are moving away from PC banking in favor of online banking.

## ONLINE SERVICES

Services vary depending on the particular bank. Some banks provide a full range of services online, such as obtaining statements and viewing transactions, opening and closing accounts, applying for mortgages, transferring funds among accounts, and bill payment. Other banks may provide fewer online services, e.g., limited to the ability to view statements and transactions. Some banks charge a nominal monthly fee while others offer the service for free. Banks generally provide consumers with a "tour" of the website to demonstrate how online banking works, and offer online customer service.

Many banks offer the customer the option of linking all of their bank accounts, such as their checking and savings accounts. This gives the customer the ability to transfer funds between accounts as needed. Many banks also offer the customer the opportunity to open new accounts and make investments online. Loan applications may also be completed online and submitted electronically. Customers can also order checks and place stop payments online. In addition, many bank websites contain a wealth of valuable information for the consumer, offer various tutorials of interest to the consumer, and provide links to other informative finance-related websites.

## ONLINE BILL PAYMENT

Online bill payment is becoming increasingly popular with consumers. Many banks which offer online banking also provide their customers with the ability to pay their bills online using their bank account. The bank generally provides a list of payees, and the customer chooses the payees from that list. If a payee is not listed, the customer must type in the payee's name, address, telephone number and the customer's account number with the payee. This information is then stored and the customer need only enter the payment amount and date the payment should be made. The customer can thereafter track the status of bill payments online at any time.

Depending on the payee, the bill will be paid either electronically or by a paper check which is printed and mailed by the bank. An increasing number of companies are now equipped to accept direct electronic payments, which are transmitted instantaneously. Nevertheless, it is still advisable to schedule payments approximately 5 days in advance to make sure the payees receive timely payments and avoid late charges.

Despite the expediency and convenience of online bill payment, many consumers are still reluctant to take advantage of this service. According to a 2002 study by the American Banker, 30% express concern over using their checking accounts for online bill payment, and 50% believe using their credit card offers better protection.

### Automatic Bill Payment

The customer can also request automatic bill payment for bills that are paid in the same amount and at the same time each month, such as an installment loan. The bank will automatically make those payments from the customer's account each month. The customer must be careful, however, to notate the monthly deduction in their checking or saving account ledger each month.

### Electronic Bills

Many companies are now offering their customers the option of receiving electronic bills (e-bills) instead of mailing a paper bill. The e-bill is transmitted to the customer over the internet. It contains all of the same information as the paper bill, and offers the customer the opportunity to pay the bill online.

### MAINTAINING PRIVACY AND SECURITY

Despite the convenience and expediency of online banking, security is still a concern and causes many consumers to be reluctant to bank over the internet. According to a 2002 survey by the Tower Group, 26% of American households do not use online banking because they are concerned over security. Concerned customers should inquire about the bank's online security procedures to make sure that their information is secure and the risk of interception by identity thieves is minimized.

For more detailed information on internet privacy issues, the reader is advised to consult this author's legal almanac entitled *Privacy and the Internet: Your Expectations & Rights Under the Law,* also published by Oceana Publications.

### Securing Online Transactions

All financial institutions require information about the consumer in order to process a transaction. Although it may be impossible to protect oneself completely from fraud and deception online, there are some steps the consumer can take to make it less likely their personal information will be intercepted, as further discussed below.

### Secure Browsers and Encryption Technology

Given the extensive amount of personal identifying and financial information involved in internet banking, the concerns relating to security issues are certainly justified. Although there are concerns relating to security with any type of online transactions, including online banking, banks are particularly careful in selecting and developing an appropriate software system with a secure online server to process their customer's banking transactions.

A browser is special software that allows the user to navigate through the internet and view various websites. Most computers come with a browser installed, e.g., Microsoft Internet Explorer and Netscape Navigator. Some browsers are available for downloading on the internet at no cost to the user. Browsers transmit a user's personal information to website operators, including but not limited to the user's ISP, and websites the user has visited.

The consumer should make sure that they use a secure browser when providing personal identifying or financial information online. A secure browser refers to software that encrypts or scrambles the information sent over the Internet. The consumer should be sure that the browser they use has the latest encryption capabilities available and should comply with industry security standards.

All banks use sophisticated encryption technology to ensure security. Once the customer is logged into the bank's website, the URL of the website changes, indicating the information being transmitted to and from the system is encrypted, i.e. scrambled, to ensure privacy and security.

### Emptying the Cache

The "cache" is an area on the computer's hard drive where copies of the websites the user visits are stored so that the browser can access them locally instead of going to the website. This helps to make browsing faster and easier. However, storage of the user's browsing record can jeopardize the user's privacy, particularly if the user shares the computer with others, or uses a public computer, e.g., in a library or internet cafe.

This browsing record can be deleted by taking the following steps:

1. Click on "edit" in the browser.

2. Scroll down to "preferences."

3. Click on the "empty cache" button.

4. Close the browser.

### Cookies

"Cookies" are bits of electronic information in the form of small text files that identify the computer used by a specific customer to a particular website. Cookies are placed on a computer's hard drive when the user visits various websites. Cookies are used by the website to tailor information to the particular customer, such as marketing information, preferences, etc. This data may include the user's name, address, and preferences and browsing patterns.

Cookies inform the website operator that the user has visited the website, and can be used to track the user online and enable the website operator to create a profile of the user without the user's knowledge. If the user has obtained a username and password to access the website, cookies remembers that information so that the user can easily access the website again without having to enter their password each time they visit the site. When the user revisits the same website, it opens the cookie file to access stored information.

The presence of cookies on a website can be detected using special software or particular browser settings. You can search the hard drive for a file with the word "cookie" in it—e.g., cookie.txt—to view the cookies that have been stored on your computer. Internet users who prefer not to have cookies stored on their hard drive can set their preferences concerning the cookies that are stored. For example, some users choose to limit third-party cookies. The user can also completely disable the ability for cookies to be placed on their hard drive.

Newer browsers allow the user to recognize websites that send cookies in advance. The user can then reject the cookies before they are placed on the computer's hard driver rather than having to delete them afterwards.

### Javascript

JavaScript is a programming language used to add features to web pages in order to make the website more interactive. Javascript is interpreted by the web browser. Unfortunately, Javascript creates some privacy risks to the user due to "privacy holes" sometimes found in javascript. For example, some "privacy holes" have permitted remote sites to read the URLs from the browser's cache, thus gaining access to the list of websites visited by the user. It is advisable, therefore, to turn Javascript off when visiting unfamiliar websites. In addition, virus detectors can identify whether a specific Javascript has a privacy hole.

### Privacy Statements

When visiting a website, it is important to check whether the website has a privacy statement, particularly if the website requests the user to enter personal information. A privacy statement describes the way in which the website collects, shares and protects the user's personal information. It is a legally binding document which the website owner must abide by or face legal action.

Internet users should carefully read the privacy policy of all websites with which they do business, including the privacy policy of their own internet service provider. Any website that asks for personal information should have a privacy policy statement. If a website does not post a privacy statement, the user is advised not to patronize that website.

A website's privacy statement should be easily accessible and understandable. Some websites post a simplified version of their privacy policy that is easy for users to read, and provide links to additional information, which may contain more complicated legal or technical information.

A well-drafted privacy policy should provide the user with the following information:

1. The information that is being collected.

2. Whether the information is personally identifiable.

3. The reasons the website collects the information.

4. The appropriateness of the data collection as it relates to the particular activity or transaction.

5. The manner in which the data is collected.

6. Whether the user has a choice regarding the type and quantity of personal information that the site collects.

7. Whether the website uses cookies.

8. Whether the website maintains web logs.

9. How the personal information collected is used by the website.

10. Whether personal information is ever used for a secondary purpose—i.e., a purpose other than that for which the user has provided the information.

11. If personal information is used for a secondary purpose, the user should be so informed.

12. Whether the visitor has consented to secondary use of personal information.

13. Whether the visitor has the option to prohibit secondary use of personal information.

14. Whether the website offers different kinds of service depending on user privacy preferences, e.g., does the website disadvantage users who exercise data collection choices.

15. Whether the user can access the information collected.

16. Whether the user can correct inaccurate data that has been collected.

17. The length of time personal information is stored.

18. The website's complaint procedures.

19. Contact information, such as an e-mail address or phone number, so the user can contact the company if they have any questions about online security or their privacy policy statement.

20. The laws governing data collection.

### The Gramm-Leach-Bliley Act (GLBA)

The Gramm-Leach-Bliley Act (GLBA) requires financial institutions to ensure the security and confidentiality of the personal information financial institutions collect from their customers, such as their names, addresses and phone numbers; bank and credit card account numbers; income and credit histories; and social security numbers.

### The Safeguards Rule

As part of its implementation of the GLBA, the Federal Trade Commission (FTC) has issued the Safeguards Rule. The Safeguards Rule requires financial institutions under FTC jurisdiction to secure customer records and information.

The text of the Safeguards Rule is set forth at Appendix 19 of this almanac.

### Covered Institutions

The Safeguards Rule applies to businesses, regardless of size, that are "significantly engaged" in providing financial products or services to consumers. This includes check-cashing businesses, data processors, mortgage brokers, nonbank lenders, personal property or real estate appraisers, professional tax prepares, courier services, and retailers that issue credit cards to consumers.

The Safeguards Rule also applies to financial companies, like credit reporting agencies and ATM operators, that receive information from other financial institutions about their customers. In addition to developing their own safeguards, financial institutions are responsible for taking steps to ensure that their affiliates and service providers safeguard customer information in their care. Poorly-managed customer data can lead to identity theft which occurs when someone steals a consumer's personal identifying information for illegal purposes, e.g., to fraudulently open new charge accounts, order merchandise, or borrow money.

### Requirements

The Safeguards Rule requires financial institutions to develop a written information security plan that describes their program to protect customer information. The plan must be appropriate to the financial institution's size and complexity, the nature and scope of its activities, and the sensitivity of the customer information it handles. As part of its plan, each financial institution must:

1. Designate one or more employees to coordinate the safeguards;

2. Identify and assess the risks to customer information in each relevant area of the company's operation, and evaluate the effectiveness of the current safeguards for controlling these risks;

3. Design and implement a safeguards program, and regularly monitor and test it;

4. Select appropriate service providers and contract with them to implement safeguards; and

5. Evaluate and adjust the program in light of relevant circumstances, including changes in the firm's business arrangements or operations, or the results of testing and monitoring of safeguards.

Each financial institution is advised to implement safeguards appropriate to its own circumstances. For example, some financial institutions may choose to describe their safeguards programs in a single document, while others may set forth their plans in several different documents, such as one to cover an information technology division and another to describe the training program for employees.

### The Financial Services Modernization Act

A new federal law, the Financial Services Modernization Act, gives consumers some rights to protect their personal financial information. It outlines the circumstances when financial service companies must allow the consumer to limit the sharing of their information, and outlines the steps consumers must take to do so. As a result of this new law, consumers will periodically receive notices from the financial institutions with which they do business, notifying them of the company's privacy policy.

## SECURITY FAILURES AND IDENTITY THEFT

Identity theft occurs when an identity thief obtains personal information about another individual and uses that information, without the individual's knowledge or consent, in order to commit fraud and gain a financial benefit. Identity theft is fast becoming the most prevalent and costly financial crime in the nation. It is estimated that more than 750,000 people have their identity stolen each year, costing consumers and the financial industry billions of dollars.

According to the FTC, in 2002, bank fraud accounted for 13% of the total identity theft complaints. New fraudulent bank accounts were opened in the victim's name in 2.7% of all cases. Fraud using a victim's existing bank account occurred in 6.2% of the cases. Fraud involving electronic fund transfers accounted for 1.9% of all cases, and 2.3% of the bank fraud complaints were unspecified as to the type of fraud involved.

If a website is not secure, as set forth above, identity thieves who are knowledgeable computer hackers may be able to access information through the bank's website. Nevertheless, security failures are more often due to the carelessness of the customer, e.g., in failing to protect passwords and sharing personal information over the internet or via email. For example, the customer should be aware of fraudulent e-mails that are purportedly sent to them from their bank requesting details about their account, such as their password. An online bank will not send a customer an e-mail containing specific information about their bank accounts, unless requested by the customer. A customer who receives such an e-mail purportedly from their bank should not reply to the e-mail or use any links in the e-mail that directs them to visit the website. If there is a URL, one should type in the URL and see where it leads.

Unfortunately, identity thieves who are able to obtain the customer's username and password are also able to access a wealth of information and services. A customer should safeguard their internet banking password very carefully. It is just as valuable as the PIN number assigned to their bank ATM card. One should not use a password that can easily be guessed by an identity thief. It is also wise to change one's password from time to time to minimize the risk that the account will be accessed.

A table of state identity theft laws is set forth at Appendix 20.

For more detailed information on identity theft, the reader is advised to consult this author's legal almanac entitled *The Law of Identity Theft*, also published by Oceana Publications.

# APPENDIX 1:
# TWENTY-FIVE LARGEST BANKING COMPANIES RANKED BY CONSOLIDATED COMPANY ASSETS

| RANK | BANK | ASSETS (IN U.S. $000,000) |
|---|---|---|
| 1 | Citigroup, Inc. | 1,097,190 |
| 2 | J.P. Morgan Chase & Co. | 758,800 |
| 3 | Bank of America Corporation | 660,458 |
| 4 | Wells Fargo & Company | 349,259 |
| 5 | Wachovia Corporation | 341,839 |
| 6 | Bank One Corporation | 277,383 |
| 7 | Washington Mutual, Inc. | 268,298 |
| 8 | FleetBoston Financial Corporation | 190,453 |
| 9 | U.S. Bancorp | 180,027 |
| 10 | National City Corporation | 118,258 |
| 11 | SunTrust Banks, Inc. | 117,323 |
| 12 | State Street Corporation | 85,794 |
| 13 | KeyCorp | 85,202 |
| 14 | Fifth Third Bancorp | 80,894 |
| 15 | BB&T Corporation | 80,217 |
| 16 | Bank of New York Company, Inc. | 77,170 |
| 17 | Golden West Financial Corporation | 68,406 |
| 18 | PNC Financial Services Group, Inc. | 66,377 |
| 19 | Comerica Incorporated | 53,301 |
| 20 | SouthTrust Corporation | 50,571 |
| 21 | Regions Financial Corporation | 47,939 |
| 22 | Charter One Financial, Inc. | 41,896 |

| RANK | BANK | ASSETS (IN U.S. $000,000) |
|------|------|---------------------------|
| 23 | AmSouth Bancorporation | 40,571 |
| 24 | UnionBanCal Corporation | 40,170 |
| 25 | Sovereign Bancorp, Inc. | 39,524 |

Source: Federal Deposit Insurance Corporation (FDIC)

# APPENDIX 2:
# APPLICABLE SECTIONS—
# UCC ARTICLE 3: NEGOTIABLE
# INSTRUMENTS

### SECTION 3-108. PAYABLE ON DEMAND OR AT DEFINITE TIME

(a) A promise or order is "payable on demand" if it (i) states that it is payable on demand or at sight, or otherwise indicates that it is payable at the will of the holder, or (ii) does not state any time of payment.

(b) A promise or order is "payable at a definite time" if it is payable on elapse of a definite period of time after sight or acceptance or at a fixed date or dates or at a time or times readily ascertainable at the time the promise or order is issued, subject to rights of (i) prepayment, (ii) acceleration, (iii) extension at the option of the holder, or (iv) extension to a further definite time at the option of the maker or acceptor or automatically upon or after a specified act or event.

(c) If an instrument, payable at a fixed date, is also payable upon demand made before the fixed date, the instrument is payable on demand until the fixed date and, if demand for payment is not made before that date, becomes payable at a definite time on the fixed date.

### SECTION 3-109. PAYABLE TO BEARER OR TO ORDER

(a) A promise or order is payable to bearer if it:

   (1) states that it is payable to bearer or to the order of bearer or otherwise indicates that the person in possession of the promise or order is entitled to payment;

   (2) does not state a payee; or

   (3) states that it is payable to or to the order of cash or otherwise indicates that it is not payable to an identified person.

(b) A promise or order that is not payable to bearer is payable to order if it is payable (i) to the order of an identified person or (ii) to an identified person or order. A promise or order that is payable to order is payable to the identified person.

(c) An instrument payable to bearer may become payable to an identified person if it is specially indorsed pursuant to Section 3-205(a). An instrument payable to an identified person may become payable to bearer if it is indorsed in blank pursuant to Section 3-205(b).

### SECTION 3-205. SPECIAL INDORSEMENT; BLANK INDORSEMENT; ANOMALOUS INDORSEMENT

(a) If an indorsement is made by the holder of an instrument, whether payable to an identified person or payable to bearer, and the indorsement identifies a person to whom it makes the instrument payable, it is a "special indorsement." When specially indorsed, an instrument becomes payable to the identified person and may be negotiated only by the indorsement of that person. The principles stated in Section 3-110 apply to special indorsements.

(b) If an indorsement is made by the holder of an instrument and it is not a special indorsement, it is a "blank indorsement." When indorsed in blank, an instrument becomes payable to bearer and may be negotiated by transfer of possession alone until specially indorsed.

### SECTION 3-302. HOLDER IN DUE COURSE

(a) Subject to subsection (c) and Section 3-106(d), "holder in due course" means the holder of an instrument if:

(1) the instrument when issued or negotiated to the holder does not bear such apparent evidence of forgery or alteration or is not otherwise so irregular or incomplete as to call into question its authenticity; and

(2) the holder took the instrument (i) for value, (ii) in good faith, (iii) without notice that the instrument is overdue or has been dishonored or that there is an uncured default with respect to payment of another instrument issued as part of the same series, (iv) without notice that the instrument contains an unauthorized signature or has been altered, (v) without notice of any claim to the instrument described in Section 3-306, and (vi) without notice that any party has a defense or claim in recoupment described in Section 3-305(a).

## SECTION 3-305. DEFENSES AND CLAIMS IN RECOUPMENT

(a) [T]he right to enforce the obligation of a party to pay an instrument is subject to the following:

(1) a defense of the obligor based on (i) infancy of the obligor to the extent it is a defense to a simple contract, (ii) duress, lack of legal capacity, or illegality of the transaction which, under other law, nullifies the obligation of the obligor, (iii) fraud that induced the obligor to sign the instrument with neither knowledge nor reasonable opportunity to learn of its character or its essential terms, or (iv) discharge of the obligor in insolvency proceedings.

## SECTION 3-401. SIGNATURE

(a) A person is not liable on an instrument unless (i) the person signed the instrument, or (ii) the person is represented by an agent or representative who signed the instrument and the signature is binding on the represented person under Section 3-402.

## SECTION 3-402. SIGNATURE BY REPRESENTATIVE

(a) If a person acting, or purporting to act, as a representative signs an instrument by signing either the name of the represented person or the name of the signer, the represented person is bound by the signature to the same extent the represented person would be bound if the signature were on a simple contract. If the represented person is bound, the signature of the representative is the "authorized signature of the represented person" and the represented person is liable on the instrument, whether or not identified in the instrument.

(b) If a representative signs the name of the representative to an instrument and the signature is an authorized signature of the represented person, the following rules apply:

(1) If the form of the signature shows unambiguously that the signature is made on behalf of the represented person who is identified in the instrument, the representative is not liable on the instrument.

(2) Subject to subsection (c), if (i) the form of the signature does not show unambiguously that the signature is made in a representative capacity or (ii) the represented person is not identified in the instrument, the representative is liable on the instrument to a holder in due course that took the instrument without notice that the representative was not intended to be liable on the instrument. With respect to any other person, the representative is liable on the instrument unless the representative proves that the original parties did not intend the representative to be liable on the instrument.

(c) If a representative signs the name of the representative as drawer of a check without indication of the representative status and the check is payable from an account of the represented person who is identified on the check, the signer is not liable on the check if the signature is an authorized signature of the represented person.

## SECTION 3-403. UNAUTHORIZED SIGNATURE

(a) Unless otherwise provided in this Article or Article 4, an unauthorized signature is ineffective except as the signature of the unauthorized signer in favor of a person who in good faith pays the instrument or takes it for value. An unauthorized signature may be ratified for all purposes of this Article.

## SECTION 3-416. TRANSFER WARRANTIES

(a) A person who transfers an instrument for consideration warrants to the transferee and, if the transfer is by indorsement, to any subsequent transferee that:

(1) the warrantor is a person entitled to enforce the instrument;

(2) all signatures on the instrument are authentic and authorized;

(3) the instrument has not been altered;

(4) the instrument is not subject to a defense or claim in recoupment of any party which can be asserted against the warrantor; and

(5) the warrantor has no knowledge of any insolvency proceeding commenced with respect to the maker or acceptor or, in the case of an unaccepted draft, the drawer.

(b) A person to whom the warranties under subsection (a) are made and who took the instrument in good faith may recover from the warrantor as damages for breach of warranty an amount equal to the loss suffered as a result of the breach, but not more than the amount of the instrument plus expenses and loss of interest incurred as a result of the breach.

## SECTION 3-601. DISCHARGE AND EFFECT OF DISCHARGE

(a) The obligation of a party to pay the instrument is discharged as stated in this Article or by an act or agreement with the party which would discharge an obligation to pay money under a simple contract.

(b) Discharge of the obligation of a party is not effective against a person acquiring rights of a holder in due course of the instrument without notice of the discharge.

## SECTION 3-602. PAYMENT

(a) Subject to subsection (b), an instrument is paid to the extent payment is made (i) by or on behalf of a party obliged to pay the instrument, and (ii) to a person entitled to enforce the instrument. To the extent of the payment, the obligation of the party obliged to pay the instrument is discharged even though payment is made with knowledge of a claim to the instrument under Section 3-306 by another person.

(b) The obligation of a party to pay the instrument is not discharged under subsection (a) if:

(1) a claim to the instrument under Section 3-306 is enforceable against the party receiving payment and (i) payment is made with knowledge by the payor that payment is prohibited by injunction or similar process of a court of competent jurisdiction, or (ii) in the case of an instrument other than a cashier's check, teller's check, or certified check, the party making payment accepted, from the person having a claim to the instrument, indemnity against loss resulting from refusal to pay the person entitled to enforce the instrument; or

(2) the person making payment knows that the instrument is a stolen instrument and pays a person it knows is in wrongful possession of the instrument.

## SECTION 3-604. DISCHARGE BY CANCELLATION OR RENUNCIATION

(a) A person entitled to enforce an instrument, with or without consideration, may discharge the obligation of a party to pay the instrument (i) by an intentional voluntary act, such as surrender of the instrument to the party, destruction, mutilation, or cancellation of the instrument, cancellation or striking out of the party's signature, or the addition of words to the instrument indicating discharge, or (ii) by agreeing not to sue or otherwise renouncing rights against the party by a signed writing.

# APPENDIX 3:
# SAMPLE PROMISSORY NOTE

_____, [State]_____, 20___

**PROMISE TO PAY.** On _____, the under-signed ("I", "Me", or "My" when used in this Note means everyone who signs this Note) promise(s) to pay to the order of

### [BANK ADDRESS]

THE SUM OF:

_____ DOLLARS $_____ with other interest from the date of this Note unless this Note is payable other than on demand and the Bank has taken interest in advance).

**DEFAULT.** Unless this Note is payable on demand, the Bank may require me to pay this Note immediately in full if: (1) I or any guarantor or endorser of the Note becomes insolvent or incompetent or dies; or (2) I or any guarantor or endorser of the Note files or has filed against us a bankruptcy or other insolvency proceeding; or (3) I break one of my promises under this Note or under any other agreement I have made with the Bank; or (4) Something else happens which, the Bank reasonably believes, affects my ability to pay the Note.

**COLLECTION COSTS.** I agree to pay all of the Bank's expenses in collecting payment of this Note, including reasonable attorney's fees or such other amount as may be permitted by law.

**INTEREST.** Interest shall be payable at the rate of _____% per year. Interest after maturity or demand, if this is a demand note, shall continue to be payable at the note rate in effect at the time of maturity or demand until this note is paid in full.

_____

_____

## [Reserve Side of Note]
## ENDORSEMENT AND GUARANTEE

I ("I", "me" or "my" shall mean everyone who signs this endorsement) agree to be equally responsible with the other person(s) signing this Note for its full repayment and will, at the request of Bank, promptly pay the entire amount owing upon a default by any other person(s) who signed the Note or this Endorsement. I also agree that my responsibility to pay this Note shall not be affected by the Bank permitting a change in the terms and time of repayment, releasing any security or the obligation of any other person for the payment of this Note or not notifying me of any dishonor of the Note or of any other action taken with respect to this Note or of any collateral that may be given to secure the Note's repayment.

# APPENDIX 4:
# APPLICABLE SECTIONS—
# UCC ARTICLE 4: BANK DEPOSITS AND
# COLLECTIONS

---

### SECTION 4-201. STATUS OF COLLECTING BANK AS AGENT AND PROVISIONAL STATUS OF CREDITS

(a) Unless a contrary intent clearly appears and before the time that a settlement given by a collecting bank for an item is or becomes final, the bank, with respect to the item, is an agent or sub-agent of the owner of the item and any settlement given for the item is provisional. . .

### SECTION 4-202. RESPONSIBILITY FOR COLLECTION OR RETURN; WHEN ACTION TIMELY

(a) A collecting bank must exercise ordinary care in:

(1) presenting an item or sending it for presentment;

(2) sending notice of dishonor or nonpayment or returning an item other than a documentary draft to the bank's transferor after learning that the item has not been paid or accepted, as the case may be;

(3) settling for an item when the bank receives final settlement; and

(4) notifying its transferor of any loss or delay in transit within a reasonable time after discovery thereof.

(b) A collecting bank exercises ordinary care under subsection (a) by taking proper action before its midnight deadline following receipt of an item, notice, or settlement. Taking proper action within a reasonably longer time may constitute the exercise of ordinary care, but the bank has the burden of establishing timeliness.

---

## SECTION 4-205. DEPOSITARY BANK HOLDER OF UNINDORSED ITEM

If a customer delivers an item to a depositary bank for collection:

(1) the depositary bank becomes a holder of the item at the time it receives the item for collection if the customer at the time of delivery was a holder of the item, whether or not the customer indorses the item, and, if the bank satisfies the other requirements of Section 3-302, it is a holder in due course; and

(2) the depositary bank warrants to collecting banks, the payor bank or other payor, and the drawer that the amount of the item was paid to the customer or deposited to the customer's account.

## SECTION 4-207. TRANSFER WARRANTIES

(a) A customer or collecting bank that transfers an item and receives a settlement or other consideration warrants to the transferee and to any subsequent collecting bank that:

(1) the warrantor is a person entitled to enforce the item;

(2) all signatures on the item are authentic and authorized;

(3) the item has not been altered;

(4) the item is not subject to a defense or claim in recoupment (Section 3-305(a)) of any party that can be asserted against the warrantor; and

(5) the warrantor has no knowledge of any insolvency proceeding commenced with respect to the maker or acceptor or, in the case of an unaccepted draft, the drawer.

(b) If an item is dishonored, a customer or collecting bank transferring the item and receiving settlement or other consideration is obliged to pay the amount due on the item (i) according to the terms of the item at the time it was transferred, or (ii) if the transfer was of an incomplete item, according to its terms when completed as stated in Sections 3-115 and 3-407. The obligation of a transferor is owed to the transferee and to any subsequent collecting bank that takes the item in good faith. A transferor cannot disclaim its obligation under this subsection by an indorsement stating that it is made "without recourse" or otherwise disclaiming liability.

(c) A person to whom the warranties under subsection (a) are made and who took the item in good faith may recover from the warrantor as damages for breach of warranty an amount equal to the loss suffered as a result of the breach, but not more than the amount of the item plus expenses and loss of interest incurred as a result of the breach.

---

(d) The warranties stated in subsection (a) cannot be disclaimed with respect to checks. Unless notice of a claim for breach of warranty is given to the warrantor within 30 days after the claimant has reason to know of the breach and the identity of the warrantor, the warrantor is discharged to the extent of any loss caused by the delay in giving notice of the claim.

(e) A cause of action for breach of warranty under this section accrues when the claimant has reason to know of the breach.

### SECTION 4-208. PRESENTMENT WARRANTIES

(a) If an unaccepted draft is presented to the drawee for payment or acceptance and the drawee pays or accepts the draft, (i) the person obtaining payment or acceptance, at the time of presentment, and (ii) a previous transferor of the draft, at the time of transfer, warrant to the drawee that pays or accepts the draft in good faith that:

(1) the warrantor is, or was, at the time the warrantor transferred the draft, a person entitled to enforce the draft or authorized to obtain payment or acceptance of the draft on behalf of a person entitled to enforce the draft;

(2) the draft has not been altered; and

(3) the warrantor has no knowledge that the signature of the purported drawer of the draft is unauthorized.

(b) A drawee making payment may recover from a warrantor damages for breach of warranty equal to the amount paid by the drawee less the amount the drawee received or is entitled to receive from the drawer because of the payment. In addition, the drawee is entitled to compensation for expenses and loss of interest resulting from the breach. . .

### SECTION 4-401. WHEN BANK MAY CHARGE CUSTOMER'S ACCOUNT

(a) A bank may charge against the account of a customer an item that is properly payable from that account even though the charge creates an overdraft. An item is properly payable if it is authorized by the customer and is in accordance with any agreement between the customer and bank.

(b) A customer is not liable for the amount of an overdraft if the customer neither signed the item nor benefitted from the proceeds of the item.

(c) A bank may charge against the account of a customer a check that is otherwise properly payable from the account, even though payment was made before the date of the check, unless the customer has given notice to the bank of the postdating describing the check with reasonable certainty. The notice is effective for the period stated in Section 4-403(b) for stop-payment orders, and must be received at such time and in such manner as to afford the bank a reasonable opportunity to act on it before the bank takes any action with respect to the check described in Section 4-303. If a bank charges against the account of a customer a check before the date stated in the notice of postdating, the bank is liable for damages for the loss resulting from its act. The loss may include damages for dishonor of subsequent items under Section 4-402.

(d) A bank that in good faith makes payment to a holder may charge the indicated account of its customer according to:

(1) the original terms of the altered item; or

(2) the terms of the completed item, even though the bank knows the item has been completed unless the bank has notice that the completion was improper.

### SECTION 4-403. CUSTOMER'S RIGHT TO STOP PAYMENT; BURDEN OF PROOF OF LOSS

(a) A customer or any person authorized to draw on the account if there is more than one person may stop payment of any item drawn on the customer's account or close the account by an order to the bank describing the item or account with reasonable certainty received at a time and in a manner that affords the bank a reasonable opportunity to act on it before any action by the bank with respect to the item described in Section 4-303. If the signature of more than one person is required to draw on an account, any of these persons may stop payment or close the account.

(b) A stop-payment order is effective for six months, but it lapses after 14 calendar days if the original order was oral and was not confirmed in writing within that period. A stop-payment order may be renewed for additional six-month periods by a writing given to the bank within a period during which the stop-payment order is effective.

### SECTION 4-404. BANK NOT OBLIGED TO PAY CHECK MORE THAN SIX MONTHS OLD

A bank is under no obligation to a customer having a checking account to pay a check, other than a certified check, which is presented more than six months after its date, but it may charge its customer's account for a payment made thereafter in good faith.

## SECTION 4-503. RESPONSIBILITY OF PRESENTING BANK FOR DOCUMENTS AND GOODS; REPORT OF REASONS FOR DISHONOR; REFEREE IN CASE OF NEED.

Unless otherwise instructed and except as provided in Article 5, a bank presenting a documentary draft:

(1) must deliver the documents to the drawee on acceptance of the draft if it is payable more than three days after presentment; otherwise, only on payment; and

(2) upon dishonor, either in the case of presentment for acceptance or presentment for payment, may seek and follow instructions from any referee in case of need designated in the draft or, if the presenting bank does not choose to utilize the referee's services, it must use diligence and good faith to ascertain the reason for dishonor, must notify its transferor of the dishonor and of the results of its effort to ascertain the reasons therefor, and must request instructions. . .

# APPENDIX 5:
## SAMPLE NOTICE OF DISHONOR

Please Take Notice That Check No. _____, dated _____
20___ drawn by you on _____ Bank in the sum of
$_____, payable to _____ or order has been dishon-
ored by nonpayment.

_____
Authorized Signature

# APPENDIX 6:
# SAMPLE STOP PAYMENT ORDER

| Date Placed | Date of Renewal | | | |
|---|---|---|---|---|
| Account Number | | | | |
| Exact Title of Account | | | | |
| Number and Street | | City and State | | |
| Payable to the order of | | | | |
| Number of Check | Date of Check | Amount | Due Date if Note or Accept. | Note of Accept. No. |

Please Stop Payment of the Described Item Drawn on or Payable at Your Office. This Written Order will become ineffective six months from the date requested unless renewed in writing.

☐ Will

A Replacement of this Item    Be Issued After Your Advice is Received.

☐ Will Not    _____

Customer Signature

**Do Not Write Below This Line—For Bank Use Only**

| | | |
|---|---|---|
| Time Received _____ | Check List<br>☐ Check Files Checked<br>☐ Current Work Checked<br>☐ Confirmation (BCH 302) Processed | Terminate Oral Order After Fourteen Days and Written Orders and Renewals After Six Months. |
| Received by &<br>Action Taken By _____ | | |
| Tabulating Check Payments (ARP Accounts Only) Notified By _____ | ☐ Customer Confirmation (BCH 302A) Sent with Advice of Oral Stop Payment | |
| Cards for Stop Payment Boards Received in P & R Dept. by_____ | ☐ Flash Cards (BCH 201) Distributed | |

# APPENDIX 7:
## APPLICABLE SECTIONS—
## UCC ARTICLE 4A: FUNDS TRANSFERS

### SECTION 4A-201. SECURITY PROCEDURE

"Security procedure" means a procedure established by agreement of a customer and a receiving bank for the purpose of (i) verifying that a payment order or communication amending or canceling a payment order is that of the customer, or (ii) detecting error in the transmission or the content of the payment order or communication. A security procedure may require the use of algorithms or other codes, identifying words or numbers, encryption, callback procedures, or similar security devices. Comparison of a signature on a payment order or communication with an authorized specimen signature of the customer is not by itself a security procedure.

### SECTION 4A-202. AUTHORIZED AND VERIFIED PAYMENT ORDERS

(b) If a bank and its customer have agreed that the authenticity of payment orders issued to the bank in the name of the customer as sender will be verified pursuant to a security procedure, a payment order received by the receiving bank is effective as the order of the customer, whether or not authorized, if (i) the security procedure is a commercially reasonable method of providing security against unauthorized payment orders, and (ii) the bank proves that it accepted the payment order in good faith and in compliance with the security procedure and any written agreement or instruction of the customer restricting acceptance of payment orders issued in the name of the customer. The bank is not required to follow an instruction that violates a written agreement with the customer or notice of which is not received at a time and in a manner affording the bank a reasonable opportunity to act on it before the payment order is accepted.

### SECTION 4A-203. UNENFORCEABILITY OF CERTAIN VERIFIED PAYMENT ORDERS

(a) If an accepted payment order is not, under Section 4A-202(a), an authorized order of a customer identified as sender, but is effective as an order of the customer pursuant to Section 4A-202(b):

> (2) The receiving bank is not entitled to enforce or retain payment of the payment order if the customer proves that the order was not caused, directly or indirectly, by a person (i) entrusted at any time with duties to act for the customer with respect to payment orders or the security procedure, or (ii) who obtained access to transmitting facilities of the customer or who obtained, from a source controlled by the customer and without authority of the receiving bank, information facilitating breach of the security procedure, regardless of how the information was obtained or whether the customer was at fault. Information includes any access device, computer software, or the like.

### SECTION 4A-207. MISDESCRIPTION OF BENEFICIARY.

(a) Subject to subsection (b), if, in a payment order received by the beneficiary's bank, the name, bank account number, or other identification of the beneficiary refers to a nonexistent or unidentifiable person or account, no person has rights as a beneficiary of the order and acceptance of the order cannot occur.

(b) If a payment order received by the beneficiary's bank identifies the beneficiary both by name and by an identifying or bank account number and the name and number identify different persons, the following rules apply:

> (1) Except as otherwise provided in subsection (c), if the beneficiary's bank does not know that the name and number refer to different persons, it may rely on the number as the proper identification of the beneficiary of the order. The beneficiary's bank need not determine whether the name and number refer to the same person.

> (2) If the beneficiary's bank pays the person identified by name or knows that the name and number identify different persons, no person has rights as beneficiary except the person paid by the beneficiary's bank if that person was entitled to receive payment from the originator of the funds transfer. If no person has rights as beneficiary, acceptance of the order cannot occur.

(c) If (i) a payment order described in subsection (b) is accepted, (ii) the originator's payment order described the beneficiary inconsistently by name and number, and (iii) the beneficiary's bank pays the person identified by number as permitted by subsection (b)(1), the following rules apply:

(1) If the originator is a bank, the originator is obliged to pay its order.

(2) If the originator is not a bank and proves that the person identified by number was not entitled to receive payment from the originator, the originator is not obliged to pay its order unless the originator's bank proves that the originator, before acceptance of the originator's order, had notice that payment of a payment order issued by the originator might be made by the beneficiary's bank on the basis of an identifying or bank account number even if it identifies a person different from the named beneficiary. Proof of notice may be made by any admissible evidence. The originator's bank satisfies the burden of proof if it proves that the originator, before the payment order was accepted, signed a writing stating the information to which the notice relates.

(d) In a case governed by subsection (b)(1), if the beneficiary's bank rightfully pays the person identified by number and that person was not entitled to receive payment from the originator, the amount paid may be recovered from that person to the extent allowed by the law governing mistake and restitution as follows:

(1) If the originator is obliged to pay its payment order as stated in subsection (c), the originator has the right to recover.

(2) If the originator is not a bank and is not obliged to pay its payment order, the originator's bank has the right to recover.

## SECTION 4A-209. ACCEPTANCE OF PAYMENT ORDER

(a) Subject to subsection (d), a receiving bank other than the beneficiary's bank accepts a payment order when it executes the order.

(b) Subject to subsections (c) and (d), a beneficiary's bank accepts a payment order at the earliest of the following times:

(1) when the bank (i) pays the beneficiary as stated in Section 4A-405(a) or 4A-405(b), or (ii) notifies the beneficiary of receipt of the order or that the account of the beneficiary has been credited with respect to the order unless the notice indicates that the bank is rejecting the order or that funds with respect to the order may not be withdrawn or used until receipt of payment from the sender of the order;

(2) when the bank receives payment of the entire amount of the sender's order pursuant to Section 4A-403(a)(1) or 4A-403(a)(2); or

(3) the opening of the next funds-transfer business day of the bank following the payment date of the order if, at that time, the amount of the sender's order is fully covered by a withdrawable credit balance in an authorized account of the sender or the bank has otherwise received full payment from the sender, unless the order was rejected before that time or is rejected within (i) one hour after that time, or (ii) one hour after the opening of the next business day of the sender following the payment date if that time is later. If notice of rejection is received by the sender after the payment date and the authorized account of the sender does not bear interest, the bank is obliged to pay interest to the sender on the amount of the order for the number of days elapsing after the payment date to the day the sender receives notice or learns that the order was not accepted, counting that day as an elapsed day. If the withdrawable credit balance during that period falls below the amount of the order, the amount of interest payable is reduced accordingly.

(c) Acceptance of a payment order cannot occur before the order is received by the receiving bank. Acceptance does not occur under subsection (b)(2) or (b)(3) if the beneficiary of the payment order does not have an account with the receiving bank, the account has been closed, or the receiving bank is not permitted by law to receive credits for the beneficiary's account.

(d) A payment order issued to the originator's bank cannot be accepted until the payment date if the bank is the beneficiary's bank, or the execution date if the bank is not the beneficiary's bank. If the originator's bank executes the originator's payment order before the execution date or pays the beneficiary of the originator's payment order before the payment date and the payment order is subsequently canceled pursuant to Section 4A-211(b), the bank may recover from the beneficiary any payment received to the extent allowed by the law governing mistake and restitution.

### SECTION 4A-210. REJECTION OF PAYMENT ORDER

(a) A payment order is rejected by the receiving bank by a notice of rejection transmitted to the sender orally, electronically, or in writing. A notice of rejection need not use any particular words and is sufficient if it indicates that the receiving bank is rejecting the order or will not execute or pay the order. Rejection is effective when the notice is given if transmission is by a means that is reasonable in the circumstances. If notice of rejection is given by a means that is not reasonable, rejection is effective when the notice is received. If an agreement of the sender and receiving bank establishes the means to be used to reject a payment order, (i) any means complying with the agreement is reasonable and (ii) any means not complying is not reasonable unless no significant delay in receipt of the notice resulted from the use of the noncomplying means.

### SECTION 4A-211. CANCELLATION AND AMENDMENT OF PAYMENT ORDER

(a) A communication of the sender of a payment order canceling or amending the order may be transmitted to the receiving bank orally, electronically, or in writing. If a security procedure is in effect between the sender and the receiving bank, the communication is not effective to cancel or amend the order unless the communication is verified pursuant to the security procedure or the bank agrees to the cancellation or amendment.

(b) Subject to subsection (a), a communication by the sender canceling or amending a payment order is effective to cancel or amend the order if notice of the communication is received at a time and in a manner affording the receiving bank a reasonable opportunity to act on the communication before the bank accepts the payment order.

(c) After a payment order has been accepted, cancellation or amendment of the order is not effective unless the receiving bank agrees or a funds-transfer system rule allows cancellation or amendment without agreement of the bank.

### SECTION 4A-401. PAYMENT DATE

"Payment date" of a payment order means the day on which the amount of the order is payable to the beneficiary by the beneficiary's bank. The payment date may be determined by instruction of the sender but cannot be earlier than the day the order is received by the beneficiary's bank and, unless otherwise determined, is the day the order is received by the beneficiary's bank.

### SECTION 4A-402. OBLIGATION OF SENDER TO PAY RECEIVING BANK.

(a) This section is subject to Sections 4A-205 and 4A-207.

(b) With respect to a payment order issued to the beneficiary's bank, acceptance of the order by the bank obliges the sender to pay the bank the amount of the order, but payment is not due until the payment date of the order.

(c) This subsection is subject to subsection (e) and to Section 4A-303. With respect to a payment order issued to a receiving bank other than the beneficiary's bank, acceptance of the order by the receiving bank obliges the sender to pay the bank the amount of the sender's order. Payment by the sender is not due until the execution date of the sender's order. The obligation of that sender to pay its payment order is excused if the funds transfer is not completed by acceptance by the beneficiary's bank of a payment order instructing payment to the beneficiary of that sender's payment order.

### SECTION 4A-405. PAYMENT BY BENEFICIARY'S BANK TO BENEFICIARY

(a) If the beneficiary's bank credits an account of the beneficiary of a payment order, payment of the bank's obligation under Section 4A404(a) occurs when and to the extent (i) the beneficiary is notified of the right to withdraw the credit, (ii) the bank lawfully applies the credit to a debt of the beneficiary, or (iii) funds with respect to the order are otherwise made available to the beneficiary by the bank.

# APPENDIX 8:
# ELECTRONIC FUNDS TRANSFER ACT

### SEC. 1693. CONGRESSIONAL FINDINGS AND DECLARATION OF PURPOSE.

#### (a) Rights and liabilities undefined.

The Congress finds that the use of electronic systems to transfer funds provides the potential for substantial benefits to consumers. However, due to the unique characteristics of such systems, the application of existing consumer protection legislation is unclear, leaving the rights and liabilities of consumers, financial institutions, and intermediaries in electronic fund transfers undefined.

#### (b) Purposes.

It is the purpose of this subchapter to provide a basic framework establishing the rights, liabilities, and responsibilities of participants in electronic fund transfer systems. The primary objective of this subchapter, however, is the provision of individual consumer rights.

### SEC. 1693A. DEFINITIONS.

As used in this subchapter—

(1) the term "accepted card or other means of access" means a card, code, or other means of access to a consumer's account for the purpose of initiating electronic fund transfers when the person to whom such card or other means of access was issued has requested and received or has signed or has used, or authorized another to use, such card or other means of access for the purpose of transferring money between accounts or obtaining money, property, labor, or services;

(2) the term "account" means a demand deposit, savings deposit, or other asset account (other than an occasional or incidental credit balance in an open end credit plan as defined in section 1602(i) of this title), as described in regulations of the Board, established pri-

marily for personal, family, or household purposes, but such term does not include an account held by a financial institution pursuant to a bona fide trust agreement;

(3) the term "Board" means the Board of Governors of the Federal Reserve System;

(4) the term "business day" means any day on which the offices of the consumer's financial institution involved in an electronic fund transfer are open to the public for carrying on substantially all of its business functions;

(5) the term "consumer" means a natural person;

(6) the term "electronic fund transfer" means any transfer of funds, other than a transaction originated by check, draft, or similar paper instrument, which is initiated through an electronic terminal, telephonic instrument, or computer or magnetic tape so as to order, instruct, or authorize a financial institution to debit or credit an account. Such term includes, but is not limited to, point-of-sale transfers, automated teller machine transactions, direct deposits or withdrawals of funds, and transfers initiated by telephone. Such term does not include—

(A) any check guarantee or authorization service which does not directly result in a debit or credit to a consumer's account:

(B) any transfer of funds, other than those processed by automated clearinghouse, made by a financial institution on behalf of a consumer by means of a service that transfers funds held at either Federal Reserve banks or other depository institutions and which is not designed primarily to transfer funds on behalf of a consumer;

(C) any transaction the primary purpose of which is the purchase or sale of securities or commodities through a broker-dealer registered with or regulated by the Securities and Exchange Commission;

(D) any automatic transfer from a savings account to a demand deposit account pursuant to an agreement between a consumer and a financial institution for the purpose of covering an overdraft or maintaining an agreed upon minimum balance in the consumer's demand deposit account; or

(E) any transfer of funds which is initiated by a telephone conversation between a consumer and an officer or employee of a financial institution which is not pursuant to a prearranged plan and under which periodic or recurring transfers are not contemplated; as determined under regulations of the Board;

(7) the term "electronic terminal" means an electronic device, other than a telephone operated by a consumer, through which a consumer may initiate an electronic fund transfer. Such term includes, but is not limited to, point-of-sale terminals, automated teller machines, and cash dispensing machines;

(8) the term "financial institution" means a State or National bank, a State or Federal savings and loan association, a mutual savings bank, a State or Federal credit union, or any other person who, directly or indirectly, holds an account belonging to a consumer;

(9) the term "preauthorized electronic fund transfer" means an electronic fund transfer authorized in advance to recur at substantially regular intervals;

(10) the term "State" means any State, territory, or possession of the United States, the District of Columbia, the Commonwealth of Puerto Rico, or any political subdivision of any of the foregoing; and

(11) the term "unauthorized electronic fund transfer" means an electronic fund transfer from a consumer's account initiated by a person other than the consumer without actual authority to initiate such transfer and from which the consumer receives no benefit, but the term does not include any electronic fund transfer (A) initiated by a person other than the consumer who was furnished with the card, code, or other means of access to such consumer's account by such consumer, unless the consumer has notified the financial institution involved that transfers by such other person are no longer authorized, (B) initiated with fraudulent intent by the consumer or any person acting in concert with the consumer, or (C) which constitutes an error committed by a financial institution.

## SEC. 1693B. REGULATIONS.

### (d) Applicability to service providers other than certain financial institutions.

#### (1) In general.

If electronic fund transfer services are made available to consumers by a person other than a financial institution holding a consumer's account, the Board shall by regulation assure that the disclosures, protections, responsibilities, and remedies created by this subchapter are made applicable to such persons and services.

### (2) State and local government electronic benefit transfer systems.

### (A) "Electronic benefit transfer system" defined.

In this paragraph, the term "electronic benefit transfer system"—

(i) means a system under which a government agency distributes needs-tested benefits by establishing accounts that may be accessed by recipients electronically, such as through automated teller machines or point-of-sale terminals; and

(ii) does not include employment-related payments, including salaries and pension, retirement, or unemployment benefits established by a Federal, State, or local government agency.

### (B) Exemption generally.

The disclosures, protections, responsibilities, and remedies established under this subchapter, and any regulation prescribed or order issued by the Board in accordance with this subchapter, shall not apply to any electronic benefit transfer system established under State or local law or administered by a State or local government.

### (C) Exception for direct deposit into recipient's account.

Subparagraph (B) shall not apply with respect to any electronic funds transfer under an electronic benefit transfer system for a deposit directly into a consumer account held by the recipient of the benefit.

### (D) Rule of construction.

No provision of this paragraph—

(i) affects or alters the protections otherwise applicable with respect to benefits established by any other provision of Federal, State, or local law; or

(ii) otherwise supersedes the application of any State or local law.

### (3) Fee disclosures at automated teller machines.

### (A) In general.

The regulations prescribed under paragraph (1) shall require any automated teller machine operator who imposes a fee on any consumer for providing host transfer services to such consumer to provide notice in accordance with subparagraph (B) to the consumer (at the time the service is provided) of—

(i) the fact that a fee is imposed by such operator for providing the service; and

(ii) the amount of any such fee.

**(B) Notice requirements.**

**(i) On the machine.**

The notice required under clause (i) of subparagraph (A) with respect to any fee described in such subparagraph shall be posted in a prominent and conspicuous location on or at the automated teller machine at which the electronic fund transfer is initiated by the consumer.

**(ii) On the screen.**

The notice required under clauses (i) and (ii) of subparagraph (A) with respect to any fee described in such subparagraph shall appear on the screen of the automated teller machine, or on a paper notice issued from such machine, after the transaction is initiated and before the consumer is irrevocably committed to completing the transaction, except that during the period beginning on November 12, 1999, and ending on December 31, 2004, this clause shall not apply to any automated teller machine that lacks the technical capability to disclose the notice on the screen or to issue a paper notice after the transaction is initiated and before the consumer is irrevocably committed to completing the transaction.

**(C) Prohibition on fees not properly disclosed and explicitly assumed by consumer.**

No fee may be imposed by any automated teller machine operator in connection with any electronic fund transfer initiated by a consumer for which a notice is required under subparagraph (A), unless—

(i) the consumer receives such notice in accordance with subparagraph (B); and

(ii) the consumer elects to continue in the manner necessary to effect the transaction after receiving such notice.

**(D) Definitions.**

For purposes of this paragraph, the following definitions shall apply:

**(i) Automated teller machine operator.**

The term "automated teller machine operator" means any person who—

(I) operates an automated teller machine at which consumers initiate electronic fund transfers; and

(II) is not the financial institution that holds the account of such consumer from which the transfer is made.

### (ii) Electronic fund transfer.

The term "electronic fund transfer" includes a transaction that involves a balance inquiry initiated by a consumer in the same manner as an electronic fund transfer, whether or not the consumer initiates a transfer of funds in the course of the transaction.

### (iii) Host transfer services.

The term "host transfer services" means any electronic fund transfer made by an automated teller machine operator in connection with a transaction initiated by a consumer at an automated teller machine operated by such operator.

## SEC. 1693C. TERMS AND CONDITIONS OF TRANSFERS.

### (a) Disclosures; time; form; contents.

The terms and conditions of electronic fund transfers involving a consumer's account shall be disclosed at the time the consumer contracts for an electronic fund transfer service, in accordance with regulations of the Board. Such disclosures shall be in readily understandable language and shall include, to the extent applicable—

(1) the consumer's liability for unauthorized electronic fund transfers and, at the financial institution's option, notice of the advisability of prompt reporting of any loss, theft, or unauthorized use of a card, code, or other means of access;

(2) the telephone number and address of the person or office to be notified in the event the consumer believes than an unauthorized electronic fund transfer has been or may be effected;

(3) the type and nature of electronic fund transfers which the consumer may initiate, including any limitations on the frequency or dollar amount of such transfers, except that the details of such limitations need not be disclosed if their confidentiality is necessary to maintain the security of an electronic fund transfer system, as determined by the Board;

(4) any charges for electronic fund transfers or for the right to make such transfers;

(5) the consumer's right to stop payment of a preauthorized electronic fund transfer and the procedure to initiate such a stop payment order;

(6) the consumer's right to receive documentation of electronic fund transfers under section 1693d of this title;

(7) a summary, in a form prescribed by regulations of the Board, of the error resolution provisions of section 1693f of this title and the consumer's rights thereunder. The financial institution shall thereafter transmit such summary at least once per calendar year;

(8) the financial institution's liability to the consumer under section 1693h of this title;

(9) under what circumstances the financial institution will in the ordinary course of business disclose information concerning the consumer's account to third persons; and

(10) a notice to the consumer that a fee may be imposed by—

(A) an automated teller machine operator (as defined in section 1693b(d)(3)(D)(i) of this title) if the consumer initiates a transfer from an automated teller machine that is not operated by the person issuing the card or other means of access; and

(B) any national, regional, or local network utilized to effect the transaction.

**(b) Notification of changes to consumer.**

A financial institution shall notify a consumer in writing at least twenty-one days prior to the effective date of any change in any term or condition of the consumer's account required to be disclosed under subsection (a) of this section if such change would result in greater cost or liability for such consumer or decreased access to the consumer's account. A financial institution may, however, implement a change in the terms or conditions of an account without prior notice when such change is immediately necessary to maintain or restore the security of an electronic fund transfer system or a consumer's account. Subject to subsection (a)(3) of this section, the Board shall require subsequent notification if such a change is made permanent.

**(c) Time for disclosures respecting accounts accessible prior to effective date of this subchapter.**

For any account of a consumer made accessible to electronic fund transfers prior to the effective date of this subchapter, the information required to be disclosed to the consumer under subsection (a) of this section shall be disclosed not later than the earlier of—

(1) the first periodic statement required by section 1693d(c) of this title after the effective date of this subchapter; or

(2) thirty days after the effective date of this subchapter.

### SEC. 1693D. DOCUMENTATION OF TRANSFERS.

**(a) Availability of written documentation to consumer; contents.**

For each electronic fund transfer initiated by a consumer from an electronic terminal, the financial institution holding such consumer's account shall, directly or indirectly, at the time the transfer is initiated, make available to the consumer written documentation of such transfer. The documentation shall clearly set forth to the extent applicable—

(1) the amount involved and date the transfer is initiated;

(2) the type of transfer;

(3) the identity of the consumer's account with the financial institution from which or to which funds are transferred;

(4) the identity of any third party to whom or from whom funds are transferred; and

(5) the location or identification of the electronic terminal involved.

**(b) Notice of credit to consumer.**

For a consumer's account which is scheduled to be credited by a preauthorized electronic fund transfer from the same payor at least once in each successive sixty-day period, except where the payor provides positive notice of the transfer to the consumer, the financial institution shall elect to provide promptly either positive notice to the consumer when the credit is made as scheduled, or negative notice to the consumer when the credit is not made as scheduled, in accordance with regulations of the Board. The means of notice elected shall be disclosed to the consumer in accordance with section 1693c of this title.

**(c) Periodic statement; contents.**

A financial institution shall provide each consumer with a periodic statement for each account of such consumer that may be accessed by means of an electronic fund transfer. Except as provided in subsections (d) and (e) of this section, such statement shall be provided at least monthly for each monthly or shorter cycle in which an electronic fund transfer affecting the account has occurred, or every three months, whichever is more frequent. The statement, which may include information regarding transactions other than electronic fund transfers, shall clearly set forth—

(1) with regard to each electronic fund transfer during the period, the information described in subsection (a) of this section, which may be provided on an accompanying document;

(2) the amount of any fee or charge assessed by the financial institution during the period for electronic fund transfers or for account maintenance;

(3) the balances in the consumer's account at the beginning of the period and at the close of the period; and

(4) the address and telephone number to be used by the financial institution for the purpose of receiving any statement inquiry or notice of account error from the consumer. Such address and telephone number shall be preceded by the caption "Direct Inquiries To:" or other similar language indicating that the address and number are to be used for such inquiries or notices.

**(d) Consumer passbook accounts.**

In the case of a consumer's passbook account which may not be accessed by electronic fund transfers other than preauthorized electronic fund transfers crediting the account, a financial institution may, in lieu of complying with the requirements of subsection (c) of this section, upon presentation of the passbook provide the consumer in writing with the amount and date of each such transfer involving the account since the passbook was last presented.

**(e) Accounts other than passbook accounts.**

In the case of a consumer's account, other than a passbook account, which may not be accessed by electronic fund transfers other than preauthorized electronic fund transfers crediting the account, the financial institution may provide a periodic statement on a quarterly basis which otherwise complies with the requirements of subsection (c) of this section.

**(f) Documentation as evidence.**

In any action involving a consumer, any documentation required by this section to be given to the consumer which indicates that an electronic fund transfer was made to another person shall be admissible as evidence of such transfer and shall constitute prima facie proof that such transfer was made.

**SEC. 1693E. PREAUTHORIZED TRANSFERS.**

(a) A preauthorized electronic fund transfer from a consumer's account may be authorized by the consumer only in writing, and a copy of such authorization shall be provided to the consumer when made. A consumer may stop payment of a preauthorized electronic fund transfer by notifying the financial institution orally or in writing at any time up to three business days preceding the scheduled date of such transfer. The financial institution may require written confirmation to be provided to it within fourteen days of an oral notification if, when the oral notification is made, the consumer is advised of such requirement and the address to which such confirmation should be sent.

(b) In the case of preauthorized transfers from a consumer's account to the same person which may vary in amount, the financial institution or designated payee shall, prior to each transfer, provide reasonable advance notice to the consumer, in accordance with regulations of the Board, of the amount to be transferred and the scheduled date of the transfer.

### SEC. 1693F. ERROR RESOLUTION.

#### (a) Notification to financial institution of error.

If a financial institution, within sixty days after having transmitted to a consumer documentation pursuant to section 1693d(a), (c), or (d) of this title or notification pursuant to section 1693d(b) of this title, receives oral or written notice in which the consumer—

(1) sets forth or otherwise enables the financial institution to identify the name and account number of the consumer;

(2) indicates the consumer's belief that the documentation, or, in the case of notification pursuant to section 1693d(b) of this title, the consumer's account, contains an error and the amount of such error; and

(3) sets forth the reasons for the consumer's belief (where applicable) that an error has occurred, the financial institution shall investigate the alleged error, determine whether an error has occurred, and report or mail the results of such investigation and determination to the consumer within ten business days. The financial institution may require written confirmation to be provided to it within ten business days of an oral notification of error if, when the oral notification is made, the consumer is advised of such requirement and the address to which such confirmation should be sent. A financial institution which requires written confirmation in accordance with the previous sentence need not provisionally recredit a consumer's account in accordance with subsection (c) of this section, nor shall the financial institution be liable under subsection (e) of this section if the written confirmation is not received within the ten-day period referred to in the previous sentence.

#### (b) Correction of error; interest.

If the financial institution determines that an error did occur, it shall promptly, but in no event more than one business day after such determination, correct the error, subject to section 1693g of this title, including the crediting of interest where applicable.

### (c) Provisional recredit of consumer's account.

If a financial institution receives notice of an error in the manner and within the time period specified in subsection (a) of this section, it may, in lieu of the requirements of subsections (a) and (b) of this section, within ten business days after receiving such notice provisionally recredit the consumer's account for the amount alleged to be in error, subject to section 1693g of this title, including interest where applicable, pending the conclusion of its investigation and its determination of whether an error has occurred. Such investigation shall be concluded not later than forty-five days after receipt of notice of the error. During the pendency of the investigation, the consumer shall have full use of the funds provisionally recredited.

### (d) Absence of error; finding; explanation.

If the financial institution determines after its investigation pursuant to subsection (a) or (c) of this section that an error did not occur, it shall deliver or mail to the consumer an explanation of its findings within 3 business days after the conclusion of its investigation, and upon request of the consumer promptly deliver or mail to the consumer reproductions of all documents which the financial institution relied on to conclude that such error did not occur. The financial institution shall include notice of the right to request reproductions with the explanation of its findings.

### (e) Treble damages.

If in any action under section 1693m of this title, the court finds that—

(1) the financial institution did not provisionally recredit a consumer's account within the ten-day period specified in subsection (c) of this section, and the financial institution (A) did not make a good faith investigation of the alleged error, or (B) did not have a reasonable basis for believing that the consumer's account was not in error; or

(2) the financial institution knowingly and willfully concluded that the consumer's account was not in error when such conclusion could not reasonably have been drawn from the evidence available to the financial institution at the time of its investigation, then the consumer shall be entitled to treble damages determined under section 1693m(a)(1) of this title.

### (f) Acts constituting error.

For the purpose of this section, an error consists of—

(1) an unauthorized electronic fund transfer;

(2) an incorrect electronic fund transfer from or to the consumer's account;

(3) the omission from a periodic statement of an electronic fund transfer affecting the consumer's account which should have been included;

(4) a computational error by the financial institution;

(5) the consumer's receipt of an incorrect amount of money from an electronic terminal;

(6) a consumer's request for additional information or clarification concerning an electronic fund transfer or any documentation required by this subchapter; or

(7) any other error described in regulations of the Board.

### SEC. 1693G. CONSUMER LIABILITY.

#### (a) Unauthorized electronic fund transfers; limit.

A consumer shall be liable for any unauthorized electronic fund transfer involving the account of such consumer only if the card or other means of access utilized for such transfer was an accepted card or other means of access and if the issuer of such card, code, or other means of access has provided a means whereby the user of such card, code, or other means of access can be identified as the person authorized to use it, such as by signature, photograph, or fingerprint or by electronic or mechanical confirmation. In no event, however, shall a consumer's liability for an unauthorized transfer exceed the lesser of—

(1) $50; or

(2) the amount of money or value of property or services obtained in such unauthorized electronic fund transfer prior to the time the financial institution is notified of, or otherwise becomes aware of, circumstances which lead to the reasonable belief that an unauthorized electronic fund transfer involving the consumer's account has been or may be effected. Notice under this paragraph is sufficient when such steps have been taken as may be reasonably required in the ordinary course of business to provide the financial institution with the pertinent information, whether or not any particular officer, employee, or agent of the financial institution does in fact receive such information. Notwithstanding the foregoing, reimbursement need not be made to the consumer for losses the financial institution establishes would not have occurred but for the failure of the consumer to report within sixty days of transmittal of the statement (or in extenuating circumstances such as extended travel or hospitalization,

within a reasonable time under the circumstances) any unauthorized electronic fund transfer or account error which appears on the periodic statement provided to the consumer under section 1693d of this title. In addition, reimbursement need not be made to the consumer for losses which the financial institution establishes would not have occurred but for the failure of the consumer to report any loss or theft of a card or other means of access within two business days after the consumer learns of the loss or theft (or in extenuating circumstances such as extended travel or hospitalization, within a longer period which is reasonable under the circumstances), but the consumer's liability under this subsection in any such case may not exceed a total of $500, or the amount of unauthorized electronic fund transfers which occur following the close of two business days (or such longer period) after the consumer learns of the loss or theft but prior to notice to the financial institution under this subsection, whichever is less.

### (b) Burden of proof.

In any action which involves a consumer's liability for an unauthorized electronic fund transfer, the burden of proof is upon the financial institution to show that the electronic fund transfer was authorized or, if the electronic fund transfer was unauthorized, then the burden of proof is upon the financial institution to establish that the conditions of liability set forth in subsection (a) of this section have been met, and, if the transfer was initiated after the effective date of section 1693c of this title, that the disclosures required to be made to the consumer under section 1693c(a)(1) and (2) of this title were in fact made in accordance with such section.

### (c) Determination of limitation on liability.

In the event of a transaction which involves both an unauthorized electronic fund transfer and an extension of credit as defined in section 1602(e) of this title pursuant to an agreement between the consumer and the financial institution to extend such credit to the consumer in the event the consumer's account is overdrawn, the limitation on the consumer's liability for such transaction shall be determined solely in accordance with this section.

### (d) Restriction on liability.

Nothing in this section imposes liability upon a consumer for an unauthorized electronic fund transfer in excess of his liability for such a transfer under other applicable law or under any agreement with the consumer's financial institution.

**(e) Scope of liability.**

Except as provided in this section, a consumer incurs no liability from an unauthorized electronic fund transfer.

### SEC. 1693H. LIABILITY OF FINANCIAL INSTITUTIONS.

**(a) Action or failure to act proximately causing damages.**

Subject to subsections (b) and (c) of this section, a financial institution shall be liable to a consumer for all damages proximately caused by—

(1) the financial institution's failure to make an electronic fund transfer, in accordance with the terms and conditions of an account, in the correct amount or in a timely manner when properly instructed to do so by the consumer, except where—

(A) the consumer's account has insufficient funds;

(B) the funds are subject to legal process or other encumbrance restricting such transfer;

(C) such transfer would exceed an established credit limit;

(D) an electronic terminal has insufficient cash to complete the transaction; or

(E) as otherwise provided in regulations of the Board;

(2) the financial institution's failure to make an electronic fund transfer due to insufficient funds when the financal institution failed to credit, in accordance with the terms and conditions of an account, a deposit of funds to the consumer's account which would have provided sufficient funds to make the transfer, and preauthorized transfer from a consumer's account when instructed to do so in accordance with the terms and conditions of the account.

**(b) Acts of God and technical malfunctions.**

A financial institution shall not be liable under subsection (a)(1) or (2) of this section if the financial institution shows by a preponderance of the evidence that its action or failure to act resulted from—

(1) an act of God or other circumstance beyond its control, that it exercised reasonable care to prevent such an occurrence, and that it exercised such diligence as the circumstances required; or

(2) a technical malfunction which was known to the consumer at the time he attempted to initiate an electronic fund transfer or, in the case of a preauthorized transfer, at the time such transfer should have occurred.

## (c) Intent

In the case of a failure described in subsection (a) of this section which was not intentional and which resulted from a bona fide error, notwithstanding the maintenance of procedures reasonably adapted to avoid any such error, the financial institution shall be liable for actual damages proved.

### (d) Exception for damaged notices.

If the notice required to be posted pursuant to section 1693b(d)(3)(B)(i) of this title by an automated teller machine operator has been posted by such operator in compliance with such section and the notice is subsequently removed, damaged, or altered by any person other than the operator of the automated teller machine, the operator shall have no liability under this section for failure to comply with section 1693b(d)(3)(B)(i) of this title.

### SEC. 1693I. ISSUANCE OF CARDS OR OTHER MEANS OF ACCESS.

#### (a) Prohibition; proper issuance.

No person may issue to a consumer any card, code, or other means of access to such consumer's account for the purpose of initiating an electronic fund transfer other than—

(1) in response to a request or application therefor; or

(2) as a renewal of, or in substitution for, an accepted card, code, or other means of access, whether issued by the initial issuer or a successor.

#### (b) Exceptions.

Notwithstanding the provisions of subsection (a) of this section, a person may distribute to a consumer on an unsolicited basis a card, code, or other means of access for use in initiating an electronic fund transfer from such consumer's account, if—

(1) such card, code, or other means of access is not validated;

(2) such distribution is accompanied by a complete disclosure, in accordance with section 1693c of this title, of the consumer's rights and liabilities which will apply if such card, code, or other means of access is validated;

(3) such distribution is accompanied by a clear explanation, in accordance with regulations of the Board, that such card, code, or other means of access is not validated and how the consumer may dispose of such code, card, or other means of access if validation is not desired; and

(4) such card, code, or other means of access is validated only in response to a request or application from the consumer, upon verification of the consumer's identity.

### (c) Validation.

For the purpose of subsection (b) of this section, a card, code, or other means of access is validated when it may be used to initiate an electronic fund transfer.

### SEC. 1693J. SUSPENSION OF OBLIGATIONS.

If a system malfunction prevents the effectuation of an electronic fund transfer initiated by a consumer to another person, and such other person has agreed to accept payment by such means, the consumer's obligation to the other person shall be suspended until the malfunction is corrected and the electronic fund transfer may be completed, unless such other person has subsequently, by written request, demanded payment by means other than an electronic fund transfer.

### SEC. 1693K. COMPULSORY USE OF ELECTRONIC FUND TRANSFERS.

No person may—

(1) condition the extension of credit to a consumer on such consumer's repayment by means of preauthorized electronic fund transfers; or

(2) require a consumer to establish an account for receipt of electronic fund transfers with a particular financial institution as a condition of employment or receipt of a government benefit.

### SEC. 1693L. WAIVER OF RIGHTS.

No writing or other agreement between a consumer and any other person may contain any provision which constitutes a waiver of any right conferred or cause of action created by this subchapter. Nothing in this section prohibits, however, any writing or other agreement which grants to a consumer a more extensive right or remedy or greater protection than contained in this subchapter or a waiver given in settlement of a dispute or action.

### SEC. 1693M. CIVIL LIABILITY.

#### (a) Individual or class action for damages; amount of award.

Except as otherwise provided by this section and section 1693h of this title, any person who fails to comply with any provision of this subchapter with respect to any consumer, except for an error resolved in accordance with section 1693f of this title, is liable to such consumer in an amount equal to the sum of—

(1) any actual damage sustained by such consumer as a result of such failure;

(2)(A) in the case of an individual action, an amount not less than $100 nor greater than $1,000; or

(2)(B) in the case of a class action, such amount as the court may allow, except that (i) as to each member of the class no minimum recovery shall be applicable, and (ii) the total recovery under this subparagraph in any class action or series of class actions arising out of the same failure to comply by the same person shall not be more than the lesser of $500,000 or 1 per centum of the net worth of the defendant; and

(3) in the case of any successful action to enforce the foregoing liability, the costs of the action, together with a reasonable attorney's fee as determined by the court.

**(b) Factors determining amount of award.**

In determining the amount of liability in any action under subsection (a) of this section, the court shall consider, among other relevant factors—

(1) in any individual action under subsection (a)(2)(A) of this section, the frequency and persistence of noncompliance, the nature of such noncompliance, and the extent to which the noncompliance was intentional; or

(2) in any class action under subsection (a)(2)(B) of this section, the frequency and persistence of noncompliance, the nature of such noncompliance, the resources of the defendant, the number of persons adversely affected, and the extent to which the noncompliance was intentional.

**(c) Unintentional violations; bona fide error.**

Except as provided in section 1693h of this title, a person may not be held liable in any action brought under this section for a violation of this subchapter if the person shows by a preponderance of evidence that the violation was not intentional and resulted from a bona fide error notwithstanding the maintenance of procedures reasonably adapted to avoid any such error.

**(d) Good faith compliance with rule, regulation, or interpretation of Board or approval of duly authorized official or employee of Federal Reserve System.**

No provision of this section or section 1693n of this title imposing any liability shall apply to—

(1) any act done or omitted in good faith in conformity with any rule, regulation, or interpretation thereof by the Board or in conformity with any interpretation or approval by an official or employee of the Federal Reserve System duly authorized by the Board to issue such interpretations or approvals under such procedures as the Board may prescribe therefor; or

(2) any failure to make disclosure in proper form if a financial institution utilized an appropriate model clause issued by the Board, notwithstanding that after such act, omission, or failure has occurred, such rule, regulation, approval, or model clause is amended, rescinded, or determined by judicial or other authority to be invalid for any reason.

**(e) Notification to consumer prior to action; adjustment of consumer's account.**

A person has no liability under this section for any failure to comply with any requirement under this subchapter if, prior to the institution of an action under this section, the person notifies the consumer concerned of the failure, complies with the requirements of this subchapter, and makes an appropriate adjustment to the consumer's account and pays actual damages or, where applicable, damages in accordance with section 1693h of this title.

**(f) Action in bad faith or for harassment; attorney's fees.**

On a finding by the court that an unsuccessful action under this section was brought in bad faith or for purposes of harassment, the court shall award to the defendant attorney's fees reasonable in relation to the work expended and costs.

**(g) Jurisdiction of courts; time for maintenance of action.**

Without regard to the amount in controversy, any action under this section may be brought in any United States district court, or in any other court of competent jurisdiction, within one year from the date of the occurrence of the violation.

**SEC. 1693N. CRIMINAL LIABILITY.**

**(a) Violations respecting giving of false or inaccurate information, failure to provide information, and failure to comply with provisions of this subchapter.**

Whoever knowingly and willfully—

(1) gives false or inaccurate information or fails to provide information which he is required to disclose by this subchapter or any regulation issued thereunder; or

(2) otherwise fails to comply with any provision of this subchapter; shall be fined not more than $5,000 or imprisoned not more than one year, or both.

**(b) Violations affecting interstate or foreign commerce.**

Whoever—

(1) knowingly, in a transaction affecting interstate or foreign commerce, uses or attempts or conspires to use any counterfeit, fictitious, altered, forged, lost, stolen, or fraudulently obtained debit instrument to obtain money, goods, services, or anything else of value which within any one-year period has a value aggregating $1,000 or more; or

(2) with unlawful or fraudulent intent, transports or attempts or conspires to transport in interstate or foreign commerce a counterfeit, fictitious, altered, forged, lost, stolen, or fraudulently obtained debit instrument knowing the same to be counterfeit, fictitious, altered, forged, lost, stolen, or fraudulently obtained; or

(3) with unlawful or fraudulent intent, uses any instrumentality of interstate or foreign commerce to sell or transport a counterfeit, fictitious, altered, forged, lost, stolen, or fraudulently obtained debit instrument knowing the same to be counterfeit, fictitious, altered, forged, lost, stolen, or fraudulently obtained; or

(4) knowingly receives, conceals, uses, or transports money, goods, services, or anything else of value (except tickets for interstate or foreign transportation) which (A) within any one-year period has a value aggregating $1,000 or more, (B) has moved in or is part of, or which constitutes interstate or foreign commerce, and (C) has been obtained with a counterfeit, fictitious, altered, forged, lost, stolen, or fraudulently obtained debit instrument; or

(5) knowingly receives, conceals, uses, sells, or transports in interstate or foreign commerce one or more tickets for interstate or foreign transportation, which (A) within any one-year period have a

value aggregating $500 or more, and (B) have been purchased or obtained with one or more counterfeit, fictitious, altered, forged, lost, stolen, or fraudulently obtained debit instrument; or

(6) in a transaction affecting interstate or foreign commerce, furnishes money, property, services, or anything else of value, which within any one-year period has a value aggregating $1,000 or more, through the use of any counterfeit, fictitious, altered, forged, lost, stolen, or fraudulently obtained debit instrument knowing the same to be counterfeit, fictitious, altered, forged, lost, stolen, or fraudulently obtained—shall be fined not more than $10,000 or imprisoned not more than ten years, or both.

**(c) "Debit instrument" defined.**

As used in this section, the term "debit instrument" means a card, code, or other device, other than a check, draft, or similar paper instrument, by the use of which a person may initiate an electronic fund transfer.

### SEC. 1693Q. RELATION TO STATE LAWS.

This subchapter does not annul, alter, or affect the laws of any State relating to electronic fund transfers, except to the extent that those laws are inconsistent with the provisions of this subchapter, and then only to the extent of the inconsistency. A State law is not inconsistent with this subchapter if the protection such law affords any consumer is greater than the protection afforded by this subchapter.

# APPENDIX 9:
# APPLICABLE SECTIONS—
# UCC ARTICLE 5: LETTERS OF CREDIT

### SECTION 5-104. FORMAL REQUIREMENTS; SIGNING

(1) Except as otherwise required in subsection (1)(c) of Section 5-102 on scope, no particular form of phrasing is required for a credit. A credit must be in writing and signed by the issuer and a confirmation must be in writing and signed by the confirming bank. A modification of the terms of a credit or confirmation must be signed by the issuer or confirming bank.

### 5-106. TIME AND EFFECT OF ESTABLISHMENT OF CREDIT

(1) Unless otherwise agreed a credit is established

(a) as regards the customer as soon as a letter of credit is sent to him or the letter of credit or an authorized written advice of its issuance is sent to the beneficiary; and

(b) as regards the beneficiary when he receives a letter of credit or an authorized written advice of its issuance.

(2) Unless otherwise agreed once an irrevocable credit is established as regards the customer it can be modified or revoked only with the consent of the customer and once it is established as regards the beneficiary it can be modified or revoked only with his consent.

### SECTION 5-107. ADVICE OF CREDIT; CONFIRMATION; ERROR IN STATEMENT TERMS

(1) Unless otherwise specified an advising bank by advising a credit issued by another bank does not assume any obligation to honor drafts drawn or demands for payment made under the credit but it does assume obligation for the accuracy of its own statement.

(2) A confirming bank by confirming a credit becomes directly obligated on the credit to the extent of its confirmation as though it were its issuer and acquires the rights of an issuer.

### SECTION 5-111. WARRANTIES ON TRANSFER AND PRESENTMENT

(1) Unless otherwise agreed the beneficiary by transferring or presenting a documentary draft or demand for payment warrants to all interested parties that the necessary conditions of the credit have been complied with. This is in addition to any warranties arising under Articles 3, 4, 7 and 8.

### SECTION 5-114. ISSUER'S DUTY AND PRIVILEGE TO HONOR; RIGHT TO REIMBURSEMENT

(1) An issuer must honor a draft or demand for payment which complies with the terms of the relevant credit regardless of whether the goods or documents conform to the underlying contract for sale or other contract between the customer and the beneficiary. The issuer is not excused from honor of such a draft or demand by reason of an additional general term that all documents must be satisfactory to the issuer, but an issuer may require that specified documents must be satisfactory to it.

### SECTION 5-115. REMEDY FOR IMPROPER DISHONOR OR ANTICIPATORY REPUDIATION

(1) When an issuer wrongfully dishonors a draft or demand for payment presented under a credit the person entitled to honor has with respect to any documents the rights of a person in the position of a seller (Section 2-707) and may recover from the issuer the face amount of the draft or demand together with incidental damages under Section 2-710 on seller's incidental damages and interest but less any amount realized by resale or other use or disposition of the subject matter of the transaction. In the event no resale or other utilization is made the documents, goods or other subject matter involved in the transaction must be turned over to the issuer on payment of judgment.

(2) When an issuer wrongfully cancels or otherwise repudiates a credit before presentment of a draft or demand for payment drawn under it the beneficiary has the rights of a seller after anticipatory repudiation by the buyer under Section 2-610 if he learns of the repudiation in time reasonably to avoid procurement of the required documents. Otherwise the beneficiary has an immediate right of action for wrongful dishonor.

# APPENDIX 10:
# THE U.S.A. PATRIOT ACT
# (H.R.3162)—SELECTED PROVISIONS

### SECTION 1. SHORT TITLE AND TABLE OF CONTENTS.

(a) SHORT TITLE—This Act may be cited as the 'Uniting and Strengthening America by Providing Appropriate Tools Required to Intercept and Obstruct Terrorism (USA PATRIOT ACT) Act of 2001'.

### ENHANCING DOMESTIC SECURITY AGAINST TERRORISM

#### SEC. 105. EXPANSION OF NATIONAL ELECTRONIC CRIME TASK FORCE INITIATIVE.

The Director of the United States Secret Service shall take appropriate actions to develop a national network of electronic crime task forces, based on the New York Electronic Crimes Task Force model, throughout the United States, for the purpose of preventing, detecting, and investigating various forms of electronic crimes, including potential terrorist attacks against critical infrastructure and financial payment systems.

### TITLE II—ENHANCED SURVEILLANCE PROCEDURES

#### SEC. 201. AUTHORITY TO INTERCEPT WIRE, ORAL, AND ELECTRONIC COMMUNICATIONS RELATING TO TERRORISM.

Section 2516(1) of title 18, United States Code, is amended—

(1) by redesignating paragraph (p), as so redesignated by section 434(2) of the Antiterrorism and Effective Death Penalty Act of 1996 (Public Law 104-132; 110 Stat. 1274), as paragraph (r); and

(2) by inserting after paragraph (p), as so redesignated by section 201(3) of the Illegal Immigration Reform and Immigrant Re-

sponsibility Act of 1996 (division C of Public Law 104-208; 110 Stat. 3009-565), the following new paragraph:

'(q) any criminal violation of section 229 (relating to chemical weapons); or sections 2332, 2332a, 2332b, 2332d, 2339A, or 2339B of this title (relating to terrorism); or'.

### SEC. 202. AUTHORITY TO INTERCEPT WIRE, ORAL, AND ELECTRONIC COMMUNICATIONS RELATING TO COMPUTER FRAUD AND ABUSE OFFENSES.

Section 2516(1)(c) of title 18, United States Code, is amended by striking 'and section 1341 (relating to mail fraud),' and inserting 'section 1341 (relating to mail fraud), a felony violation of section 1030 (relating to computer fraud and abuse),'.

### SEC. 203. AUTHORITY TO SHARE CRIMINAL INVESTIGATIVE INFORMATION.

(b) AUTHORITY TO SHARE ELECTRONIC, WIRE, AND ORAL INTERCEPTION INFORMATION—

(1) LAW ENFORCEMENT—Section 2517 of title 18, United States Code, is amended by inserting at the end the following:

'(6) Any investigative or law enforcement officer, or attorney for the Government, who by any means authorized by this chapter, has obtained knowledge of the contents of any wire, oral, or electronic communication, or evidence derived therefrom, may disclose such contents to any other Federal law enforcement, intelligence, protective, immigration, national defense, or national security official to the extent that such contents include foreign intelligence or counterintelligence (as defined in section 3 of the National Security Act of 1947 (50 U.S.C. 401a)), or foreign intelligence information (as defined in subsection (19) of section 2510 of this title), to assist the official who is to receive that information in the performance of his official duties. Any Federal official who receives information pursuant to this provision may use that information only as necessary in the conduct of that person's official duties subject to any limitations on the unauthorized disclosure of such information.'.

### SEC. 204. CLARIFICATION OF INTELLIGENCE EXCEPTIONS FROM LIMITATIONS ON INTERCEPTION AND DISCLOSURE OF WIRE, ORAL, AND ELECTRONIC COMMUNICATIONS.

Section 2511(2)(f) of title 18, United States Code, is amended—

(1) by striking 'this chapter or chapter 121' and inserting 'this chapter or chapter 121 or 206 of this title'; and

(2) by striking 'wire and oral' and inserting 'wire, oral, and electronic'.

### SEC. 209. SEIZURE OF VOICE-MAIL MESSAGES PURSUANT TO WARRANTS.

Title 18, United States Code, is amended—

(1) in section 2510—

(A) in paragraph (1), by striking beginning with 'and such' and all that follows through 'communication'; and

(B) in paragraph (14), by inserting 'wire or' after 'transmission of'; and

(2) in subsections (a) and (b) of section 2703—

(A) by striking 'CONTENTS OF ELECTRONIC' and inserting 'CONTENTS OF WIRE OR ELECTRONIC' each place it appears;

(B) by striking 'contents of an electronic' and inserting 'contents of a wire or electronic' each place it appears; and

(C) by striking 'any electronic' and inserting 'any wire or electronic' each place it appears.

### SEC. 210. SCOPE OF SUBPOENAS FOR RECORDS OF ELECTRONIC COMMUNICATIONS.

Section 2703(c)(2) of title 18, United States Code, as redesignated by section 212, is amended—

(1) by striking 'entity the name, address, local and long distance telephone toll billing records, telephone number or other subscriber number or identity, and length of service of a subscriber' and inserting the following: 'entity the—

'(A) name;

'(B) address;

'(C) local and long distance telephone connection records, or records of session times and durations;

'(D) length of service (including start date) and types of service utilized;

'(E) telephone or instrument number or other subscriber number or identity, including any temporarily assigned network address; and

'(F) means and source of payment for such service (including any credit card or bank account number), of a subscriber'; and

(2) by striking 'and the types of services the subscriber or customer utilized,'.

### SEC. 211. CLARIFICATION OF SCOPE.

Section 631 of the Communications Act of 1934 (47 U.S.C. 551) is amended—

(1) in subsection (c)(2)—

(A) in subparagraph (B), by striking 'or';

(B) in subparagraph (C), by striking the period at the end and inserting '; or'; and

(C) by inserting at the end the following:

'(D) to a government entity as authorized under chapters 119, 121, or 206 of title 18, United States Code, except that such disclosure shall not include records revealing cable subscriber selection of video programming from a cable operator.'; and

(2) in subsection (h), by striking 'A governmental entity' and inserting 'Except as provided in subsection (c)(2)(D), a governmental entity'.

### SEC. 212. EMERGENCY DISCLOSURE OF ELECTRONIC COMMUNICATIONS TO PROTECT LIFE AND LIMB.

(a) DISCLOSURE OF CONTENTS—

(1) IN GENERAL—Section 2702 of title 18, United States Code, is amended—

(A) by striking the section heading and inserting the following:

'Sec. 2702. Voluntary disclosure of customer communications or records';

(B) in subsection (a)—

(i) in paragraph (2)(A), by striking 'and' at the end;

(ii) in paragraph (2)(B), by striking the period and inserting '; and'; and

(iii) by inserting after paragraph (2) the following:

'(3) a provider of remote computing service or electronic communication service to the public shall not knowingly divulge a record or other information pertaining to a subscriber to or customer of such service (not including the contents of communications covered by paragraph (1) or (2)) to any governmental entity.';

(C) in subsection (b), by striking 'EXCEPTIONS- A person or entity' and inserting 'EXCEPTIONS FOR DISCLOSURE OF COMMUNICATIONS—A provider described in subsection (a)';

(D) in subsection (b)(6)—

.(i) in subparagraph (A)(ii), by striking 'or';

(ii) in subparagraph (B), by striking the period and inserting '; or'; and

(iii) by adding after subparagraph (B) the following:

'(C) if the provider reasonably believes that an emergency involving immediate danger of death or serious physical injury to any person requires disclosure of the information without delay.'; and

(E) by inserting after subsection (b) the following:

'(c) EXCEPTIONS FOR DISCLOSURE OF CUSTOMER RECORDS- A provider described in subsection (a) may divulge a record or other information pertaining to a subscriber to or customer of such service (not including the contents of communications covered by subsection (a)(1) or (a)(2))—

'(1) as otherwise authorized in section 2703;

'(2) with the lawful consent of the customer or subscriber;

'(3) as may be necessarily incident to the rendition of the service or to the protection of the rights or property of the provider of that service;

'(4) to a governmental entity if the provider reasonably believes that an emergency involving immediate danger of death or serious physical injury to any person justifies disclosure of the information; or

'(5) to any person other than a governmental entity.'.

(2) TECHNICAL AND CONFORMING AMENDMENT—The table of sections for chapter 121 of title 18, United States Code, is amended by striking the item relating to section 2702 and inserting the following:

'2702. Voluntary disclosure of customer communications or records.'.

(b) REQUIREMENTS FOR GOVERNMENT ACCESS—

(1) IN GENERAL—Section 2703 of title 18, United States Code, is amended—

(A) by striking the section heading and inserting the following:

'Sec. 2703. Required disclosure of customer communications or records';

(B) in subsection (c) by redesignating paragraph (2) as paragraph (3);

(C) in subsection (c)(1)—

(i) by striking '(A) Except as provided in subparagraph (B), a provider of electronic communication service or remote computing service may' and inserting 'A governmental entity may require a provider of electronic communication service or remote computing service to';

(ii) by striking 'covered by subsection (a) or (b) of this section) to any person other than a governmental entity.

'(B) A provider of electronic communication service or remote computing service shall disclose a record or other information pertaining to a subscriber to or customer of such service (not including the contents of communications covered by subsection (a) or (b) of this section) to a governmental entity' and inserting ')';

(iii) by redesignating subparagraph (C) as paragraph (2);

(iv) by redesignating clauses (i), (ii), (iii), and (iv) as subparagraphs (A), (B), (C), and (D), respectively;

(v) in subparagraph (D) (as redesignated) by striking the period and inserting '; or'; and

(vi) by inserting after subparagraph (D) (as redesignated) the following:

'(E) seeks information under paragraph (2).'; and

(D) in paragraph (2) (as redesignated) by striking 'subparagraph (B)' and insert 'paragraph (1)'.

(2) TECHNICAL AND CONFORMING AMENDMENT- The table of sections for chapter 121 of title 18, United States Code, is amended by striking the item relating to section 2703 and inserting the following:

'2703. Required disclosure of customer communications or records.'.

---

**SEC. 213. AUTHORITY FOR DELAYING NOTICE OF THE EXECUTION OF A WARRANT.**

Section 3103a of title 18, United States Code, is amended—

(1) by inserting '(a) IN GENERAL—' before 'In addition'; and

(2) by adding at the end the following:

'(b) DELAY—With respect to the issuance of any warrant or court order under this section, or any other rule of law, to search for and seize any property or material that constitutes evidence of a criminal offense in violation of the laws of the United States, any notice required, or that may be required, to be given may be delayed if—

'(1) the court finds reasonable cause to believe that providing immediate notification of the execution of the warrant may have an adverse result (as defined in section 2705);

'(2) the warrant prohibits the seizure of any tangible property, any wire or electronic communication (as defined in section 2510), or, except as expressly provided in chapter 121, any stored wire or electronic information, except where the court finds reasonable necessity for the seizure; and

'(3) the warrant provides for the giving of such notice within a reasonable period of its execution, which period may thereafter be extended by the court for good cause shown.'.

**SEC. 217. INTERCEPTION OF COMPUTER TRESPASSER COMMUNICATIONS.**

Chapter 119 of title 18, United States Code, is amended—

(1) in section 2510—

(A) in paragraph (18), by striking 'and' at the end;

(B) in paragraph (19), by striking the period and inserting a semicolon; and

(C) by inserting after paragraph (19) the following:

'(20) 'protected computer' has the meaning set forth in section 1030; and

'(21) 'computer trespasser'—

'(A) means a person who accesses a protected computer without authorization and thus has no reasonable expectation of privacy in any communication transmitted to, through, or from the protected computer; and

'(B) does not include a person known by the owner or operator of the protected computer to have an existing contractual relationship with the owner or operator of the protected computer for access to all or part of the protected computer.'; and

(2) in section 2511(2), by inserting at the end the following:

'(i) It shall not be unlawful under this chapter for a person acting under color of law to intercept the wire or electronic communications of a computer trespasser transmitted to, through, or from the protected computer, if—

'(I) the owner or operator of the protected computer authorizes the interception of the computer trespasser's communications on the protected computer;

'(II) the person acting under color of law is lawfully engaged in an investigation;

'(III) the person acting under color of law has reasonable grounds to believe that the contents of the computer trespasser's communications will be relevant to the investigation; and

'(IV) such interception does not acquire communications other than those transmitted to or from the computer trespasser.'.

### SEC. 223. CIVIL LIABILITY FOR CERTAIN UNAUTHORIZED DISCLOSURES.

(a) Section 2520 of title 18, United States Code, is amended—

(1) in subsection (a), after 'entity', by inserting ', other than the United States,';

(2) by adding at the end the following:

'(f) ADMINISTRATIVE DISCIPLINE—If a court or appropriate department or agency determines that the United States or any of its departments or agencies has violated any provision of this chapter, and the court or appropriate department or agency finds that the circumstances surrounding the violation raise serious questions about whether or not an officer or employee of the United States acted willfully or intentionally with respect to the violation, the department or agency shall, upon receipt of a true and correct copy of the decision and findings of the court or appropriate department or agency promptly initiate a proceeding to determine whether disciplinary action against the officer or employee is warranted. If the head of the department or agency involved determines that disciplinary action is not warranted, he or she shall notify the Inspector General with jurisdiction over the department or agency concerned and shall provide the Inspector General with the reasons for such determination.'; and

(3) by adding a new subsection (g), as follows:

'(g) IMPROPER DISCLOSURE IS VIOLATION—Any willful disclosure or use by an investigative or law enforcement officer or governmental entity of information beyond the extent permitted by section 2517 is a violation of this chapter for purposes of section 2520(a).'.

# APPENDIX 11:
# SAMPLE JOINT SURVIVORSHIP
# ACCOUNT SIGNATURE CARD

| ACCOUNT/TITLE/NAMES(PRIMARY SIGNER) | CHECKING ACCOUNT NO. | | |
|---|---|---|---|
| 1. | | ☐ Joint ☐ Indiv. | |
| 2. | SAVINGS ACCOUNT NO. TYPE 10 | | |
| | | ☐ Joint ☐ Indiv. | |
| 3. | PASSBOOK ACCOUNT NO. TYPE 20 | | |
| | | ☐ Joint ☐ Indiv. | |
| ADDRESS (PRIMARY SIGNER) | PHONE NO.    NO. OF SIGS REQUIRED | | |
| 1. | | | |
| CITY AND STATE          ZIP CODE | DATE OF BIRTH | | |
| 1. | | | |
| SIGNATURES: | SOCIAL SECURITY NO. | | |
| 1. | | | |
| 2. | SOCIAL SECURITY NO. | | |
| 3. | SOCIAL SECURITY NO. | | |

| AUTHORIZED SIGNATURES SUBJECT TO THE TERMS AND CONDITIONS ON THE BACK HEREON. | DISTRIBUTION OF DEPOSIT | | |
|---|---|---|---|
| | DDA | SAV | PSB |
| EMPLOYED BY | TP | BUSINESS PHONE | |
| 1. | | | |
| 2. | | | |
| 3. | | | |
| DATE OPENED | OPENED BY | | |

# APPENDIX 12:
# SAMPLE CORPORATE
# BANKING RESOLUTION

I, the undersigned, Secretary of _____, a corporation duly organized under the laws of the State of _____, hereby certify to the Bank that at a meeting of the Board of Directors of said corporation, duly called and held on the _____ day of _____, 20____, a quorum being present throughout, the following resolution was duly and unanimously adopted and entered upon the regular minute book of the said corporation, that the same is in accordance with the Charter and By-Laws of said corporation, and is now in full force and effect:

**[Deposits and Withdrawals]**

"RESOLVED:

1. That the _____ Bank (hereinafter referred to as the "Bank") be and hereby is designated as a depository of this corporation, and the officers and agents of this corporation be and hereby are, and each of them hereby is, authorized to deposit any of the funds of this corporation in the Bank, either at its head office or at any of its branches. The Bank is hereby authorized to pay, cash or otherwise honor and charge to this corporation any and all checks, drafts, notes, acceptances and other instruments, items, and orders for the payment or withdrawal of monies, credits, items and property at any time held by the Bank for the account of this corporation, including those which may cause an overdraft, when made, signed, drawn, accepted or indorsed on behalf of this corporation by any person then holding the following offices or by any of the following named signatories: (See Note Below).

2. That the Bank is hereby authorized to pay any such instrument, item or order, or make any such charge, and also receive the same

from the payee or any other holder, without limit as to amount and without inquiry as to the circumstances of issue or the disposition of proceeds even if drawn to the individual order of any signing person, or payable to the Bank or other for his account, or tendered in payment of his individual obligation, and whether drawn against an account in the name of this corporation, or in the name of any officer or agent of this corporation as such, and, at the option of the Bank, even if the account shall not be in credit to the full amount of such instrument, order or charge.

3. That the Bank is hereby authorized to accept for deposit for the account of this corporation for credit, or for collection, or otherwise, any and all instruments or items indorsed by any person or by hand-stamped impression in the name of this corporation or without indorsement.

### [Loans, Credits and Security]

4. That the persons then holding the following offices or the following named signatories: (See Note Below).

are hereby authorized on behalf of this corporation: to borrow money and to obtain credit for this corporation from the Bank on any terms and to make and deliver notes, drafts, acceptances, applications for letters of credit, instruments of guarantee, agreements or undertakings and any other obligation of this corporation therefor in form satisfactory to the Bank, and as security therefor, to grant a security interest in, and to assign, pledge, deliver, create any lien or encumbrance upon, withdraw, exchange or substitute, instruments, stocks, bonds and other securities, mortgages, bills receivable and accounts, commercial and chattel paper, bills of lading, warehouse receipts and other documents of title, goods, insurance policies, certificates, general intangibles and any other property whatever held by or belonging to this corporation, with full authority to indorse, assign or guarantee the same in the name of this corporation; to execute and deliver security agreements and all instruments of assignment, transfer, hypothecation, powers of attorney, mortgage, pledge and trust; to discount any bills receivable or other instruments or commercial and chattel paper held by this corporation with full authority to indorse the same in the name of this corporation; to subordinate and assign any obligations and debts owed to this corporation by another or others, and in connection therewith, to execute and deliver instruments of subordination sand assignment in form satisfactory to the Bank; to withdraw from the Bank and give receipt for, or to authorize the Bank to deliver to bearer or one or more designated persons, all or any instruments, documents, securities, or other property held by the Bank, whether held as collateral security, or for safekeeping or for any other purpose; to give any instructions to the Bank for the purchase, receipt, sale, delivery, exchange or other disposition of any stocks, bonds, or other securities and foreign exchange or the proceeds thereof; to execute and deliver all instruments, agreements or documents required by the Bank in connection with any of the foregoing matters, and to affix thereto the seal of this corporation.

5. That the Bank may be promptly notified in writing by the Secretary or any other officer of this corporation of any change in this resolution, such notice to be given to each office of the Bank in which any account of this corporation may be maintained; that until the Bank has actually received such notice in writing, this resolution and the authority hereby conferred shall remain in full force and effect; that the Bank is authorized to act in pursuance of this resolution, and that until it has actually so received such notice, it shall be indemnified and saved harmless from any loss suffered or liability incurred by it in continuing to act in pursuance of this resolution, even though this resolution may have been changed; that the Secretary or any Assistant Secretary or any other officer of this corporation is hereby authorized and directed to certify, under the seal of this corporation or not, with like effect in the latter case, to the Bank, this resolution, the names of the officers, agents and signatories, and specimens of their respective signatures; and that the Bank may conclusively assume that persons at any time certified to it to be officers, agents or signatories of this corporation continue as such until receipt by the Bank of written notice to the contrary.

6. That all controversies and questions concerning the intendment and legal effect of any of the provisions of this resolution shall be governed by and construed under the in accordance with the laws of the State of _____ .

7. That any and all transactions heretofore entered into between this corporation and the Bank, including, but not limited to, transactions such as those hereinbefore described in these resolutions and all acts that have been heretofore done and documents heretofore executed and delivered to the Bank to carry out the purposes of any of the foregoing, executed and delivered on behalf of this corporation by any officer or agent of this corporation, are hereby expressly ratified, confirmed, and approved and the Bank is hereby authorized to rely upon these resolutions.

I FURTHER CERTIFY that the present officers of said corporation and the officers respectively held by them are as follows:

NAME                                        TITLE

_____          _____

_____          _____

IN WITNESS WHEREOF, I have hereunto set my hands as Secretary of said corporation and affixed the corporate seal this _____ day of _____, 20____ and I do further acknowledge, on behalf of said corporation, that the foregoing resolution also constitutes an agreements by said corporation with the Bank with respect to the matters therein set forth.

_____
As Secretary of Said Corporation

_____
Other Officer*

_____
Title

(Corporate Seal)

_____

NOTE: *Clients are requested to insert in the spaces above, titles only of the signing officers, or the names of other authorized persons. Also, to indicate fully in what manner they are to sign, i.e., singly, any two, jointly, etc., as for insurance: the President, Secretary and Treasurer or any "one" or "two" of them (or indicate any special combination).*

*\* In case the Secretary or other recording officer is authorized to sign checks, notes, etc., by the above resolution this certificate must also be signed by a second officer of the corporation.*

# APPENDIX 13:
# DIRECTORY OF STATE CONSUMER
# PROTECTION AGENCIES

| STATE | ADDRESS | TELEPHONE NUMBER |
|---|---|---|
| Alabama | Consumer Protection Division<br>Office of the Attorney General<br>11 S. Union Street<br>Montgomery, AL 36130 | 205-261-7334 |
| Alaska | Consumer Protection Section<br>Office of the Attorney Genera,<br>1031 W. 4th Avenue, Suite 110-B<br>Anchorage, AK 99501 | 907-279-0428 |
| Arizona | Financial Fraud Division<br>Office of the Attorney General<br>1275 W. Washington St.<br>Phoenix, AZ 85007 | 602-542-3702 |
| Arkansas | Consumer Protection Division<br>Office of the Attorney General<br>200 Tower Building, 4th & Center<br>Streets, Little Rock, AR 72201 | 501-682-2007 |
| California | Public Inquiry Unit<br>Office of the Attorney General<br>1515 K Street, Suite 511<br>Sacramento, CA 94244-2550 | 916-322-3360 |
| California | Consumer Protection Division<br>Los Angeles City Attorney's Office<br>200 N. Main Street, 1600 City Hall East<br>Los Angeles, CA 90012 | 213-485-4515 |
| Colorado | Consumer Protection Unit<br>Office of the Attorney General<br>1525 Sherman Street, 3rd Floor<br>Denver, CO 80203 | 303-866-5167 |

| STATE | ADDRESS | TELEPHONE NUMBER |
|---|---|---|
| Connecticut | Department of Consumer Protection<br>165 Capitol Avenue<br>Hartford, CT 06106 | 203-566-4999 |
| Delaware | Division of Consumer Affairs<br>Department of Community Affairs<br>820 N. French Street, 4th Floor<br>Wilmington, DE 19801 | 302-571-3250 |
| District of Columbia | Department of Consumer &<br>Regulatory Affairs<br>614 H Street NW<br>Washington, DC 20001 | 202-737-7000 |
| Florida | Division of Consumer Services<br>218 Mayo Building<br>Tallahassee, FL 32399 | 904-488-2226 |
| Georgia | Governor's Office of Consumer Affairs<br>2 Martin Luther King Jr. Drive<br>SE Plaza Level, E Tower<br>Atlanta, GA 30334 | 404-656-7000 |
| Hawaii | Office of Consumer Protection<br>828 Fort St. Mall<br>Honolulu, HI 96812-3767 | 808-548-2560 |
| Idaho | None Listed | |
| Illinois | Consumer Protection Division<br>Office of the Attorney General<br>100 W. Randolph Street<br>12th Floor, Chicago, IL 60601 | 312-917-3580 |
| Indiana | Consumer Protection Division<br>Office of the Attorney General<br>219 State House<br>Indianapolis, IN 46204 | 317-232-6330 |
| Iowa | Consumer Protection Division<br>Office of the Attorney General<br>1300 E. Walnut Street, 2nd Floor<br>Des Moines, IA 50319 | 515-281-5926 |
| Kansas | Consumer Protection Division<br>Office of the Attorney General<br>Kansas Judicial Center, 2nd Floor<br>Topeka, KS 66612 | 913-296-3761 |
| Kentucky | Consumer Protection Division<br>Office of the Attorney General<br>209 St. Clair Street<br>Frankfort, KY 40601 | 502-564-2200 |

| STATE | ADDRESS | TELEPHONE NUMBER |
|---|---|---|
| Louisiana | Consumer Protection Section<br>Office of the Attorney General<br>State Capitol Building<br>P.O. Box 94005<br>Baton Rouge, LA 70804 | 504-342-7013 |
| Maine | Consumer and Antitrust Division<br>Office of the Attorney General<br>State House Station #6<br>Augusta, ME 04333 | 207-289-3716 |
| Maryland | Consumer Protection Division<br>Office of the Attorney General<br>7 N. Calvert Street, 3rd Floor<br>Baltimore, MD 21202 | 301-528-8662 |
| Massachusetts | Consumer Protection Division<br>Office of the Attorney General<br>One Ashburton Place, Room 1411<br>Boston, MA 02108 | 617-727-7780 |
| Michigan | Consumer Protection Division<br>Office of the Attorney General<br>670 Law Building<br>Lansing, MI 48913 | 517-373-1140 |
| Minnesota | Office of Consumer Services<br>Office of the Attorney General<br>117 University Avenue<br>St. Paul, MN 55155 | 612-296-2331 |
| Mississippi | Consumer Protection Division<br>Office of the Attorney General<br>P.O. Box 220<br>Jackson, MS 39205 | 601-359-3680 |
| Missouri | Trade Offense Division<br>Office of the Attorney General<br>P.O. Box 899<br>Jefferson City, MO 65102 | 314-751-2616 |
| Montana | Consumer Affairs Unit<br>Department of Commerce<br>1424 9th Avenue<br>Helena, MT 59620 | 406-444-4312 |
| Nebraska | Consumer Protection Division<br>Department of Justice<br>2115 State Capitol<br>P.O. Box 98920<br>Lincoln, NE 68509 | 402-471-4723 |
| Nevada | Department of Commerce<br>State Mail Room Complex<br>Las Vegas, NV 89158 | 702-486-4150 |

| STATE | ADDRESS | TELEPHONE NUMBER |
|---|---|---|
| New Hampshire | Consumer Protection and Antitrust Division Office of the Attorney General State House Annex Concord, NH 03301 | 603-271-3641 |
| New Jersey | Division of Consumer Affairs 1100 Raymond Boulevard Room 504 Newark, NJ 07102 | 201-648-4010 |
| New Mexico | Consumer and Economic Crime Division Office of the Attorney General P.O. Box Drawer 1508 Santa Fe, NM 87504 | 505-872-6910 |
| New York | Consumer Protection Board 99 Washington Avenue Albany, NY 12210 | 518-474-8583 |
| New York | Consumer Protection Board 250 Broadway, 17th Floor New York, NY 10007-2593 | 212-587-4908 |
| North Carolina | Consumer Protection Section Office of the Attorney General P.O. Box 629 Raleigh, NC 27602 | 919-733-7741 |
| North Dakota | Consumer Fraud Division Office of the Attorney General State Capitol Building Bismarck, ND 58505 | 701-224-2210 |
| Ohio | Consumer Frauds and Crimes Section Office of the Attorney General 30 E. Broad Street, 25th Floor Columbus, OH 43266-0410 | 614-466-4986 |
| Oklahoma | Consumer Affairs Office of the Attorney General 112 State Capitol Building Oklahoma City, OK 73105 | 405-521-3921 |
| Oregon | Financial Fraud Section Office of the Attorney General Justice Building Salem, OR 97310 | 503-378-4320 |
| Pennsylvania | Bureau of Consumer Protection Office of the Attorney General Strawberry Square, 14th Floor Harrisburg, PA 17120 | 717-787-9707 |

| STATE | ADDRESS | TELEPHONE NUMBER |
|---|---|---|
| Rhode Island | Consumer Protection Division<br>Office of the Attorney General<br>72 Pine Street<br>Providence, RI 02903 | 401-277-2104 |
| South Carolina | Department of Consumer Affairs<br>P.O. Box 5757<br>Columbia, SC 29250 | 803-734-9452 |
| South Dakota | Division of Consumer Affairs<br>Office of the Attorney General<br>State Capitol Building<br>Pierre, SD 57501 | 605-773-4400 |
| Tennessee | Division of Consumer Affairs<br>Department of Commerce & Insurance<br>500 James Robertson Parkway<br>5th Floor<br>Nashville, TN 37219 | 615-741-4737 |
| Texas | Consumer Protection Division<br>Office of the Attorney General<br>Box 12548, Capitol Station<br>Austin, TX 78711 | 512-463-2070 |
| Utah | Division of Consumer Protection<br>Department of Business Regulation<br>160 E. Third South<br>P.O. Box 45802<br>Salt Lake City, UT 84145 | 801-530-6601 |
| Vermont | Public Protection Division<br>Office of the Attorney General<br>109 State Street<br>Montpelier, VT 05602 | 802-828-3171 |
| Virginia | Division of Consumer Counsel<br>Office of the Attorney General<br>Supreme Court Building<br>101 N. 8th Street<br>Richmond, VA 23219 | 804-786-2116 |
| Washington | Consumer and Business Fair Practices<br>Division, 710 2nd Avenue, Suite 1300<br>Seattle, WA 98104 | 206-464-7744 |
| West Virginia | Consumer Protection Division<br>Office of the Attorney General<br>812 Quarrier Street, 6th Floor<br>Charleston, WV 25301 | 304-348-8986 |
| Wisconsin | Office of Consumer Protection<br>Department of Justice<br>P.O. Box 7856<br>Madison, WI 53707 | 608-266-1852 |

| STATE | ADDRESS | TELEPHONE NUMBER |
|---|---|---|
| Wyoming | Office of the Attorney General 123 State Capitol Building Cheyenne, WY 82002 | 307-777-6286 |

Source: Consumers Resource Handbook U.S. Office of Consumer Affairs.

# APPENDIX 14:
# FAILED FINANCIAL INSTITUTIONS
# (OCTOBER 2000—APRIL 2004)

| FINANCIAL INSTITUTION | CITY | STATE | CLOSING DATE |
|---|---|---|---|
| Reliance Bank | White Plains | New York | March 19, 2004 |
| Guaranty National Bank of Tallahassee | Tallahassee | Florida | March 12, 2004 |
| Dollar Savings Bank | Newark | New Jersey | February 14, 2004 |
| Pulaski Savings Bank | Philadelphia | Pennsylvania | November 14, 2003 |
| The First National Bank of Blanchardville | Blanchardville | Wisconsin | May 9, 2003 |
| Southern Pacific Bank | Torrance | California | February 7, 2003 |
| The Farmers Bank of Cheneyville | Cheneyville | Louisiana | December 17, 2002 |
| The Bank of Alamo | Alamo | Tennessee | November 8, 2002 |
| AmTrade International Bank of Georgia | Atlanta | Georgia | September 30, 2002 |
| Universal Federal Savings Bank | Chicago | Illinois | June 27, 2002 |
| Connecticut Bank of Commerce | Stamford | Connecticut | June 26, 2002 |
| New Century Bank | Shelby Township | Michigan | March 28, 2002 |

| FINANCIAL INSTITUTION | CITY | STATE | CLOSING DATE |
|---|---|---|---|
| Net 1st National Bank | Boca Raton | Florida | March 1, 2002 |
| NextBank, N.A. | Phoenix | Arizona | February 7, 2002 |
| Oakwood Deposit Bank Company | Oakwood | Ohio | February 1, 2002 |
| Bank of Sierra Blanca | Sierra Blanca | Texas | January 18, 2002 |
| Hamilton Bank, N.A. | Miami | Florida | January 11, 2002 |
| Sinclair National Bank | Gravette | Arkansas | September 7, 2001 |
| Superior Bank, FSB | Hinsdale | Illinois | July 27, 2001 |
| The Malta National Bank | Malta | Ohio | May 3, 2001 |
| First Alliance Bank &.Trust Company | Manchester | New Hampshire | February 2, 2001 |
| National State Bank of Metropolis | Metropolis | Illinois | December 14, 2000 |
| Bank of Honolulu | Honolulu | Hawaii | October 13, 2000 |

Source: Federal Deposit Insurance Corporation (FDIC)

# APPENDIX 15:
# FEDERAL DEPOSIT INSURANCE
# CORPORATION—REGIONAL OFFICES

| REGION COVERED | ADDRESS |
|---|---|
| Alabama, Florida, Georgia, North Carolina, South Carolina, Virginia, West Virginia | FDIC, Attn: Deposit Insurance One Atlanta Center, Suite 1500 1201 W Peachtree St. NE Atlanta, Georgia 30309-3449 |
| Connecticut, Maine, Massachusetts, New Hampshire, Rhode Island, Vermont | FDIC, Attn: Deposit Insurance Westwood Executive Center 200 Lowder Brook Drive Westwood, Massachusetts 02090 |
| Illinois, Indiana, Michigan, Ohio, Wisconsin | FDIC, Attn: Deposit Insurance 500 West Monroe, Suite 3600 Chicago, Illinois 60661-3630 |
| Colorado, New Mexico, Oklahoma, Texas | FDIC, Attn: Deposit Insurance 1910 Pacific Avenue, Suite 2000 Dallas, Texas 75201 |
| Iowa, Kansas, Minnesota, Missouri, Nebraska, North Dakota, South Dakota | FDIC, Attn: Deposit Insurance 2345 Grand Avenue, Suite 1500 Kansas City, Missouri 64108 |
| Arkansas, Kentucky, Louisiana, Mississippi, Tennessee | FDIC, Attn: Deposit Insurance 5100 Poplar Avenue, Suite 1900 Memphis, Tennessee 38137 |
| Delaware, District of Columbia, Maryland, New Jersey, New York, Pennsylvania, Puerto Rico, Virgin Islands | FDIC, Attn: Deposit Insurance 452 Fifth Avenue, 19th Floor New York, New York 10018 |
| Alaska, Arizona, California, Guam, Hawaii, Idaho, Montana, Nevada, Oregon, Utah, Washington, Wyoming | FDIC, Attn: Deposit Insurance 25 Ecker Street, Suite 2300 San Francisco, California 94105 |

Source: Federal Deposit Insurance Corporation (FDIC)

# APPENDIX 16:
# TOP 25 ONLINE BANKS

| RANK | BANK |
|------|------|
| 1 | Bank of America |
| 2 | Wells Fargo |
| 3 | JP Morgan |
| 4 | Key Corp |
| 5 | First Union |
| 6 | Nation's Bank |
| 7 | Chase Manhattan |
| 8 | Citicorp |
| 9 | Fleet Financial Group |
| 10 | Norwest Bank |
| 11 | Bank Boston |
| 12 | Crestar Financial |
| 13 | Bankers Trust |
| 14 | US Bancorp |
| 15 | Huntington Bancshares |
| 16 | Bank One |
| 17 | First Chicago |
| 18 | PNC Bank |
| 19 | Mellon Bank |
| 20 | Barnett Bank |
| 21 | Centura Banks |
| 22 | Union Bank |
| 23 | Firstar |
| 24 | Comerica |
| 25 | Republic New York |

Source: Internet Valley

# APPENDIX 17:
# PROJECTED NUMBER OF ONLINE
# BANKING HOUSEHOLDS (2004-2008)

| Year | Number of Households Banking Online (millions) |
|------|-----------------------------------------------|
| 2004 | 35.3 |
| 2005 | 40.9 |
| 2006 | 46.2 |
| 2007 | 51.3 |
| 2008 | 56.0 |

Source: Jupiter Research, November 2003

# APPENDIX 18:
# PROJECTED NUMBER OF ONLINE BANKING HOUSEHOLDS (2004-2008)

| Year | Percentage of Households Making Online Payments |
|------|--------------------------------------------------|
| 2004 | 57% |
| 2005 | 64% |
| 2006 | 71% |
| 2007 | 78% |
| 2008 | 85% |

Source: Jupiter Research, November 2003

# APPENDIX 19:
# THE SAFEGUARDS RULE

---

**FEDERAL TRADE COMMISSION [16 CFR PART 314]**

**PART 314–STANDARDS FOR SAFEGUARDING CUSTOMER INFORMATION**

### § 314.1 Purpose and scope.

(a) Purpose. This part ("rule"), which implements sections 501 and 505(b)(2) of the Gramm-Leach-Bliley Act, sets forth standards for developing, implementing, and maintaining reasonable administrative, technical, and physical safeguards to protect the security, confidentiality, and integrity of customer information.

(b) Scope. This rule applies to the handling of customer information by all financial institutions over which the Federal Trade Commission ("FTC" or "Commission") has jurisdiction. This rule refers to such entities as "you." The rule applies to all customer information in your possession, regardless of whether such information pertains to individuals with whom you have a customer relationship, or pertains to the customers of other financial institutions that have provided such information to you.

### § 314.2 Definitions.

(a) In general. Except as modified by this rule or unless the context otherwise requires, the terms used in this rule have the same meaning as set forth in the Commission's rule governing the Privacy of Consumer Financial Information, 16 CFR part 313.

(b) "Customer information" means any record containing nonpublic personal information as defined in 16 CFR 313.3(n), about a customer of a financial institution, whether in paper, electronic, or other form, that is handled or maintained by or on behalf of you or your affiliates.

(c) "Information security program" means the administrative, technical, or physical safeguards you use to access, collect, distribute, pro-

---

cess, protect, store, use, transmit, dispose of, or otherwise handle customer information.

(d) "Service provider" means any person or entity that receives, maintains, processes, or otherwise is permitted access to customer information through its provision of services directly to a financial institution that is subject to the rule.

### § 314.3 Standards for safeguarding customer information.

(a) Information security program. You shall develop, implement, and maintain a comprehensive information security program that is written in one or more readily accessible parts and contains administrative, technical, and physical safeguards that are appropriate to your size and complexity, the nature and scope of your activities, and the sensitivity of any customer information at issue. Such safeguards shall include the elements set forth in section 314.4 and shall be reasonably designed to achieve the objectives of this rule, as set forth in paragraph (b) of this section.

(b) Objectives. The objectives of section 501(b) of the Act, and of this rule, are to:

(1) Insure the security and confidentiality of customer information;

(2) Protect against any anticipated threats or hazards to the security or integrity of such information; and

(3) Protect against unauthorized access to or use of such information that could result in substantial harm or inconvenience to any customer.

### § 314.4 Elements.

In order to develop, implement, and maintain your information security program, you shall:

(a) Designate an employee or employees to coordinate your information security program.

(b) Identify reasonably foreseeable internal and external risks to the security, confidentiality, and integrity of customer information that could result in the unauthorized disclosure, misuse, alteration, destruction or other compromise of such information, and assess the sufficiency of any safeguards in place to control these risks. At a minimum, such a risk assessment should include consideration of risks in each relevant area of your operations, including:

(1) employee training and management;

(2) information systems, including network and software design, as well as information processing, storage, transmission and disposal; and

(3) detecting, preventing and responding to attacks, intrusions, or other systems failures.

(c) Design and implement information safeguards to control the risks you identify through risk assessment, and regularly test or otherwise monitor the effectiveness of the safeguards' key controls, systems, and procedures.

(d) Oversee service providers, by:

(1) taking reasonable steps to select and retain service providers that are capable of maintaining appropriate safeguards for the customer information at issue; and

(2) requiring your service providers by contract to implement and maintain such safeguards.

(e) Evaluate and adjust your information security program in light of the results of the testing and monitoring required by paragraph (c); any material changes to your operations or business arrangements; or any other circumstances that you know or have reason to know may have a material impact on your information security program.

## § 314.5 Effective date.

(a) Each financial institution subject to the Commission's jurisdiction must implement an information security program pursuant to this rule no later than one year from the date on which the Final Rule is published in the Federal Register.

(b) Two-year grandfathering of service contracts. Until two years from the date on which the Final Rule is published in the Federal Register, a contract you have entered into with a nonaffiliated third party to perform services for you or functions on your behalf satisfies the provisions of section 314.4(d) of this part, even if the contract does not include a requirement that the service provider maintain appropriate safeguards, as long as you entered into the contract not later than 30 days from the date on which the Final Rule is published in the Federal Register.

By direction of the Commission.

Donald S. Clark Secretary

# APPENDIX 20:
# STATE IDENTITY THEFT LEGISLATION

## ALABAMA [2001 AL. PUB. ACT 312]

**Identity theft.**

(a) A person commits the crime of identity theft if, without the authorization, consent, or permission of the victim, and with the intent to defraud for his or her own benefit or the benefit of a third person, he or she does any of the following:

(1) Obtains, records, or accesses identifying information that would assist in accessing financial resources, obtaining identification documents, or obtaining benefits of the victim.

(2) Obtains goods or services through the use of identifying information of the victim.

(3) Obtains identification documents in the victim's name.

(b) Identity theft in which there is a financial loss of greater than two hundred fifty dollars ($250) or the defendant has previously been convicted of identity theft constitutes identity theft in the first degree. Identity theft in the first degree is a Class C felony.

(c) Identity theft in which the defendant has not previously been convicted of identity theft and there is no financial loss or the financial loss is two hundred fifty dollars ($250) or less constitutes identity theft in the second degree. Identity theft in the second degree is a Class A misdemeanor.

(d) This section shall not apply when a person obtains the identity of another person to misrepresent his age for the sole purpose of obtaining alcoholic beverages, tobacco, or another privilege denied to minors.

## ALASKA [ALASKA STAT. § 11.46.180]

### Theft by deception.

(a) A person commits theft by deception if, with intent to deprive another of property or to appropriate property of another to oneself or a third person, the person obtains the property of another by deception.

(b) In a prosecution based on theft by deception, if the state seeks to prove that the defendant used deception by promising performance which the defendant did not intend to perform or knew would not be performed, that intent or knowledge may not be established solely by or inferred solely from the fact that the promise was not performed.

(c) As used in this section, "deception" has the meaning ascribed to it in AS 11.81.900 but does not include falsity as to matters having no pecuniary significance or "puffing" by statements unlikely to deceive reasonable persons in the group addressed.

## ARIZONA [ARIZ. REV. STAT. § 13-2008]

### Taking identity of another person; classification

A. A person commits taking the identity of another person if the person knowingly takes, uses, sells or transfers any personal identifying information of another person, without the consent of that other person, with the intent to obtain, use, sell or transfer the other person's identity for any unlawful purpose or to cause loss to a person.

B. A peace officer in any jurisdiction in which an element of the offense is committed or a result of the offense occurs may take a report.

C. If a defendant is alleged to have committed multiple violations of this section within the same county, the prosecutor may file a complaint charging all of the violations and any related charges under other sections that have not been previously filed in the justice of the peace precinct in which the greatest number of violations are alleged to have occurred.

D. Taking the identity of another person is class 4 felony.

## ARKANSAS [ARK. CODE AN. § 5-37-227]

### Financial identity fraud.

(a)(1) A person commits financial identity fraud if, with the intent to unlawfully appropriate financial resources of another person to his or her own use or to the use of a third party, and without the authorization of that person, he or she:

(A) Obtains or records identifying information that would assist in accessing the financial resources of the other person; or

(B) Accesses or attempts to access the financial resources of the other person through the use of the identifying information, as defined in subdivision (a)(2) of this section.

(a)(2) "Identifying information", as used in this section, includes, but is not limited to:

(A) Social security numbers;

(B) Driver's license numbers;

(C) Checking account numbers;

(D) Savings account numbers;

(E) Credit card numbers;

(F) Debit card numbers;

(G) Personal identification numbers;

(H) Electronic identification numbers;

(I) Digital signatures; or

(J) Any other numbers or information that can be used to access a person's financial resources.

(b) The provisions of this section do not apply to any person who obtains another person's driver's license or other form of identification for the sole purpose of misrepresenting his or her age.

(c) Financial identity fraud is a Class D felony.

(d)(1) A violation of this section shall constitute an unfair or deceptive act or practice as defined by the Deceptive Trade Practices Act, § 4-88-101 et seq.

(d)(2) All remedies, penalties, and authority granted to the Attorney General or other persons under the Deceptive Trade Practices Act, § 4-88-101 et seq., shall be available to the Attorney General or other persons for the enforcement of this section.

## CALIFORNIA [CAL. PENAL CODE §§ 530.5; 5-530.6; 5-530.7] PENAL CODE

### Section 530.5

(a) Every person who willfully obtains personal identifying information, as defined in subdivision (b), of another person, and uses that information for any unlawful purpose, including to obtain, or attempt to obtain, credit, goods, services, or medical information in the name of the other person without the consent of that person, is guilty of a public offense, and upon conviction therefor, shall be punished either by imprisonment in a county jail not to exceed one year, a fine not to exceed one thousand dollars ($1,000), or both that imprisonment and fine, or by imprisonment in the state prison, a fine not to exceed ten thousand dollars ($10,000), or both that imprisonment and fine.

(b) "Personal identifying information," as used in this section, means the name, address, telephone number, driver's license number, social security number, place of employment, employee identification number, mother's maiden name, demand deposit account number, savings account number, or credit card number of an individual person.

(c) In any case in which a person willfully obtains personal identifying information of another person without the authorization of that person, and uses that information to commit a crime in addition to a violation of subdivision (a), and is convicted of that crime, the court records shall reflect that the person whose identity was falsely used to commit the crime did not commit the crime.

### Section 530.6

(a) A person who has learned or reasonably suspects that his or her personal identifying information has been unlawfully used by another, as described in subdivision (a) of Section 530.5, may initiate a law enforcement investigation by contacting the local law enforcement agency that has jurisdiction over his or her actual residence, which shall take a police report of the matter, provide the complainant with a copy of that report, and begin an investigation of the facts or, if the suspected crime was committed in a different jurisdiction, refer the matter to the law enforcement agency where the suspected crime was committed for an investigation of the facts.

(b) A person who reasonably believes that he or she is the victim of identity theft may petition a court for an expedited judicial determination of his or her factual innocence, where the perpetrator of the identity theft was arrested for or convicted of a crime under the victim's identity, or where the victim's identity has been mistakenly associated with a record of criminal conviction. Any judicial determination of factual innocence made pursuant to this section may be heard and determined upon declarations, affidavits, police reports, or other material, relevant, and reliable information submitted by the parties. Where the court determines that the petition is meritorious and that there is no reasonable cause to believe that the petitioner committed the offense for which the perpetrator of the identity theft was arrested or convicted, the court shall find the petitioner factually innocent of that offense. If the petitioner is found factually innocent, the court shall issue an order certifying this determination. The Judicial Council of California shall develop a form for use in issuing an order pursuant to these provisions. A court issuing a determination of factual innocence pursuant to this section may at any time vacate that determination if the petition, or any information submitted in support of the petition, is found to contain any material misrepresentation or fraud.

### Section 530.7

(a) In order for a victim of identity theft to be included in the data base established pursuant to subdivision (c), he or she shall submit to the Department of Justice a court order obtained pursuant to any provision of law, a full set of fingerprints, and any other information prescribed by the department.

(b) Upon receiving information pursuant to subdivision (a), the Department of Justice shall verify the identity of the victim against any driver's license or other identification record maintained by the Department of Motor Vehicles.

(c) The Department of Justice shall establish and maintain a data base of individuals who have been victims of identity theft. The department shall provide a victim of identity theft or his or her authorized representative access to the data base in order to establish that the individual has been a victim of identity theft. Access to the data base shall be limited to criminal justice agencies, victims of identity theft, and individuals and agencies authorized by the victims.

(d) The Department of Justice shall establish and maintain a toll-free telephone number to provide access to information under subdivision (c).

(e) This section shall be operative September 1, 2001.

### COLORADO [COLO. REV. STAT. §§ 18-5-102; 18-5-113]

#### Section 18-5-102—Forgery.

(1) A person commits forgery, if, with intent to defraud, such person falsely makes, completes, alters, or utters a written instrument which is or purports to be, or which is calculated to become or to represent if completed:

(a) Part of an issue of money, stamps, securities, or other valuable instruments issued by a government or government agency; or

(b) Part of an issue of stock, bonds, or other instruments representing interests in or claims against a corporate or other organization or its property; or

(c) A deed, will, codicil, contract, assignment, commercial instrument, promissory note, check, or other instrument which does or may evidence, create, transfer, terminate, or otherwise affect a legal right, interest, obligation, or status; or

(d) A public record or an instrument filed or required by law to be filed or legally fileable in or with a public office or public servant; or

(e) A written instrument officially issued or created by a public office, public servant, or government agency; or

(f) Part of an issue of tokens, transfers, certificates, or other articles manufactured and designed for use in transportation fees upon public conveyances, or as symbols of value usable in place of money for the purchase of property or services available to the public for compensation; or

(g) Part of an issue of lottery tickets or shares designed for use in the lottery held pursuant to part 2 of article 35 of title 24, C.R.S.; or

(h) A document-making implement that may be used or is used in the production of a false identification document or in the production of another document-making implement to produce false identification documents.

(2) Forgery is a class 5 felony.

### Section 18-5-113—Criminal impersonation.

(1) A person commits criminal impersonation if he knowingly assumes a false or fictitious identity or capacity, and in such identity or capacity he:

(a) Marries, or pretends to marry, or to sustain the marriage relation toward another without the connivance of the latter; or

(b) Becomes bail or surety for a party in an action or proceeding, civil or criminal, before a court or officer authorized to take the bail or surety; or

(c) Confesses a judgment, or subscribes, verifies, publishes, acknowledges, or proves a written instrument which by law may be recorded, with the intent that the same may be delivered as true; or

(d) Does an act which if done by the person falsely impersonated, might subject such person to an action or special proceeding, civil or criminal, or to liability, charge, forfeiture, or penalty; or

(e) Does any other act with intent to unlawfully gain a benefit for himself or another or to injure or defraud another.

(2) Criminal impersonation is a class 6 felony.

## CONNECTICUT [1999 GEN. STAT. § 53]

### Identity Theft

(a) A person is guilty of identity theft when such person intentionally obtains personal identifying information of another person without the authorization of such other person and uses that information for any unlawful purpose including, but not limited to, obtaining, or attempting to obtain, credit, goods, services or medical information in the name of such other person without the consent of such other person. As used in this section, "personal identifying information" means a motor vehicle operator's license number, Social Security number, employee identification number, mother's maiden name, demand deposit number, savings account number or credit card number.

(b) The victim of an identity theft may report the theft to the police department of their residence. The police department of the victim's residence shall receive the complaint and coordinate, if necessary, with any other police department the investigation of the identity theft and crimes committed or attempted as a result of the identity theft. Any subsequent prosecution of the identity theft and crimes committed or attempted, within the state, as a result of the identity theft may be prosecuted in the judicial district of the victim's residence.

(c) Identity theft is a Class D felony.

## DELAWARE [DEL. CODE AN. TIT. 11 § 854]

### Identity theft; class E felony; class D felony.

(a) A person commits identity theft when the person knowingly or recklessly obtains, produces, possesses, uses, sells, gives or transfers personal identifying information belonging or pertaining to another person without the consent of the other person and with intent to use the information to commit or facilitate any crime set forth in this title.

(b) A person commits identity theft when the person knowingly or recklessly obtains, produces, possesses, uses, sells, gives or transfers personal identifying information belonging or pertaining to another person without the consent of the other person, thereby knowingly or recklessly facilitating the use of the information by a third person to commit or facilitate any crime set forth in this title.

(c) For the purposes of this section, "personal identifying information" includes name, address, birth date, Social Security number, driver's license number, telephone number, financial services account number, savings account number, checking account number, credit card number, debit card number, identification document or false identification document, electronic identification number, educational record, health care record, financial record, credit record, employment record, e-mail address, computer system password, mother's maiden name or similar personal number, record or information.

(d) Identity theft is a class E felony, unless the victim is 62 years of age or older, in which case identity theft is a class D felony.

(e) When a person is convicted of or pleads guilty to identity theft, the sentencing judge shall order full restitution for monetary loss, including documented loss of wages and reasonable attorney fees, suffered by the victim.

(f) Prosecution under this section does not preclude prosecution or sentencing under any other section of this Code.

## FLORIDA [FLA. STAT. AN. § 817.568]

### Criminal use of personal identification information.

(1) As used in this section, the term:

(a) "Access device" means any card, plate, code, account number, electronic serial number, mobile identification number, personal identification number, or other telecommunications service, equipment, or instrument identifier, or other means of account access that can be used, alone or in conjunction with another access device, to obtain money, goods, services, or any other thing of value, or that can be used to initiate a transfer of funds, other than a transfer originated solely by paper instrument.

(b) "Authorization" means empowerment, permission, or competence to act.

(c) "Harass" means to engage in conduct directed at a specific person that is intended to cause substantial emotional distress to such person and serves no legitimate purpose. "Harass" does not mean to use personal identification information for accepted commercial purposes. The term does not include constitutionally protected conduct such as organized protests or the use of personal identification information for accepted commercial purposes.

(d) "Individual" means a single human being and does not mean a firm, association of individuals, corporation, partnership, joint venture, sole proprietorship, or any other entity.

(e) "Person" means a "person" as defined in s. 1.01(3).

(f) "Personal identification information" means any name or number that may be used, alone or in conjunction with any other information, to identify a specific individual, including any:

1. Name, social security number, date of birth, official state-issued or United States-issued driver's license or identification number, alien registration number, government passport number, employer or taxpayer identification number, or Medicaid or food stamp account number;

2. Unique biometric data, such as fingerprint, voice print, retina or iris image, or other unique physical representation;

3. Unique electronic identification number, address, or routing code; or

4. Telecommunication identifying information or access device.

(2)(a) Any person who willfully and without authorization fraudulently uses, or possesses with intent to fraudulently use, personal identification information concerning an individual without first obtaining that individual's consent, commits the offense of fraudulent use of personal identification information, which is a felony of the third degree, punishable as provided in s. 775.082, s. 775.083, or s. 775.084.

(2)(b) Any person who willfully and without authorization fraudulently uses personal identification information concerning an individual without first obtaining that individual's consent commits a felony of the second degree, punishable as provided in s. 775.082, s. 775.083, or s. 775.084, if the pecuniary benefit, the value of the services received, the payment sought to be avoided, or the amount of the injury or fraud perpetrated is $75,000 or more.

(3) Any person who willfully and without authorization possesses, uses, or attempts to use personal identification information concerning an individual without first obtaining that individual's consent, and who does so for the purpose of harassing that individual, commits the offense of harassment by use of personal identification information, which is a misdemeanor of the first degree, punishable as provided in s. 775.082 or s. 775.083.

(4) If an offense prohibited under this section was facilitated or furthered by the use of a public record, as defined in s. 119.011, the offense is reclassified to the next higher degree as follows:

(a) A misdemeanor of the first degree is reclassified as a felony of the third degree.

(b) A felony of the third degree is reclassified as a felony of the second degree.

(c) A felony of the second degree is reclassified as a felony of the first degree.

## GEORGIA [GA. CODE AN. §§ 16-9-121; 16-9-127]

### Section 16-9-121

A person commits the offense of financial identity fraud when without the authorization or permission of another person and with the intent unlawfully to appropriate financial resources of that other person to his or her own use or to the use of a third party he or she:

(1) Obtains or records identifying information which would assist in accessing the financial resources of the other

(2) Accesses or attempts to access the financial resources of the other person through the use of identifying information. Such identifying information shall include but not be limited to:

(A) Social security numbers; not be limited to:

(B) Driver's license numbers; not be limited to:

(C) Checking account numbers; not be limited to:

(D) Savings account numbers; not be limited to:

(E) Credit card numbers; not be limited to:

(F) Debit card numbers; not be limited to:

(G) Personal identification numbers; not be limited to:

(H) Electronic identification numbers; not be limited to:

(I) Digital signatures; or

(J) Any other numbers or information which can be used to access a person's financial resources.

### Section 16-9-127

The prohibitions set forth in Code Section 16-9-121 shall not apply to:

(1) The lawful obtaining of credit information in the course of a bona fide consumer or commercial transaction;

(2) The lawful, good faith exercise of a security interest or a right to offset by a creditor or a financial institution; or

(3) The lawful, good faith compliance by any party when required by any warrant, levy, garnishment, attachment, court order, or other judicial or administrative order, decree, or directive.

## HAWAII [HAW. REV. STAT. § 708]

### Identity theft in the first degree.

(1) A person commits the offense of identity theft in the first degree if that person makes or causes to be made, either directly or indirectly, a transmission of any personal information of another by any oral statement, any written statement, or any statement conveyed by any electronic means, with the intent to:

(a) Facilitate the commission of a murder in any degree, a class A felony, kidnapping, unlawful imprisonment in any degree, extortion in any degree, any offense under chapter 134, criminal property damage in the first or second degree, escape in any degree, any offense under part VI of chapter 710, any offense under section 711-1103, or any offense under chapter 842; or

(b) Commit the offense of theft in the first degree from the person whose personal information is used, or from any other person or entity.

(2) Identity theft in the first degree is a class A felony.

### Identity theft in the second degree.

(1) A person commits the offense of identity theft in the second degree if that person makes or causes to be made, either directly or indirectly, a transmission of any personal information of another by any oral statement, any written statement, or any statement conveyed by any electronic means, with the intent to commit the offense of theft in the second degree from the person whose personal information is used, or from any other person or entity.

(2) Identity theft in the second degree is a class B felony.

### Identity theft in the third degree.

(1) A person commits the offense of identity theft in the third degree if that person makes or causes to be made, either directly or indirectly, a transmission of any personal information of another by any oral statement, any written statement, or any statement conveyed by any electronic means, with the intent to commit the offense of theft in the third or fourth degree from the person whose personal information is used, or from any other person or entity.

(2) Identity theft in the third degree is a class C felony.

## IDAHO [IDAHO CODE 18-3126]

### Misappropriation of Personal Identifying Information.

It is unlawful for any person to obtain or record personal identifying information of another person without the authorization of that person, with the intent that the information be used to obtain, or attempt to obtain, credit, money, goods or services in the name of the other person without the consent of that person.

## ILLINOIS [720 ILL. COMP. STAT. 5/16G-15; 5/16G-20]

### Section 5/16G-15. Financial identity theft.

(a) A person commits the offense of financial identity theft when he or she knowingly uses any personal identifying information or personal identification document of another person to fraudulently obtain credit, money, goods, services, or other property in the name of the other person.

(b) Knowledge shall be determined by an evaluation of all circumstances surrounding the use of the other person's identifying information or document.

(c) When a charge of financial identity theft of credit, money, goods, services, or other property exceeding a specified value is brought the value of the credit, money, goods, services, or other property is an element of the offense to be resolved by the trier of fact as either exceeding or not exceeding the specified value.

(d) Sentence.

(1) Financial identity theft of credit, money, goods,services, or other property not exceeding $300 in value is a Class A misdemeanor. A person who has been previously convicted of financial identity theft of less than $300 who is convicted of a second or subsequent offense of financial identity theft of less than $300 is guilty of a Class 4 felony. A person who has been convicted of financial identity theft of less than $300 who has been previously convicted of any type of theft, robbery, armed robbery, burglary, residential burglary, possession of burglary tools, home invasion, home repair fraud, aggravated home repair fraud, or financial exploitation of an elderly or disabled person is guilty of a Class 4 felony. When a person has any such prior conviction, the information or indictment charging that person shall state the prior conviction so as to give notice of the State's intention to treat the charge as a felony. The fact of the prior conviction is not an element of the offense and may not be disclosed to the jury during trial unless otherwise permitted by issues properly raised during the trial.

(2) Financial identity theft of credit, money, goods, services, or other property exceeding $300 and not exceeding $2,000 in value is a Class 4 felony.

(3) Financial identity theft of credit, money, goods, services, or other property exceeding $2,000 and not exceeding $10,000 in value is a Class 3 felony.

(4) Financial identity theft of credit, money, goods, services, or other property exceeding $10,000 and not exceeding $100,000 in value is a Class 2 felony.

(5) Financial identity theft of credit, money, goods, services, or other property exceeding $100,000 in value is a Class 1 felony.

### Section 16G-20. Aggravated financial identity theft.

(a) A person commits the offense of aggravated financial identity theft when he or she commits the offense of financial identity theft as set forth in subsection (a) of Section 16G-15 against a person 60 years of age or older or a disabled person as defined in Section 16-1.3 of this Code.

(b) Knowledge shall be determined by an evaluation of all circumstances surrounding the use of the other person's identifying information or document.

(c) When a charge of aggravated financial identity theft of credit, money, goods, services, or other property exceeding a specified value is brought the value of the credit, money, goods, services, or other property is an element of the offense to be resolved by the trier of fact as either exceeding or not exceeding the specified value.

(d) A defense to aggravated financial identity theft does not exist merely because the accused reasonably believed the victim to be a person less than 60 years of age.

(e) Sentence.

(1) Aggravated financial identity theft of credit, money, goods, services, or other property not exceeding $300 in value is a Class 4 felony.

(2) Aggravated financial identity theft of credit, money, goods, services, or other property exceeding $300 and not exceeding $10,000 in value is a Class 3 felony.

(3) Aggravated financial identity theft of credit, money, goods, services, or other property exceeding $10,000 in value and not exceeding $100,000 in value is a Class 2 felony.

(4) Aggravated financial identity theft of credit, money, goods, services, or other property exceeding $100,000 in value is a Class 1 felony.

(5) A person who has been previously convicted of aggravated financial identity theft regardless of the value of the property involved who is convicted of a second or subsequent offense of aggravated financial identity theft regardless of the value of the property involved is guilty of a Class X felony.

## INDIANA [IND. CODE AN. § 35-43-5-4]

A person who:

(1) with intent to defraud, obtains property by:

(A) using a credit card, knowing that the credit card was unlawfully obtained or retained;

(B) using a credit card, knowing that the credit card is forged, revoked, or expired;

(C) using, without consent, a credit card that was issued to another person;

(D) representing, without the consent of the credit card holder, that the person is the authorized holder of the credit card; or

(E) representing that the person is the authorized holder of a credit card when the card has not in fact been issued;

(2) being authorized by an issuer to furnish property upon presentation of a credit card, fails to furnish the property and, with intent to defraud the issuer or the credit card holder, represents in writing to the issuer that the person has furnished the property;

(3) being authorized by an issuer to furnish property upon presentation of a credit card, furnishes, with intent to defraud the issuer or the credit card holder, property upon presentation of a credit card, knowing that the credit card was unlawfully obtained or retained or that the credit card is forged, revoked, or expired;

(4) not being the issuer, knowingly or intentionally sells a credit card;

(5) not being the issuer, receives a credit card, knowing that the credit card was unlawfully obtained or retained or that the credit card is forged, revoked, or expired;

(6) with intent to defraud, receives a credit card as security for debt;

(7) receives property, knowing that the property was obtained in violation of subdivision (1) of this section;

(8) with intent to defraud the person's creditor or purchaser, conceals, encumbers, or transfers property;

(9) with intent to defraud, damages property;

(10) knowingly and with intent to defraud, makes, utters, presents, or causes to be presented to an insurer or an insurance claimant, a claim statement that contains false, incomplete, or misleading information concerning the claim; or

(11) knowingly or intentionally:

(A) sells;

(B) rents;

(C) transports; or

(D) possesses a recording for commercial gain or personal financial gain that does not conspicuously display the true name and address of the manufacturer of the recording;

commits fraud, a Class D felony.

## IOWA [IOWA CODE § 715A.8]

### Identity theft.

1. For purposes of this section, *"identification information"* means the name, address, date of birth, telephone number, driver's license number, nonoperator's identification number, social security number, place of employment, employee identification number, parent's legal surname prior to marriage, demand deposit account number, savings or checking account number, or credit card number of a person.

2. A person commits the offense of identity theft if the person with the intent to obtain a benefit fraudulently obtains identification information of another person and uses or attempts to use that information to obtain credit, property, or services without the authorization of that other person.

3. If the value of the credit, property, or services exceeds one thousand dollars, the person commits a class "D" felony. If the value of the credit, property, or services does not exceed one thousand dollars, the person commits an aggravated misdemeanor.

4. A violation of this section is an unlawful practice under section 714.16.

## KANSAS [KAN. STAT. AN. §21-4018]

### Identity theft.

(a) Identity theft is knowingly and with intent to defraud for economic benefit, obtaining, possessing, transferring, using or attempting to obtain, possess, transfer or use, one or more identification documents or personal identification number of another person other than that issued lawfully for the use of the possessor.

(b) "Identification documents" means the definition as provided in K.S.A. 21-3830, and amendments thereto.

(c) Identity theft is a severity level 7, person felony.

(d) This section shall be part of and supplemental to the Kansas criminal code.

### KENTUCKY [KY. REV. STAT. AN. § 514.160]

#### Theft of identity.

(1) A person is guilty of the theft of the identity of another when, without the other's consent, he or she knowingly possesses or uses any identifying information of the other person, such as one's name, Social Security number, birth date, personal identification number or code, which is kept in documents, photo or electrical copies, computer storage, or any other form of document retrieval and storage, and the theft is committed with the intent to represent that he or she is the other person for the purpose of:

(a) Depriving the other person of property;

(b) Obtaining benefits or property to which he or she would otherwise not be entitled;

(c) Making financial or credit transactions using the other person's identity;

(d) Avoiding detection; or

(e) Commercial or political benefit.

(2) Theft of identity is a Class D felony.

(3) This section shall not apply when a person obtains the identity of another to misrepresent his or her age for the purpose of obtaining alcoholic beverages, tobacco, or another privilege denied to minors.

(4) This section does not apply to credit or debit card fraud under KRS 434.550 to 434.730.

(5) Where the offense consists of theft by obtaining or trafficking in the personal identity of another person, the venue of the prosecution may be in either the county where the offense was committed or the county where the other person resides.

(6) A person found guilty of violating any provisions of this section shall forfeit any lawful claim to the identifying information, property,

or other realized benefit of the other person as a result of such violation.

## LOUISIANA [LA. REV. STAT. AN. § 14.67.16]

### Identity theft

A. As used in this Section the following terms have the following meanings:

(1) "Personal identifying information" shall include but not be limited to an individual's:

(a) Social security number.

(b) Driver's license number.

(c) Checking account number.

(d) Savings account number.

(e) Credit card number.

(f) Debit card number.

(g) Electronic identification number.

(h) Digital signatures.

(i) Birth certificate.

(j) Date of birth.

(k) Mother's maiden name.

(l) Armed forces identification number.

B. Identity theft is the intentional use or attempted use with fraudulent intent by any person of any personal identifying information of another person to obtain, whether contemporaneously or not, credit, money, goods, services, or anything else of value without the authorization or consent of the other person.

C.(1) Whoever commits the crime of identity theft when credit, money, goods, services, or anything else of value is obtained which amounts to a value of one thousand dollars or more, shall be imprisoned, with or without hard labor, for not more than ten years, or may be fined not more than ten thousand dollars, or both.

C.(2) Whoever commits the crime of identity theft when credit, money, goods, services, or anything else of value is obtained which amounts to a value of five hundred dollars or more, but less than one thousand dollars, shall be imprisoned, with or without hard labor, for not more than five years, or may be fined not more than five thousand dollars, or both.

C.(3) Whoever commits the crime of identity theft when credit, money, goods, services, or anything else of value is obtained which amounts to a value of three hundred dollars or more, but less than five hundred dollars, shall be imprisoned, with or without hard labor, for not more than three years, or may be fined not more than three thousand dollars, or both.

C.(4) Whoever commits the crime of identity theft when credit, money, goods, services, or anything else of value is obtained which amounts to a value less than three hundred dollars, shall be imprisoned for not more than six months, or may be fined not more than five hundred dollars, or both. If the offender in such cases has been convicted under this Section two or more times previously, upon any subsequent conviction he shall be imprisoned, for not more than three years, with or without hard labor, or may be fined not more than three thousand dollars, or both.

D. When there has been a theft by a number of distinct acts of the offender, the aggregate of the amount of the theft shall determine the grade of the offense.

E. In addition to the foregoing penalties, a person convicted under this Section may be ordered to make full restitution to the victim and any other person who has suffered a financial loss as a result of the offense. If a person ordered to make restitution pursuant to this Section is found to be indigent and therefore unable to make restitution in full at the time of conviction, the court shall order a periodic payment plan consistent with the person's financial ability.

F. The provisions of this Section shall not apply to any person who obtains another's driver's license or other form of identification for the sole purpose of misrepresenting his age.

## MAINE [ME. REV. STAT. AN. TIT. 17-A § 354-1; 2A]

### Theft by deception.

1. A person is guilty of theft if he obtains or exercises control over property of another as a result of deception and with an intention to deprive him thereof.

2. For purposes of this section, deception occurs when a person intentionally:

A. Creates or reinforces an impression that is false and that the person does not believe to be true, including false impressions as to identity, law, value, knowledge, opinion, intention or other state of mind; except that an intention not to perform a promise, or knowledge that a promise will not be performed, may not be inferred from the fact alone that the promise was not performed.

## MARYLAND [MD. CODE AN. ART. 27 § 231]

(a) In this section, "personal identifying information" means the name, address, telephone number, driver's license number, Social Security number, place of employment, employee identification number, mother's maiden name, bank or other financial institution account number, date of birth, personal identification number, or credit card number of another person.

(b) A person may not knowingly, willfully, and with fraudulent intent obtain or aid another person in obtaining personal identifying information of an individual, without the consent of that individual, for the purpose of using that information or selling or transferring that information to obtain any benefit, credit, goods, services, or other item of value in the name of that individual.

(c) A person may not knowingly and willfully assume the identity of another:

(1) With fraudulent intent to obtain any benefit, credit, goods, services, or other item of value;

(2) With fraudulent intent to avoid the payment of a debt or other legal obligation; or

(3) To avoid prosecution for a crime.

(d) A person who violates this section is guilty of a misdemeanor and on conviction is subject to a fine not exceeding $5,000 or imprisonment in the penitentiary not exceeding 1 year or both.

(e) In addition to the restitution provided under Title 11, Subtitle 6 of the Criminal Procedure Article, a court may order a person who pleads guilty or nolo contendere or is found guilty under this section to make restitution to the victim for reasonable costs incurred, including reasonable attorney's fees:

(1) For clearing the victim's credit history or credit rating; and

(2) In connection with any civil or administrative proceeding to satisfy a debt, lien, judgment, or other obligation of the victim that arose as a result of the violation of this section.

(f) A sentence under this section may be imposed separate from and consecutive to or concurrent with a sentence for any offense based on the act or acts establishing the violation of this section.

## MASSACHUSETTS [MASS. GEN. LAWS CH. 268 § 37E]

(a) For purposes of this section, the following words shall have the following meanings:

"Harass"—willfully and maliciously engage in an act directed at a specific person or persons, which act seriously alarms or annoys such person or persons and would cause a reasonable person to suffer substantial emotional distress.

"Personal identifying information"—any name or number that may be used, alone or in conjunction with any other information, to assume the identity of an individual, including any name, address, telephone number, driver's license number, social security number, place of employment, employee identification number, mother's maiden name, demand deposit account number, savings account number, credit card number or computer password identification.

"Pose"—to falsely represent oneself, directly or indirectly, as another person or persons.

"Victim"—any person who has suffered financial loss or any entity that provided money, credit, goods, services or anything of value and has suffered financial loss as a direct result of the commission or attempted commission of a violation of this section.

(b) Whoever, with intent to defraud, poses as another person without the express authorization of that person and uses such person's personal identifying information to obtain or to attempt to obtain money, credit, goods, services, anything of value, any identification card or other evidence of such person's identity, or to harass another shall be guilty of identity fraud and shall be punished by a fine of not more than $5,000 or imprisonment in a house of correction for not more than two and one-half years, or by both such fine and imprisonment.

(c) Whoever, with intent to defraud, obtains personal identifying information about another person without the express authorization of such person, with the intent to pose as such person or who obtains personal identifying information about a person without the express authorization of such person in order to assist another to pose as such person in order to obtain money, credit, goods, services, anything of value, any identification card or other evidence of such person's identity, or to harass another shall be guilty of the crime of identity fraud and shall be punished by a fine of not more than $5,000 or imprisonment in a house of correction for not more than two and one-half years, or by both such fine and imprisonment.

(d) A person found guilty of violating any provisions of this section shall, in addition to any other punishment, be ordered to make restitution for financial loss sustained by a victim as a result of such violation. Financial loss may include any costs incurred by such victim in correcting the credit history of such victim or any costs incurred in connection with any civil or administrative proceeding to satisfy any debt or other obligation of such victim, including lost wages and attorney's fees.

### MICHIGAN [MICH. COMP. LAWS § 750.285]

**Obtaining personal identity information of another with intent to unlawfully use information; violation as felony; nonapplicability to discovery process; definitions.**

(1) A person shall not obtain or attempt to obtain personal identity information of another person with the intent to unlawfully use that information for any of the following purposes without that person's authorization:

(a) To obtain financial credit.

(b) To purchase or otherwise obtain or lease any real or personal property.

(c) To obtain employment.

(d) To obtain access to medical records or information contained in medical records.

(e) To commit any illegal act.

(2) A person who violates this section is guilty of a felony punishable by imprisonment for not more than 5 years or a fine of not more than $10,000.00, or both.

(3) This section does not prohibit the person from being charged with, convicted of, or sentenced for any other violation of law committed by that person using information obtained in violation of this section.

(4) This section does not apply to a person who obtains or attempts to obtain personal identity information of another person pursuant to the discovery process of a civil action, an administrative proceeding, or an arbitration proceeding.

(5) As used in this section:

(a) "Financial transaction device" means that term as defined in section 157m.

(b) "Medical records" includes, but is not limited to, medical and mental health histories, reports, summaries, diagnoses and prognoses, treatment and medication information, notes, entries, and x-rays and other imaging records.

(c) "Personal identity information" means any of the following information of another person:

(i) A social security number.

(ii) A driver license number or state personal identification card number.

(iii) Employment information.

(iv) Information regarding any financial account held by another person including, but not limited to, any of the following:

(A) A savings or checking account number.

(B) A financial transaction device account number.

(C) A stock or other security certificate or account number.

(D) A personal information number for an account described in sub-subparagraphs (A) to (C).

## MINNESOTA [MINN. STAT. AN. §609.527]

### Identity theft.

#### Subdivision 1. Definitions.

(a) As used in this section, the following terms have the meanings given them in this subdivision.

(b) "Direct victim" means any person or entity described in section 611A.01, paragraph (b), whose identity has been transferred, used, or possessed in violation of this section.

(c) "Identity" means any name, number, or data transmission that may be used, alone or in conjunction with any other information, to identify a specific individual, including any of the following:

(1) a name, social security number, date of birth, official government-issued driver's license or identification number, go identification number;

(2) unique electronic identification number, address, account number, or routing code; or

(3) telecommunication identification information or access device.

(d) "Indirect victim" means any person or entity described in section 611A.01, paragraph (b), other than a direct victim.

(e) "Loss" means value obtained, as defined in section 609.52, subdivision 1, clause (3), and expenses incurred by a direct or indirect victim as a result of a violation of this section.

(f) "Unlawful activity" means:

(1) any felony violation of the laws of this state or any felony violation of a similar law of another state or the United States; and

(2) any nonfelony violation of the laws of this state involving theft, theft by swindle, forgery, fraud, or giving false information to a public official, or any nonfelony violation of a similar law of another state or the United States.

### Subdivision. 2. Crime.

A person who transfers, possesses, or uses an identity that is not the person's own, with the intent to commit, aid, or abet any unlawful activity is guilty of identity theft and may be punished as provided in subdivision

### Subdivision. 3. Penalties.

A person who violates subdivision 2 may be sentenced as follows:

(1) if the offense involves a single direct victim and the total, combined loss to the direct victim and any indirect victims is $250 or less, the person may be sentenced as provided in section 609.52, subdivision 3, clause (5);

(2) if the offense involves a single direct victim and the total, combined loss to the direct victim and any indirect victims is more than $250 but not more than $500, the person may be sentenced as provided in section 609.52, subdivision 3, clause (4);

(3) if the offense involves two or three direct victims or the total, combined loss to the direct and indirect victims is more than $500 but not more than $2,500, the person may be sentenced as provided in section 609.52, subdivision 3, clause (3); and

(4) if the offense involves four or more direct victims, or if the total, combined loss to the direct and indirect victims is more than $2,500, the person may be sentenced as provided in section 609.52, subdivision 3, clause (2).

**Subdivision. 4. Restitution.**

A direct or indirect victim of an identity theft crime shall be considered a victim for all purposes, including any rights that accrue under chapter 611A and rights to court-ordered restitution.

## MISSISSIPPI [MISS. CODE AN. § 97-19-85]

**Fraudulent use of identity, social security number or other identifying information to obtain thing of value.**

(1) Any person who shall make or cause to be made any false statement or representation as to his or another person's identity, social security account number or other identifying information for the purpose of fraudulently obtaining or with the intent to obtain goods, services or any thing of value, shall be guilty of a misdemeanor and upon conviction thereof shall be fined not more than Five Thousand Dollars ($5,000.00) or imprisoned for a term not to exceed one (1) year, or both.

(2) A person is guilty of fraud under subsection (1) who:

(a) Shall furnish false information wilfully, knowingly and with intent to deceive anyone as to his true identity or the true identity of another person;

(b) Wilfully, knowingly, and with intent to deceive, uses a social security account number to establish and maintain business or other records; or

(c) With intent to deceive, falsely represents a number to be the social security account number assigned to him or another person, when in fact the number is not the social security account number assigned to him or such other person; or

(d) Knowingly alters a social security card, buys or sells a social security card or counterfeit or altered social security card, counterfeits a social security card, or possesses a social security card or counterfeit social security card with intent to sell or alter it.

## MISSOURI [MO. REV. STAT. § 570; 223]

**Identity theft—penalty—restitution.**

1. A person commits the crime of identity theft if he knowingly and with the intent to deceive or defraud obtains, possesses, transfers, uses, or attempts to obtain, transfer or use, one or more means of identification not lawfully issued for his use.

2. Identity theft is punishable by up to six months in jail for the first offense; up to one year in jail for the second offense; and one to five years imprisonment for the third or subsequent offense.

3. In addition to the provisions of subsection 2 of this section, the court may order that the defendant make restitution to any victim of the offense. Restitution may include payment for any costs, including attorney fees, incurred by the victim:

(1) In clearing the credit history or credit rating of the victim; and

(2) In connection with any civil or administrative proceeding to satisfy any debt, lien, or other obligation of the victim arising from the actions of the defendant.

## MONTANA [H.B. 331, 2001 LEG.]

### Section 1. Theft of identity.

(1) A person commits the offense of theft of identity if the person purposely or knowingly obtains personal identifying information of another person and uses that information for any unlawful purpose, including to obtain or attempt to obtain credit, goods, services, financial information, or medical information in the name of the other person without the consent of the other person.

(2)(a) A person convicted of the offense of theft of identity if no economic benefit was gained or was attempted to be gained or if an economic benefit of less than $1,000 was gained or attempted to be gained shall be fined an amount not to exceed $1,000, imprisoned in the county jail for a term not to exceed 6 months, or both.

(2)(b) A person convicted of the offense of theft of identity if an economic benefit of $1,000 or more was gained or attempted to be gained shall be fined an amount not to exceed $10,000, imprisoned in a state prison for a term not to exceed 10 years, or both.

(3) As used in this section, "personal identifying information" includes but is not limited to the name, date of birth, address, telephone number, driver's license number, social security number or other federal government identification number, place of employment, employee identification number, mother's maiden name, financial institution account number, credit card number, or similar identifying information relating to a person.

(4) If restitution is ordered, the court may include, as part of its determination of an amount owed, payment for any costs incurred by the victim, including attorney fees and any costs incurred in clearing the credit history or credit rating of the victim or in connection with any

civil or administrative proceeding to satisfy any debt, lien, or other obligation of the victim arising as a result of the actions of the defendant.

## NEVADA [NEV. REV. STAT. §205.463-465]

**Obtaining and using personal identifying information of another person to harm person or for unlawful purpose.**

1. Except as otherwise provided in subsection 2, a person who knowingly:

(a) Obtains any personal identifying information of another person; and

(b) Uses the personal identifying information to harm that other person or for any unlawful purpose, including, without limitation, to obtain credit, a good, a service or anything of value in the name of that person, is guilty of a category B felony and shall be punished by imprisonment in the state prison for a minimum term of not less than 1 year and a maximum term of not more than 20 years, and may be further punished by a fine of not more than $100,000.

2. A person who knowingly:

(a) Obtains any personal identifying information of another person; and

(b) Uses the personal identifying information to avoid or delay being prosecuted for an unlawful act, is guilty of a category E felony and shall be punished as provided in NRS 193.130.

3. In addition to any other penalty, the court shall order a person convicted of violating subsection 1 to pay restitution, including, without limitation, any attorney's fees and costs incurred to:

(a) Repair the credit history or rating of the person whose personal identifying information he obtained and used in violation of subsection 1; and

(b) Satisfy a debt, lien or other obligation incurred by the person whose personal identifying information he obtained and used in violation of subsection 1.

4. As used in this section, "personal identifying information" has the meaning ascribed to it in NRS 205.465.

## NEW HAMPSHIRE [N.H. REV. STAT. AN. § 638.26]

**Identity Fraud.**

I. A person is guilty of identity fraud when the person:

(a) Poses as another person with the purpose to defraud in order to obtain money, credit, goods, services, or anything else of value;

(b) Obtains or records personal identifying information about another person without the express authorization of such person, with the intent to pose as such person;

(c) Obtains or records personal identifying information about a person without the express authorization of such person in order to assist another to pose as such person; or

(d) Poses as another person, without the express authorization of such person, with the purpose of obtaining confidential information about such person that is not available to the general public.

II. (a) Identity fraud is:

(1) A class A felony if the value of the property or services obtained exceeds $1,000.

(2) A class B felony in all other cases.

II. (b) The value may be determined according to the provisions of RSA 637:2, V.

III. A person found guilty of violating any provisions of this section shall, in addition to the penalty under paragraph II, be ordered to make restitution for economic loss sustained by a victim as a result of such violation.

### NEW JERSEY [N.J. STAT. AN. § 2C:21-17]

**Impersonation; theft of identity; disorderly persons offense, crime.**

a. A person is guilty of an offense when he:

(1) Impersonates another or assumes a false identity and does an act in such assumed character or false identity for purpose of obtaining a pecuniary benefit for himself or another or to injure or defraud another;

(2) Pretends to be a representative of some person or organization and does an act in such pretended capacity for the purpose of obtaining a benefit for himself or another or to injure or defraud another;

(3) Impersonates another, assumes a false identity or makes a false or misleading statement regarding the identity of any person, in an oral or written application for services, for the purpose of obtaining services; or

(4) Obtains any personal identifying information pertaining to another person and uses that information, or assists another person in using the information, in order to assume the identity of or represent themselves as another person, without that person's authorization

and with the purpose to fraudulently obtain or attempt to obtain a pecuniary benefit or services, or avoid the payment of debt or other legal obligation or avoid prosecution for a crime by using the name of the other person.

As used in this paragraph: "personal identifying information" means, but is not limited to, the name, address, telephone number, social security number, place of employment, employee identification number, demand deposit account number, savings account number, credit card number or mother's maiden name of an individual person.

b. A person is guilty of an offense if, in the course of making an oral or written application for services, he impersonates another, assumes a false identity or makes a false or misleading statement with the purpose of avoiding payment for prior services. Purpose to avoid payment for prior services may be presumed upon proof that the person has not made full payment for prior services and has impersonated another, assumed a false identity or made a false or misleading statement regarding the identity of any person in the course of making oral or written application for services.

c. (1) A person who violates subsection a. or b. of this section is guilty of a crime of the second degree if the pecuniary benefit, the value of the services received, the payment sought to be avoided or the injury or fraud perpetrated on another is $75,000 or more. If the pecuniary benefit, the value of the services received, the payment sought to be avoided or the injury or fraud perpetrated on another is at least $500 but is less than $75,000, the offender is guilty of a crime of the third degree. If the pecuniary benefit, the value of the services received, the payment sought to be avoided or the injury or fraud perpetrated on another is at least $200 but is less than $500, the offender is guilty of a crime of the fourth degree.

c. (2) If the pecuniary benefit, the value of the services received, the payment sought to be avoided or the injury or fraud perpetrated on another is less than $200,or if the benefit or services received or the injury or fraud perpetrated on another has no pecuniary value, or if the person was unsuccessful in an attempt to receive a benefit or services or to injure or perpetrate a fraud on another, then the person is guilty of a disorderly persons offense.

d. A violation of R.S.39:3-37 for using the personal information of another to obtain a driver's license or register a motor vehicle or a violation of R.S.33:1-81 or section 6 of P.L.1968. c.313 (C.33:1-81.7) for using the personal information of another to illegally purchase an alcoholic beverage shall not constitute an offense under this section if the actor received only that benefit or service and did not perpetrate or attempt to perpetrate any additional injury or fraud on another.

## NEW MEXICO [H.B. 317, 2001 LEG. 45TH SESS.]

### Theft of Identity.

A. Theft of identity consists of willfully obtaining, recording or transferring personal identifying information of another person without the authorization or consent of that person and with the intent to defraud that person or another.

B. As used in this section, "personal identifying information" means information that alone or in conjunction with other information identifies a person, including the person's name, address, telephone number, driver's license number, social security number, place of employment, maiden name of the person's mother, demand deposit account number, checking or savings account number, credit card or debit card number, personal identification number, passwords or any other numbers or information that can be used to access a person's financial resources.

C. Whoever commits theft of identity is guilty of a misdemeanor.

D. Prosecution pursuant to this section shall not prevent prosecution pursuant to any other provision of the law when the conduct also constitutes a violation of that other provision.

E. In a prosecution brought pursuant to this section, the theft of identity shall be considered to have been committed in the county where the person whose identifying information was appropriated resided at the time of the offense, or in which any part of the offense took place, regardless of whether the defendant was ever actually present in the county.

F. A person found guilty of theft of identity shall, in addition to any other punishment, be ordered to make restitution for any financial loss sustained by a person injured as the direct result of the theft of identity. In addition to out-of-pocket costs, restitution may include payment for costs, including attorney fees, incurred by that person in clearing his credit history or credit rating or costs incurred in connection with a civil or administrative proceeding to satisfy a debt, lien, judgment or other obligation of that person arising as a result of the theft of identity.

G. The sentencing court shall issue written findings of fact and may issue orders as are necessary to correct a public record that contains false information as a result of the theft of identity.

## NORTH CAROLINA [N.C. GEN. STAT. § 14-113.20]

### Financial identity fraud.

(a) A person who knowingly obtains, possesses, or uses personal identifying information of another person without the consent of that other person, with the intent to fraudulently represent that the person is the other person for the purposes of making financial or credit transactions in the other person's name or for the purpose of avoiding legal consequences is guilty of a felony punishable as provided in G.S. 14-113.22(a).

(b) The term "identifying information" as used in this section includes the following:

(1) Social security numbers.

(2) Drivers license numbers.

(3) Checking account numbers.

(4) Savings account numbers.

(5) Credit card numbers.

(6) Debit card numbers.

(7) Personal Identification (PIN) Code as defined in G.S. 14-113.8(6).

(8) Electronic identification numbers.

(9) Digital signatures.

(10) Any other numbers or information that can be used to access a person's financial resources.

(c) It shall not be a violation under this section for a person to do any of the following:

(1) Lawfully obtain credit information in the course of a bona fide consumer or commercial transaction.

(2) Lawfully exercise, in good faith, a security interest or a right of offset by a creditor or financial institution.

(3) Lawfully comply, in good faith, with any warrant, court order, levy, garnishment, attachment, or other judicial or administrative order, decree, or directive, when any party is required to do so.

## NORTH DAKOTA [N.D. CENT. CODES § 12.1-23-11]

### Unauthorized use of personal identifying information—Penalty.

1. As used in this section, "personal identifying information" means any of the following information:

a. An individual's name;

b. An individual's address;

c. An individual's telephone number;

d. The distinguishing operator's license number assigned to an individual by the department of transportation under section 39-04-14;

e. An individual's social security number;

f. An individual's employer or place of employment;

g. An identification number assigned to the individual by the individual's employer;

h. The maiden name of the individual's mother; or

i. The identifying number of a depository account in a financial institution.

2. A person is guilty of a class C felony if the person uses or attempts to use any personal identifying information of an individual to obtain credit, money, goods, services, or anything else of value without the authorization or consent of the individual and by representing that person is the individual or is acting with the authorization or consent of the individual.

## OHIO [OHIO REV. CODE AN. § 2913.49]

(A) As used in this section, "Personal Identifying Information" includes, but is not limited to, the following: the name, address, telephone number, driver's license, driver's license number, commercial driver's license, commercial driver's license number, state identification card, state identification card number, social security card, social security card number, place of employment, employee identification number, mother's maiden name, demand deposit account number, savings account number, money market account number, mutual fund account number, other financial account number, personal identification number, password or credit card number of a living or dead individual.

(B) No person shall obtain, possess, or use any personal identifying information of any living or dead individual with the intent to fraudulently obtain credit, property, or services or avoid the payment of a debt or any other legal obligation.

(C) No person shall create, obtain, possess, or use the personal identifying information of any living or dead individual with the intent to aid or abet another person in violating Division (B) of this section.

## OKLAHOMA [OKLA. STAT. TIT. 21 § 1533.1]

It is unlawful for any person to willfully and with fraudulent intent obtain the name, address, social security number, date of birth, or any other personal identifying information of another person, living or dead, with intent to use, sell, or allow any other person to use or sell such personal identifying information to obtain or attempt to obtain credit, goods, property, or service in the name of the other person without the consent of that person. It is unlawful for any person to use with fraudulent intent the personal identity of another person, living or dead, or any information relating to the personal identity of another person, living or dead, to obtain or attempt to obtain credit or anything of value. Any person convicted of violating any provision of this section shall be guilty of identity theft. Identity theft is a felony offense.

## OREGON [OR. REV. STAT. § 165.800]

### Identity theft.

(1) A person commits the crime of identity theft if the person, with the intent to deceive or to defraud, obtains, possesses, transfers, creates, utters or converts to the person's own use the personal identification of another person.

(2) Identity theft is a Class C felony.

(3) It is an affirmative defense to violating subsection (1) of this section that the person charged with the offense:

(a) Was under 21 years of age at the time of committing the offense and the person used the personal identification of another person solely for the purpose of purchasing alcohol;

(b) Was under 18 years of age at the time of committing the offense and the person used the personal identification of another person solely for the purpose of purchasing tobacco products; or

(c) Used the personal identification of another person solely for the purpose of misrepresenting the person's age to gain access to a:

(A) Place the access to which is restricted based on age; or

(B) Benefit based on age.

(4) As used in this section:

(a) "Another person" means a real or imaginary person.

(b) "Personal identification" includes, but is not limited to, any written document or electronic data that does, or purports to, provide information concerning:

(A) A person's name, address or telephone number;

(B) A person's driving privileges;

(C) A person's Social Security number or tax identification number;

(D) A person's citizenship status or alien identification number;

(E) A person's employment status, employer or place of employment;

(F) The identification number assigned to a person by a person's employer;

(G) The maiden name of a person or a person's mother;

(H) The identifying number of a person's depository account at a financial institution, as defined in ORS 706.008, or a credit card account;

(I) A person's signature or a copy of a person's signature;

(J) A person's electronic mail name, electronic mail signature, electronic mail address or electronic mail account;

(K) A person's photograph;

(L) A person's date of birth; and

(M) A person's personal identification number.

## PENNSYLVANIA [18 PA. CONS. STAT § 4120]

### Identity theft.

(a) Offense Defined.—A person commits the offense of identity theft of another person if he possesses or uses identifying information of another person without the consent of that other person to further any unlawful purpose.

(b) Separate Offenses.—Each time a person possesses or uses identifying information in violation of subsection (a) constitutes a separate offense under this section.

(c) Grading.—The offenses shall be graded as follows:

1. A first offense under this section is a misdemeanor of the first degree, and a second and or subsequent offense under this section is a felony of the third degree.

2. When a person commits an offense under subsection (a) and the victim of the offense is 60 years of age or older, the grading of the offense shall be one grade higher than specified in paragraph (1).

(d) Concurrent Jurisdiction to Prosecute.—In addition to the authority conferred upon the attorney general by the act of October 15, 1980 (P.L.950, No.164), known as the Commonwealth Attorneys Act, the Attorney General shall have the authority to investigate and to institute criminal proceedings for any violation of this section or any series of such violations involving more than one county of this commonwealth or another state. No person charged with a violation of this section by the attorney general shall have standing to challenge the authority of the attorney general to investigate or prosecute the case, and, if any such challenge is made, the challenge shall be dismissed and no relief shall be made available in the courts of this Commonwealth to the person making the challenge.

(e) Use of Police Reports.—A report to a law enforcement agency by a person stating that the person's identifying information has been lost or stolen or that the person's identifying information has been used without the person's consent shall be prima facie evidence that the identifying information was possessed or used without the person's consent.

(f) Definitions.—As used in this section, the following words and phrases shall have the meaning given to them in this subsection:

"Document"—Any writing, including, but not limited to, birth certificate, social security card, driver's license, nondriver government-issued identification card, baptismal certificate, access device card, employee identification card, school identification card or other identifying information recorded by any other method, including, but not limited to, information stored on any computer, computer disc, computer printout, computer system, or part thereof, or by any other mechanical or electronic means.

"Identifying information"—Any document, photographic, pictorial or computer image of another person, or any fact used to establish identity, including, but not limited to, a name, birth date, social security number, driver'S license number, nondriver governmental identification number, telephone number, checking account number, savings account number, student identification number or employee or payroll number.

**RHODE ISLAND [R.I. GEN. LAWS. § 11-49.1-1; 11-49.1-2; 11-49.1-3; 11-49.1-4]**

### Section 11-49.1-1. Short title.

This chapter shall be known and may be cited as the "Impersonation and Identity Fraud Act."

### Section 11-49.1-2. Definitions.

As used in this chapter:

(1) "Document-making implement" means any implement, impression, electronic device, or computer hardware or software that is specifically configured or primarily used for making an identification document, a false identification document, or another document-making implement;

(2) "Identification document" means a document made or card issued by or under the authority of the United States government, a state, political subdivision of a state, a foreign government, political subdivision of a foreign government, or an international governmental or an international quasi-governmental organization which, when completed with information concerning a particular individual, is of a type intended or commonly accepted for the purpose of identification of individuals;

(3) "Means of identification" means any name or number that may be used, alone or in conjunction with any other information, to identify a specific individual, including any:

(i) Name, social security number, date of birth, official state or government issued driver's license or identification number, alien registration number, government passport number, employer, or taxpayer identification number;

(ii) Unique biometric data, such as fingerprint, voice print, retina or iris image, or other unique physical representation;

(iii) Unique electronic identification number, address, or routing code; or

(iv) Telecommunication identifying information or access device as defined in 18 U.S.C. § 1029(e).

(4) "Produce" means to manufacture, alter, authenticate, or assemble an identification document; and

(5) "State" includes any state of the United States, the District of Columbia, the Commonwealth of Puerto Rico, and any other commonwealth, possession, or territory of the United States.

### Section 11-49.1-3 Identity fraud.

(a) Any person who:

(1) knowingly and without lawful authority produces an identification document or a false identification document;

(2) knowingly transfers an identification document or a false identification document knowing that the document was stolen or produced without lawful authority;

(3) knowingly possesses with intent to use unlawfully or transfer unlawfully five (5) or more identification documents (other than those issued lawfully for the use of the possessor) or false identification documents;

(4) knowingly possesses an identification document (other than one issued lawfully for the use of the possessor) or a false identification document, with the intent the document be used to defraud the United States, the state of Rhode Island, any political subdivision of them, or any public or private entity;

(5) knowingly transfers or possesses a document-making implement with the intent the document-making implement will be used in the production of a false identification document or another document-making implement which will be so used;

(6) knowingly possesses a false identification document that is or appears to be a genuine identification document of the United States, the state of Rhode Island, any political subdivision of them, or any public or private entity, which is stolen or produced without lawful authority knowing that the document was stolen or produced without lawful authority; or

(7) knowingly transfers or uses with intent to defraud, without lawful authority, a means of identification of another person with the intent to commit, or to aid or abet, any unlawful activity that constitutes a violation of federal, state or local law; is guilty of a felony and is subject to the penalties set forth in § 11-49.1-4.

(b) The provisions of this section do not apply to any person who has not reached his or her twenty-first (21st) birthday who misrepresents or misstates his or her age through the presentation of any document in order to enter any premises licensed for the retail sale of alcoholic beverages for the purpose of purchasing or having served or delivered to him or her alcoholic beverages, or attempting to purchase or have another person purchase for him or her any alcoholic beverage, pursuant to § 3-8-6.

### Section 11-49.1-4. Penalties.

(a) Every person who violates the provisions of § 11-49.1-3 shall be imprisoned for not more than three (3) years and may be fined not more than five thousand dollars ($5,000) or both for a first conviction.

(b) Every person who violates the provisions of § 11-49.1-3 may be imprisoned for not less than three (3) years nor more than five (5) years and shall be fined not more than ten thousand dollars ($10,000) or both for a second conviction.

(c) Every person who violates the provisions of § 11-49.1-3 shall be imprisoned for not less than five (5) years nor more than ten (10) years and shall be fined not less than fifteen thousand dollars ($15,000) or both for a third or subsequent conviction.

## SOUTH CAROLINA [S.D. CODIFIED LAWS § 16-13-510]

### Personal Financial Security Act

(A) It is unlawful for a person to commit the offense of financial identity fraud.

(B) A person is guilty of financial identity fraud when he, without the authorization or permission of another person and with the intent of unlawfully appropriating the financial resources of that person to his own use or the use of a third party:

(1) obtains or records identifying information which would assist in accessing the financial records of the other person; or

(2) accesses or attempts to access the financial resources of the other person through the use of identifying information as defined in subsection (C).

(C) Identifying information includes, but is not limited to:

(1) social security numbers;

(2) driver's license numbers;

(3) checking account numbers;

(4) savings account numbers;

(5) credit card numbers;

(6) debit card numbers;

(7) personal identification numbers;

(8) electronic identification numbers;

(9) digital signatures; or

(10) other numbers or information which may be used to access a person's financial resources.

(D) A person who violates the provisions of this section is guilty of a felony and, upon conviction, must be fined in the discretion of the court or imprisoned not more than ten years, or both. The court may order restitution to the victim pursuant to the provisions of Section 17-25-322.

## SOUTH DAKOTA [S.D. CODIFIED LAWS § 22-30A-3.1]

### Identity theft defined—Violation as misdemeanor.

A person commits the offense of identity theft if the person without the authorization or permission of another person and with the intent to deceive or defraud:

(1) Obtains, possesses, transfers, uses, attempts to obtain, or records identifying information not lawfully issued for that person's use; or

(2) Accesses or attempts to access the financial resources of that person through the use of identifying information.

A violation of this section is a Class 1 misdemeanor.

## TENNESSEE [TENN. CODE AN. § 39-14-150]

### Identity theft.

(a) A person commits identity theft who knowingly transfers or uses, without lawful authority, a means of identification of another person with the intent to commit, or otherwise promote, carry on, or facilitate any unlawful activity.

(b) As used in this section, "means of identification" means any name or number that may be used, alone or in conjunction with any other information, to identify a specific individual, including:

(1) Name, social security number, date of birth, official state or government issued driver license or identification number, alien registration number, passport number, employer or taxpayer identification number;

(2) Unique biometric data, such as fingerprint, voice print, retina or iris image, or other unique physical representation;

(3) Unique electronic identification number, address, routing code or other personal identifying data which enables an individual to obtain merchandise or service or to otherwise financially encumber the legitimate possessor of the identifying data; or

(4) Telecommunication identifying information or access device.

(c) A violation of this section is a Class D felony.

## TEXAS [TEX. PENAL CODE § 32.51]

### Fraudulent Use or Possession of Identifying Information

In this section:

(1) "Identifying information" means information that alone or in conjunction with other information identifies an individual, including an individual's:

(A) name, social security number, date of birth, and government-issued identification number;

(B) unique biometric data, including the individual's fingerprint, voice print, and retina or iris image;

(C) unique electronic identification number, address, and routing code; and

(D) telecommunication identifying information or access device.

(2) "Telecommunication access device" means a card, plate, code, account number, personal identification number, electronic serial number, mobile identification number, or other telecommunications service, equipment, or instrument identifier or means of account access that alone or in conjunction with another telecommunication access device may be used to:

(A) obtain money, goods, services, or other thing of value; or

(B) initiate a transfer of funds other than a transfer originated solely by paper instrument.

(b) A person commits an offense if the person obtains, possesses, transfers, or uses identifying information of another person without the other person's consent and with intent to harm or defraud another.

(c) An offense under this section is a state jail felony.

(d) If a court orders a defendant convicted of an offense under this section to make restitution to the victim of the offense, the court may order the defendant to reimburse the victim for lost income or other expenses, other than attorney's fees, incurred as a result of the offense.

(e) If conduct that constitutes an offense under this section also constitutes an offense under any other law, the actor may be prosecuted under this section or the other law.

## UTAH [UTAH CODE AN. §§ 76-6-1101; 76-6-1102]

### 76-6-1101. Identity fraud.

This part is known as the "Identity Fraud Act."

### 76-6-1102. Identity fraud crime.

(1) For purposes of this part, "personal identifying information" may include:

(a) name;

(b) address;

(c) telephone number;

(d) driver's license number;

(e) Social Security number;

(f) place of employment;

(g) employee identification numbers or other personal identification numbers;

(h) mother's maiden name;

(i) electronic identification numbers;

(j) digital signatures or a private key; or

(k) any other numbers or information that can be used to access a person's financial resources or medical information in the name of another person without the consent of that person except for numbers or information that can be prosecuted as financial transaction card offenses under Sections 76-6-506 through 76-6-506.4.

(2) A person is guilty of identity fraud when that person knowingly or intentionally:

(a) obtains personal identifying information of another person without the authorization of that person; and

(b) uses, or attempts to use, that information with fraudulent intent, including to obtain, or attempt to obtain, credit, goods, services, any other thing of value, or medical information in the name of another person without the consent of that person.

(3) Identity fraud is:

(a) a class B misdemeanor if the value of the credit, goods, services, or any other thing of value is less than $300;

(b) a class A misdemeanor if:

(i) a value cannot be determined and the personal identifying information has been used without the consent of that person to obtain medical information or to obtain employment; or

(ii) the value of the credit, goods, services, or any other thing of value is or exceeds $300 but is less than $1,000;

(c) a third degree felony if the value of the credit, goods, services, or any other thing of value is or exceeds $1,000 but is less than $5,000; or

(d) a second degree felony if the value of the credit, goods, services, or any other thing of value is or exceeds $5,000.

(4) Multiple violations within a 90-day period may be aggregated into a single offense, and the degree of the offense is determined by the total value of all credit, goods, services, or any other thing of value used, or attempted to be used, through the multiple violations.

## VIRGINIA [VA. CODE AN. § 18-2-186.3]

### Identity fraud; penalty; victim assistance.

A. It shall be unlawful for any person, without the authorization or permission of the person who is the subject of the identifying information, with the intent to defraud, for his own use or the use of a third person, to:

1. Obtain, record or access identifying information which is not available to the general public that would assist in accessing financial resources, obtaining identification documents, or obtaining benefits of such other person; or

2. Obtain goods or services through the use of identifying information of such other person; or

3. Obtain identification documents in such other person's name.

B. It shall be unlawful for any person to use identification documents or identifying information of another to avoid summons, arrest, prosecution, or to impede a criminal investigation.

C. As used in this section, "identifying information" shall include but not be limited to: (i) name; (ii) date of birth; (iii) social security number; (iv) driver's license number; (v) bank account numbers; (vi) credit or debit card numbers; (vii) personal identification numbers (PIN); (viii) electronic identification codes; (ix) automated or electronic signatures; (x) biometric data; (xi) fingerprints; (xii) passwords; or (xiii) any other numbers or information that can be used to access a person's financial resources, obtain identification, act as identification, or obtain goods or services.

D. Violations of this section shall be punishable as a Class 1 misdemeanor. Any violation resulting in financial loss of greater than $200 shall be punishable as a Class 6 felony. Any second or subsequent conviction shall be punishable as a Class 6 felony. Any violation resulting in the arrest and detention of the person whose identification documents or identifying information were used to avoid summons, arrest, prosecution, or to impede a criminal investigation shall be punishable as a Class 6 felony. In any proceeding brought pursuant to this section, the crime shall be considered to have been committed in any locality where the person whose identifying information was appropriated resides, or in which any part of the offense took place, regardless of whether the defendant was ever actually in such locality.

E. Upon conviction, in addition to any other punishment, a person found guilty of this offense shall be ordered by the court to make restitution as the court deems appropriate to any person whose identifying information was appropriated. Such restitution may include the person's actual expenses associated with correcting inaccuracies or errors in his credit report or other identifying information.

F. Upon the request of a person whose identifying information was appropriated, the Attorney General may provide assistance to the victim in obtaining information necessary to correct inaccuracies or errors in his credit report or other identifying information; however, no legal representation shall be afforded such person.

## WASHINGTON [WASH. REV. CODE § 9.35.020]

### Identity theft.

(1) No person may knowingly obtain, possess, use, or transfer a means of identification or financial information of another person, living or dead, with the intent to commit, or to aid or abet, any crime.

(2)(a) Violation of this section when the accused or an accomplice uses the victim's means of identification or financial information and obtains an aggregate total of credit, money, goods, services, or anything else of value in excess of one thousand five hundred dollars in value shall constitute identity theft in the first degree. Identity theft in the first degree is a class B felony.

(2)(b) Violation of this section when the accused or an accomplice uses the victim's means of identification or financial information and obtains an aggregate total of credit, money, goods, services, or anything else of value that is less than one thousand five hundred dollars in value, or when no credit, money, goods, services, or anything of value is obtained shall constitute identity theft in the second degree. Identity theft in the second degree is a class C felony.

(3) A person who violates this section is liable for civil damages of five hundred dollars or actual damages, whichever is greater, including costs to repair the victim's credit record, and reasonable attorneys' fees as determined by the court.

(4) In a proceeding under this section, the crime will be considered to have been committed in any locality where the person whose means of identification or financial information was appropriated resides, or in which any part of the offense took place, regardless of whether the defendant was ever actually in that locality.

(5) The provisions of this section do not apply to any person who obtains another person's driver's license or other form of identification for the sole purpose of misrepresenting his or her age.

(6) In a proceeding under this section in which a person's means of identification or financial information was used without that person's authorization, and when there has been a conviction, the sentencing court may issue such orders as are necessary to correct a public record that contains false information resulting from a violation of this section.

## WEST VIRGINIA [W. VA. CODE § 61-3-54]

### Taking identity of another person; penalty.

Any person who knowingly takes the name, birth date, social security number or other identifying information of another person, without the consent of that other person, with the intent to fraudulently represent that he or she is the other person for the purpose of making financial or credit transactions in the other person's name, is guilty of a felony, and upon conviction, shall be punished by confinement in the penitentiary not more than five years, or fined not more than one thousand dollars, or both: *Provided*, That the provisions of this section do not apply to any person who obtains another person's drivers license or other form of identification for the sole purpose of misrepresenting his or her age.

## WISCONSIN [WIS. STAT. § 943.201]

### Misappropriation of personal identifying information or personal identification documents.

(1) In this section:

(a) "Personal identification document" means a birth certificate or a financial transaction card, as defined in s. 943.41 (1) (em).

(b) "Personal identifying information" means any of the following information:

1. An individual's name.

2. An individual's address.

3. An individual's telephone number.

4. The unique identifying driver number assigned to the individual by the department of transportation under s. 343.17 (3) (a) 4.

5. An individual's social security number.

6. An individual's employer or place of employment.

7. An identification number assigned to an individual by his or her employer.

8. The maiden name of an individual's mother.

9. The identifying number of a depository account, as defined in s. 815.18 (2) (e), of an individual.

(2) Whoever intentionally uses or attempts to use any personal identifying information or personal identification document of an individual to obtain credit, money, goods, services or anything else of value without the authorization or consent of the individual and by representing that he or she is the individual or is acting with the authorization or consent of the individual is guilty of a Class D felony.

# GLOSSARY

AD BLOCKER—Software placed on a user's personal computer that prevents advertisements from being displayed on the Web.

ACCELERATION CLAUSE—A clause in a loan agreement that makes the loan due and payable if any of the provisions are violated.

ACCEPTANCE—A draft or bill of exchange used in financing domestic and international trade in staple commodities. In a bank acceptance, a bank substitutes its own credit for its customer's credit and accepts drafts drawn under a letter of credit.

ACCOUNT—Any deposit or credit account with a bank, including a demand, time, savings, passbook, share draft, or like account, other than an account evidenced by a certificate of deposit.

ACCRUED INTEREST—Interest owing but not yet paid.

AFFIRMATIVE CUSTOMIZATION—Refers to a site's or an Internet service provider's use of personal data to tailor or modify the content or design of the site to specifications affirmatively selected by a particular individual.

AGGREGATE INFORMATION—Information that is related to a website visitor but is not about that individually personally, e.g., information kept about which pages on a website are most popular to a visitor but which cannot be traced to the individual personally.

ANNUAL PERCENTAGE RATE (APR)—The actual cost of borrowing money, expressed in the form of an annual rate to make it easy for one to compare the cost of borrowing money among several lenders.

ANONYMITY—A situation in which the user's true identity is not known.

ANONYMIZER—A service that prevents Web sites from seeing a user's Internet Protocol (IP) address. The service operates as an intermediary to protect the user's identity.

ANONYMOUS REMAILER—A special e-mail server that acts as a middleman and strips outgoing e-mail of all personally identifying information, then forwards it to its destination, usually with the IP address of the remailer attached.

ASSIGNEE—A person to whom an assignment is made.

ASSIGNMENT—A transfer or making over to another of the whole of any property, real or personal, or of any estate or right therein. It includes transfers of all kinds of property including negotiable instruments.

ASSIGNOR—A person who assigns or transfers property to another.

AUTHENTICATE—Process of verifying that the person attempting to send a message or access data is who he or she claims to be.

AUTHORIZE—To grant or deny a person access to data or systems.

BAD CHECK—A check which is dishonored on presentation for payment because of no, or insufficient, funds or closed bank account.

BALANCE—The amount credited to the depositor's account that he is entitled to withdraw as well as the plus or minus difference between total debits and credits standing to the account of a bank at the clearing house.

BANK—A sum of money placed with a bank or banker on deposit, by a customer and subject to be drawn out on the latter's check.

BANK DRAFT—A check drawn by a bank against funds deposited to its account in another bank.

BANKING DAY—The part of a day on which a bank is open to the public for carrying on substantially all of its banking functions.

BANK NOTE—A promissory note issued by a bank payable to bearer on demand without interest and acceptable as money.

BANKRUPT—The state or condition of one who is unable to pay his debts as they are, or become, due.

BANKRUPTCY—The legal process under federal law intended to insure fairness and equality among creditors of a bankrupt person, also known as a debtor, and to enable the debtor to start fresh by retaining certain property exempt from liabilities and unhampered by preexisting debts.

BANK STATEMENT—A periodic statement showing a depositor all deposits recorded, checks paid and canceled, charges made, and balance left in his account.

BANNER AD—Advertisement for a product or company that is placed on a Web page in order to sell site visitors a good or service. Clicking on a banner will take the visitor to a site to learn more about that product or service.

BBBOnline—Refers to the Better Business Bureau's Online privacy seal program. BBBOnline certifies sites that meet baseline privacy standards. The program requires its licensees to implement certain fair information practices and to submit to various types of compliance monitoring in order to display a privacy seal on their websites.

BEARER—A person holding a check, draft, bill, note or other instrument, especially if marked payable to bearer.

BLOCKING SOFTWARE—A computer program that allows parents, teachers, or guardians to "block" access to certain websites and other information available over the Internet.

BOND—An interest-bearing certificate of debt that promises under seal that the issuer, usually a government or a corporation, will pay the amount of the bond to its holder at a specified date.

BOOKMARK—An online function that lets the user access their favorite web sites quickly.

BROWSER—Special software that allows the user to navigate several areas of the internet and view a website.

CACHE—A place on the computer's hard drive where the browser stores information from pages or sites that the user has visited so that returning to those pages or sites is faster and easier.

CASH ITEMS—Items, usually checks or coupons, accepted for tentative credit to a depositor's account, subject to rejection if the items are not paid.

CASHIER'S CHECK—A check drawn by a bank upon its own funds and signed by an authorized officer.

CERTIFICATE OF DEPOSIT—A written acknowledgment by a bank of a deposit payable upon the return of the certificate on a specified date. The deposit is usually interest-bearing and may not be withdrawn in any way before maturity.

CERTIFICATION—A stamped and signed assurance by a bank on which a check is drawn that sufficient funds are on deposit to cover the check.

CHECK—A bill of exchange drawn on a checking account payable on demand.

CHECKING ACCOUNT—A bank account against which checks may be drawn.

CIPHERTEXT—Scrambled, unreadable contents of an encrypted message or file.

CLEARING—A system whereby banks offset claims and counterclaims for checks and other items held against each other so that only balances need be settled.

CLEARING CORPORATION—With respect to investment securities, generally refers to a person that is registered as a clearing agency under the federal securities laws; a federal reserve bank; or any other person that provides clearance or settlement services with respect to financial assets.

CLEARINGHOUSE—A place where representatives of commercial banks in the same locality get together to do their clearing and settle the resulting balances. It is all done automatically through computers.

COLLATERAL—A pledge of specific property as security for repayment of a loan at a certain time. It can be sold if the loan is defaulted.

COLLECTION ITEMS—Drafts, notes acceptances, and other items received by a bank that must be collected before proceeds can be credited to a depositor's account.

COMAKER—One who signs the note of another, either for value or accommodation. In either situation he is liable to the payee.

COMMERCIAL BANK—Commercial banks accept and hold demand deposits, which provide excess reserves to extend credit to borrowing customers, creating money in the process. Although they accept time and savings deposits, their essential and unique function is to deal with demand deposits.

COMMERCIAL PAPER—All sorts of short-term negotiable instruments stemming from business transactions.

COMPOUND INTEREST—Interest upon principal plus accrued interest.

CONSENT—Explicit permission, given to a website by a visitor, to handle personal information in specified ways. "Informed consent" implies that the company fully discloses its information practices prior to obtaining personal data or permission to use it.

CONSUMER CREDIT—Loans and sale credit extended to individuals to finance the purchase of goods and services arising out of consumer needs and desires.

COOKIE—When the user visits a site, a notation may be fed to a file known as a "cookie" in their computer for future reference. If the user revisits the site, the "cookie" file allows the web site to identify the user as a "return" guest and offers the user products tailored to their interests or tastes.

CORRESPONDENT BANK—A bank that carries a deposit balance with another bank or maintains reciprocal services with a bank in another city.

COUNTERSIGN—The addition of a signature to an instrument to attest its authenticity.

CREDIT—An advance of cash, merchandise, service, or something of value in the present in return for a promise to pay for it at some future date, usually with an agreed interest. If the credit period is less than a year, it is called short-term. Over that it may be called intermediate or long-term, depending on the length of the credit period. Long-term credit for over five years is often obtained in the sale of stocks, bonds or mortgages.

CREDIT REPORT—The document issued by a credit reporting agency setting forth a credit rating and pertinent financial data concerning a person or a company, which is used by banks, lenders, merchants, and suppliers in evaluating a credit risk.

CREDIT UNION—A cooperative association whose members pool their savings by purchasing shares.

CRIMINAL IMPERSONATION—As it pertains to identity theft, means to knowingly assume a false or fictitious identity or capacity, and in that identity or capacity, doing any act with intent to unlawfully gain a benefit or injure or defraud another.

CUSTOMER—With respect to a bank, means a person, including a bank, having an account with a bank or from whom a bank has agreed to receive payment orders.

CURRENCY—Generally used to describe paper money, it includes coin, government notes, and bank notes in circulation as a medium of exchange.

CYBERSPACE—Another name for the internet.

DECRYPT—To decode data from its protected, scrambled form so it can be read.

DATA SPILL—The result of a poorly designed form on a website which may cause an information leak to web servers of other companies, such as an ad network or advertising agency.

DEMAND DEPOSIT—Funds in a checking account subject to withdrawal on demand.

DEPOSIT ACCOUNT—A demand, time, savings, passbook or like account maintained with a bank, savings and loan association, credit union or like organization, other than an account evidenced by a certificate of deposit.

DIGITAL CERTIFICATE—Process using encryption technology whereby a document can be digitally stamped or certified as to its place of origin, and a certification authority supports and legitimizes the certificates.

DIGITAL SIGNATURE—A digital certification or stamp that uses encryption technology to authenticate an individual's signature is legitimate.

DIGITAL STORM—Analytic tools currently being developed by the FBI to sift and link data from disparate sources.

DISCLOSURE—The act of disclosing or revealing that which is secret or not fully understood. The Truth in Lending Act provides that there be disclosure to the consumer of certain information deemed basic to an intelligent assessment of a credit transaction.

DISCOUNT—A discount transaction is one where interest is deducted from the principal amount of a loan at the time the credit is arranged.

DIVIDENDS—A stockholder's share in the earnings of his company.

DISCOUNT RATE—The percentage of the face amount of commercial paper which a holder pays when he transfers such paper to a financial institution for cash or credit.

DOCUMENTARY DRAFT—A draft to be presented for acceptance or payment if specified documents, certificated securities, instructions for uncertificated securities, or other certificates, statements, or the like are to be received by the drawee or other payor before acceptance or payment of the draft.

DOWNLOAD—The transfer of files or software from a remote computer to the user's computer.

DOWNSTREAM DATA USAGE—Refers to companies' practice of disclosing personal information collected from users to other parties downstream to facilitate a transaction.

DRAFT—A written order signed by the drawer directing the drawee to pay a specified sum of money to the payee or his order.

DRAWEE—A person ordered in a draft to make payment.

DYNAMIC IP ADDRESS—An IP address that changes every time a user logs on, or dials-up, to a computer.

ELIGIBLE PAPER—Negotiable notes qualified for discount and purchase by a central bank.

E-MAIL—Computer-to-computer messages between one or more individuals via the Internet.

ENCRYPTION—The scrambling of digital information so that it is unreadable to the average user. A computer must have "digital keys" to unscramble and read the information.

ENYCRYPTION SOFTWARE—Often used as a security measure, encryption software scrambles data so that it is unreadable to interceptors without the appropriate information to read the data.

ENDORSEMENT OR INDORSEMENT—The technical act of signing one's name without qualifications to the back of a negotiable instrument for the purpose of a transfer.

ETHERNET—A commonly used networking technology that links computers together.

EXCHANGES—Items on banks presented for collection in a regional clearing house.

FEDERAL TRADE COMMISSION—An agency of the federal government created in 1914 for the purpose of promoting free and fair competition in interstate commerce through the prevention of general trade restraints such as price-fixing agreements, false advertising, boycotts, illegal combinations of competitors and other unfair methods of competition.

FILE TRANSFER PROTOCOL (FTP)—A way to transfer files from one computer to another.

FILTER—Software the user can buy that lets the user block access to websites and content that they may find unsuitable.

FINANCE CHARGE—Any charge assessed for an extension of credit, including interest.

FINANCIAL INFORMATION—Refers to information identifiable to an individual that concerns the amount and conditions of an individual's assets, liabilities, or credit, including (a) Account numbers and balances; (b) Transactional information concerning an account; and (c) Codes, passwords, social security numbers, tax identification numbers, driver's license or permit numbers, state identification numbers and other information held for the purpose of account access or transaction initiation.

FINANCIAL INFORMATION DEPOSITORY—Refers to a person engaged in the business of providing services to customers who have a credit, deposit, trust, stock, or other financial account or relationship with the person.

FINANCING AGENCY—A bank, finance company or other person who in the ordinary course of business makes advances against goods or documents of title or who by arrangement with either the seller or the buyer intervenes in ordinary course to make or collect payment due or claimed under the contract for sale. Includes also a bank or other person who similarly intervenes between persons who are in the position of seller and buyer in respect to the goods.

FIREWALL—A hardware or software device that controls access to computers on a Local Area Network (LAN). It examines all traffic routed between the two networks—inbound and outbound—to see if it meets certain criteria. If it does it is routed between the networks, otherwise it is stopped. It can also manage public access to private networked resources such as host applications.

FLOAT—Items in transit not yet collected.

FRAUD—A false representation of a matter of fact, whether by words or by conduct, by false or misleading allegations, or by concealment of that which should have been disclosed, which deceives and is intended to deceive another so that he shall act upon it to his legal injury.

FUNDS TRANSFER—The series of transactions, beginning with the originator's payment order, made for the purpose of making payment to the beneficiary of the order.

FUNDS TRANSFER BUSINESS DAY—The part of a day during which a receiving bank is open for the receipt, processing, and transmittal of payment orders and cancellations and amendments of payment orders.

FUNDS TRANSFER SYSTEM—A wire transfer network, automated clearinghouse, or other communication system of a clearinghouse or other association of banks through which a payment order by a bank may be transmitted to the bank to which the order is addressed.

GENUINE—Free of forgery or counterfeiting.

GOOD FAITH—In the case of a merchant, means honesty in fact and the observance of reasonable commercial standards of fair dealing in the trade.

GRACE PERIOD—The period beyond the due date set forth in the contract during which time payment may be made without incurring a penalty.

GUARANTY—An undertaking to answer for the payment of a debt or performance of a duty in the event of another's default.

GUID—Acronym for Globally Unique Identifier, a unique code used to identify a computer, user, file, etc., for tracking purposes.

HOLDER—As it refers to a negotiable instrument, it means the person in possession if the instrument is payable to bearer, or the identified person if such person is in possession. As it refers to a document of title, it means the person in possession if the goods are deliverable to bearer or to the order of the person in possession.

HOLDER IN DUE COURSE—One who has taken an instrument, complete and regular on its face, before it was overdue, in good faith and for value, without notice of any infirmity in the instrument or defect in the title of the person negotiating.

HOME PAGE—The first page or document web users see when connecting to a web server or when visiting a website.

HONOR—To pay or to accept and pay.

HOST NAME—Each computer is given a name which typically includes the user name and the organizational owner of the computer.

HYPERLINK—An image or portion of text on a web page that is linked to another web page The user clicks on the link to go to another web page or another place on the same page.

HYPERTEXT MARKUP LANGUAGE (HTML)—The standard language used for creating documents on the Internet.

HYPERTEXT TRANSFER PROTOCOL (HTTP)—The standard language that computers connected to the Internet use to communicate with each other.

INDIRECT LIABILITY—A secondary liability assumed by an endorser or guarantor of an obligation for which someone else is primarily liable.

INDIVIDUAL ACCOUNT—An account owned by one person.

INDORSEMENT—The act of a payee, drawee, accommodation indorser or holder of a bill, note, check or other negotiable instrument, in writing his name upon the back of the same, with or without further or qualifying words, whereby the property in the same is assigned and transferred to another.

INDORSER—One who signs his name as payee on the back of a check to obtain the cash or credit represented on its face.

INSTANT MESSAGE (IM)—A chat-like technology on an online service that notifies a user when another is online, allowing for simultaneous communication.

INSTRUCTION—With respect to investment securities, refers to a notification communicated to the issuer of an uncertificated security which directs that the transfer of the security be registered or that the security be redeemed.

INSTRUMENT—Refers to a negotiable instrument under UCC-Article 3, or a certificated security under UCC-Article 8, or any other writing which evidences a right to the payment of money and is not itself a security agreement or lease and is of a type which is in ordinary course of business transferred by delivery with any necessary indorsement or assignment.

INSURED INSTITUTION—A bank or savings association that is insured by the FDIC.

INTEREST—The compensation paid for the use of money or credit.

INTERNET—The universal network that allows computers to talk to other computers in words, text, graphics, and sound, anywhere in the world.

IP—Refers to "Internet Protocol"—the standards by which computers talk to each other over the Internet.

IP ADDRESS—A number or series of numbers that identify a computer linked to the Internet and which is generally written as four numbers separated by periods, e.g. 12.24.36.48.

ISP—Refers to "Internet Service Provider"—a service that allows the user to connect to the internet.

IRREVOCABLE TRUST ACCOUNT—An account for which the grantor has released all control. This type of account is established by a formal trust agreement, will, or court order.

ITEM—With respect to a bank, an instrument, promise or order to pay money handled by a bank for collection or payment.

JAVASCRIPT—A programming language used to add features to web pages in order to make the website more interactive.

JOINT ACCOUNT—An account in the name of two or more persons.

KEYWORD—A word the user enters into a search engine to begin the search for specific information or websites.

KITING—Writing checks for amounts in excess of funds in a checking account. The drawer takes advantage of the time needed by the bank to collect the checks. The term also refers to altering a check by raising the amount.

LETTER OF CREDIT—An engagement by a bank or other person, made at the request of a customer, that the issuer will honor drafts or other demands for payment upon compliance with the conditions specified in the credit.

LIEN—A charge against or interest in goods to secure payment of a debt or performance of an obligation.

LOAN—The grant of a temporary use of money by a lender to be repaid later, usually with interest.

LOAN PRINCIPAL—The amount of the debt not including interest or any other additions.

MAKER—The person who executes a note or other promise to pay. Drawer and maker are often interchangeable terms.

MATURITY—The due date of a mortgage, bond, stock, draft, or similar instrument.

MEANS OF IDENTIFICATION—As it pertains to identity theft, refers to any name or number that may be used, alone or in conjunction with any other information, to identify a specific individual, including a current or former name of the person, telephone number, an electronic address, or identifier of the individual or a member of his or her family, including the ancestor of the person; information relating to a change in name, address, telephone number, or electronic address or identifier of the individual or his or her family; a social security, driver's license, or tax identification number of the individual or a member of his or her family; and other information that could be used to identify the person, including unique biometric data.

MEDIA ACCESS CONTROL—The unique Ethernet card ID number found in network computers.

MIDNIGHT DEADLINE—With respect to a bank, refers to midnight on its next banking day following the banking day on which it receives the relevant item or notice, or from which the time for taking action commences to run, whichever is later.

MODEM—An internal or external device that connects the computer to a phone line and, if the user wishes, to a company that can link the user to the internet.

MONEY—A medium of exchange authorized or adopted by a domestic or foreign government, including a monetary unit of account established by an intergovernmental organization or by agreement between two or more nations.

MONEY ORDER—A draft sold by a bank for a fee. A Postal Money Order is sold by the Post Office.

MORTGAGE—A pledge of property for debt in which the lender (mortgagee) may foreclose the security if the debtor (mortgagor) fails to meet the terms of the contract.

MOUSE—A small device attached to the computer by a cord, which lets the user give commands to the computer by clicking.

NEGOTIABLE INSTRUMENT—An unconditional but transferable written order or promise to pay money by the drawer to order or to bearer or drawee at a determinable time.

NON-DEPOSIT INVESTMENT PRODUCT—An investment account that is not insured by the FDIC. Mutual Funds, Stocks, Annuities, and Treasury notes are all Non-Deposit Investment Products and would not be insured by the FDIC, even if purchased at or through an insured institution.

NON-NEGOTIABLE—Not capable of passing title or property by indorsement and delivery.

NO PROTEST—A waiver of formal protest of a negotiable instrument, which is also deemed to be a waiver of presentment and dishonor.

NOTE—An instrument containing an express and absolute promise of signer to pay to a specified person or order, or bearer, a definite sum of money at a specified time.

NOTICE—A person has notice of a fact when (a) he has actual knowledge of it; (b) he has received a notice or notification of it; or (c) from all the facts and circumstances known to him at the time in question he has reason to know that it exists.

NOTICE OF DISHONOR—A notice of dishonor may be given to any person who may be liable on the instrument by or on behalf or the holder or any party who has himself received notice, or any other party who can be compelled to pay the instrument.

ONLINE PROFILING—The practice of aggregating information about consumers' preferences and interests, gathered primarily by tracking their online movements and actions, with the purpose of creating targeted advertisement using the resulting profiles.

ONLINE SERVICE—An ISP with added information, entertainment and shopping features.

OPERATING SYSTEM—The main program that runs on a computer.

OPERATOR—The person who is responsible for maintaining and running a website.

ORDER—A written instruction to pay money signed by the person giving the instruction.

OVERDRAFT—The amount owing to a bank that has paid an item drawn against insufficient funds.

P3P—Acronym for Platform for Privacy Preferences Project—a proposed browser feature that would analyze privacy policies and allow a user to control what personal information is revealed to a particular site.

PARTY—As it refers to negotiable instruments, means a party to an instrument.

PASSBOOK—A book furnished by the bank in which the depositor keeps a record of his account. A savings bank passbook contains a record of deposits, withdrawals, and interest credited.

PASSWORD—A personal code that the user selects to access their account with their ISP.

PAYEE—The person in whose favor a bill of exchange, promissory note, or check is made or drawn.

PAYMENT ORDER—An instruction of a sender to a receiving bank, transmitted orally, electronically, or in writing, to pay, or to cause another bank to pay, a fixed or determinable amount of money to a beneficiary.

PAYOR—One who pays or who is to make a payment.

PERSONAL INFORMATION—As it relates to identity theft, refers to information associated with an actual person or a fictitious person that is a name, an address, a telephone number, an electronic mail address, a driver's license number, a social security number, an employer, a place of employment, information related to employment, an employee identification number, a mother's maiden name, an identifying number of a depository account, a bank account number, a password used for accessing information, or any other name, number, or code that is used, alone or in conjunction with other information, to confirm the identity of an actual or a fictitious person.

PII—Acronym for Personally Identifiable Information—refers to information such as name, mailing address, phone number or e-mail address.

POSTDATED CHECK—A check dated ahead. It is not payable until the date specified.

PREFERENCE DATA—Data which may be collected by a site or a service provider about an individual's likes and dislikes.

PRESENT VALUE—The amount as of a date certain of one or more sums payable in the future, discounted to the date certain.

PRETEXTING—The practice of fraudulently obtaining personal financial information, such as account numbers and balances, by calling financial institutions under the pretext of being a customer.

PRIME RATE—Preferential rate of interest on loans given to large and regular borrowers by banks.

PRINCIPAL—The face amount of a note or other evidence of debt on which interest is figured.

PRIVACY POLICY—A statement on a website describing what information about the user is collected by the site and how it is used; also known as a privacy statement or privacy notice.

PRIVACY SEAL PROGRAM—A program that certifies a site's compliance with the standards of privacy protection. Only those sites that comply with the standards are able to claim certification.

PRIVATE KEY—A data file assigned to a single individual to use in decrypting messages previously encrypted through use of that person's key.

PROMISE—A written undertaking to pay money signed by the person undertaking to pay.

PROMISSORY NOTE—A written promise by the maker to pay a certain sum of money to the payee or his order on demand or on a fixed date.

PROTEST—A written certification, usually by a notary, that he has presented a negotiable instrument and that the instrument was dishonored by refusal to accept or pay.

PROXY SERVER—A system that caches items from other servers to speed up access.

PSEUDONYMITY—A situation in which the user has taken on an assumed identity.

PUBLIC KEY—A data file assigned to a specific person but which others can use to send the person encrypted messages. Because public keys don't contain the components necessary to decrypt messages, they are safe to distribute to others.

QUERY STRING—The extended string of a URL after the standard website address.

REMITTING BANK—Any payor or intermediary bank remitting for an item.

REMITTUR—A person who purchases an instrument from its issuer if the instrument is payable to an identified person other than the purchaser.

RETURN ITEM—An item returned unpaid by a payor bank.

REVOCABLE TRUST ACCOUNT—An account that evidences an intention that the funds pass to a named beneficiary upon the death of the owner. May or may not have a separate trust document.

RIGHT AND CAPACITY—The manner in which funds are owned or held (e.g. Individual, Joint, Trust, Retirement).

SAFE DEPOSIT BOX—A place rented by a customer to keep valuables to which only he has access.

SCREEN NAME—The name the user selects to be known by when the user communicates online.

SEARCH ENGINE—A function that lets the user search for information and websites. Search engines or search functions may be found on many web sites.

SECURE ANONYMOUS RETAILER—Refers to a website that will strip a consumer's identifying information so they can surf other Web sites and send e-mail anonymously.

SECURED PARTY—A lender, seller or other person in whose favor there is a security interest, including a person to whom accounts or chattel paper have been sold.

SECURITY—Refers to (A) an obligation of an issuer or a share, participation, or other interest in an issuer or in property or an enterprise of an issuer which: (i) is represented by a security certificate in bearer or registered form; (ii) is one of a class or series or by its terms is divisible into a class or series of shares, participations, interests, or obligations; and (iii) is a type, dealt in or traded on securities exchanges or securities markets; or (B) is a medium for investment and by its terms expressly provides that it is a security governed by UCC-Article 8.

SECURITIES INTERMEDIARY—Refers to a clearing corporation; or a person, including a bank or broker, that in the ordinary course of its business maintains securities accounts for others and is acting in that capacity.

SERVER—A host computer that stores information and/or software programs and makes them available to users of other computers.

SETTLE—With respect to a bank, means to pay in cash, by clearinghouse settlement, in a charge or credit, or by remittance, or otherwise as agreed.

SIGHT DRAFT—A bill of exchange or draft payable on presentation.

SIGNATURE—A signature includes a symbol, trade name, or any word or mark. It may be with pencil, ink, crayon, or any means to record a signature or figures, or a mark may be in lieu of the proper name and a party intending may bind himself effectively by using such.

SIGNED—Any symbol executed or adopted by a party with present intention to authenticate a writing.

SPAM—E-mail from a company or charity that is unsolicited and sent to many people at one time, usually for advertising purposes; also known as junk e-mail.

STALE CHECK—A check that has been kept a long time before presentation to the bank for cashing. It can be refused.

STOP PAYMENT ORDER—An order by a depositor to his bank to refuse payment of an item specified by him.

SURETY—Guarantor.

SURVIVORSHIP ACCOUNT—An account in the name of two or more persons which on the death of one belongs to the survivor or survivors.

SUSPEND PAYMENTS—With respect to a bank, means that it has been closed by order of the supervisory authorities, that a public officer has been appointed to take it over, or that it ceases or refuses to make payments in the ordinary course of business.

TELLER'S CHECK—A bank draft signed by the teller of the drawer bank often given for money withdrawn from a savings bank.

THIRD PARTY COOKIE—A cookie that is placed by a party other than the user or the Web site being viewed, such as advertising or marketing groups who are trying to gather data on general consumer use third party cookies.

TIME DEPOSIT—Deposits withdrawable at a specified future date or after the lapse of a specified period of time.

TRACKER GIF—Electronic images, usually not visible to site visitors, that allow a Web site to count those who have visited that page or to access certain cookies; also known as a "Clear GIF".

TRUSTMARK—An online seal awarded by TRUSTe to websites that agree to post their privacy practices openly via privacy statements, as well as adhere to enforcement procedures that ensure that those privacy promises are met.

TRAVELER'S CHECKS—Checks issued by banks and express companies promising to pay on demand even amounts of money. The buyer signs the check on purchase and countersigns it for payment.

UNAUTHORIZED SIGNATURE—A signature made without actual, implied, or apparent authority, including a forgery.

UNCERTIFIED SECURITY—A security that is not represented by a certificate.

UNIFORM COMMERCIAL CODE (UCC)—A code of laws governing commercial transactions, such as sales of goods, commercial paper, bank deposits and collections, letter of credit, bulk transfers, warehouse receipts, bills of lading, investment securities and secured transactions, which was drafted by the National Conference of Commissioners on Uniform State Laws and designed to bring uniformity to the laws of the various states.

UNIQUE IDENTIFIERS—Non-financial identifiers issued for purposes of consistently identifying the individual.

UPLOAD—Copying or sending data or documents from one computer to another computer.

URL (Uniform Resource Locator)—The address that lets the user locate a particular site. For example, http://www.ftc.gov is the URL for the Federal Trade Commission. Government URLs end in .gov and non-profit organizations and trade associations end in .org. Commercial companies generally end in .com, although additional suffixes or domains may be used as the number of internet businesses grows.

USURY—Interest in excess of the legal rate charged to a borrower for the use of money.

VICTIM—As it relates to identity theft, refers to any person who has suffered financial loss or any entity that provided money, credit, goods, services or anything of value and has suffered financial loss as a direct result of the commission or attempted commission of a violation of this section.

VIRUS—A file maliciously planted in the user's computer that can damage files and disrupt their system.

WAIVER—An intentional and voluntary surrender of a known right.

WEB BUG—A graphic in a website or enhanced e-mail message that enables a third party to monitor who is reading the page or message.

WEBSITE—An internet destination where the user can look at and retrieve data. All the web sites in the world, linked together, make up the World Wide Web or the "Web."

WORLD WIDE WEB—A part of the Internet housing websites that provide text, graphics, video and audio information on millions of topics.

# BIBLIOGRAPHY

Better Business Bureau On-Line (Date Visited: May 2004) <http://www.bbbonline.org>.

*Black's Law Dictionary, Fifth Edition*. St. Paul, MN: West Publishing Company, 1979.

Center for Democracy and Technology (Date Visited: May 2004) <http://www.consumerprivacyguide.org>.

Consumer Information Center (Date Visited: May 2004) <http://www.pueblo.gsa.gov>.

Consumer Sentinel (Date Visited: May 2004) <http://www.consumer.gov/sentinel>.

Cornell Law School Legal Information Institute. (Date Visited: May 2004) <http://www.law.cornell.edu/>.

Federal Bureau of Investigation Internet Fraud Complaint Center (Date Visited: May 2004) <http://www.ifccfbi.gov>.

Federal Deposit Insurance Corporation (Date Visited: May 2004) <http://www.fdic.gov>.

Federal Trade Commission (Date Visited: May 2004) <http://www.ftc.gov>.

Identity Theft Resource Center (Date Visited: May 2004) <http://www.idtheftcenter.org>.

National Conference of Commissioners on Uniform State Laws—Official Site. (Date Visited: May 2004) <http://www.law.upenn.edu/bll/ulc/ulc.htm/>.

National Consumer's League (Date Visited: May 2004) <http://natlconsumersleague.org>.

National Infrastructure Protection Center (Date Visited: May 2004) <http://www.nipc.gov>.

Online Privacy Alliance (Date Visited: May 2004) <http://www.privacy allliance.com>.

Online Public Education Network (Date Visited: May 2004) <http://www.internetalliance.org>.

Privacy Rights Clearinghouse (Date Visited: May 2004) <http://www. privacyrights.org>.

TRUSTe (Date Visited: May 2004) <http://www.truste.org>.

United States Department of Justice (Date Visited: May 2004) <http://www.usdoj.gov/criminal/fraud/idtheft.html>.

United States General Accounting Office (Date Visited: May 2004) <http://www.gao.gov>.

United States Office of the Attorney General (Date Visited: May 2004) <http://www.oag.gov>.

United States Secret Service (Date Visited: May 2004) <http://www.treas.gov/usss>.